Messiah in the Mishkan

Messiah in the Mishkan

From Shadow to Substance and Beyond

CHRIS WOODALL

WIPF & STOCK · Eugene, Oregon

MESSIAH IN THE MISHKAN
From Shadow to Substance and Beyond

Wipf & Stock
An Imprint of Wipf and Stock Publishers
199 W. 8th Ave., Suite 3
Eugene, OR 97401

www.wipfandstock.com

PAPERBACK ISBN: 979-8-3852-0500-4
HARDCOVER ISBN: 979-8-3852-0501-1
EBOOK ISBN: 979-8-3852-0502-8

11/15/23

Especial gratitude must be extended to the many loyal streams that lovingly and sacrificially continue to feed into this otherwise arid rural river bed.

Contents

Permissions

Introduction

In the late autumn of 1980, I was a first-year student at the Bible College of Wales. Friday evenings were usually given over to whichever missionary was currently on furlough to deliver a talk (with obligatory slides) of their work in the farthest reaches of wherever. The benediction was not so much a prayer as an appeal for volunteers and/or financial aid. I had no particular inclination in either direction, so would often find my attention drifting elsewhere once the lights were dimmed. This Friday evening, however, was one of those rare occasions when my mind and spirit found harmony with those of the guest speaker.

I had never previously heard of Theodore Epp. I'm ashamed to admit, I cannot even remember his topic for the night, except to say that it was the first time in my four years as a Christian that I had been truly captivated by the Old Testament. As was the norm for such occasions, Epp brought with him a selection of books from his back catalogue, prominently displayed on a table to the left of our seating area. I'd say there were probably half a dozen different titles with around ten copies of each. They all interested me, but my funds allowed no more than a cursory glance.

After the meeting, the male students convened in the college library to discuss the talk. (Female students may have done something similar elsewhere, but we were not encouraged to be inquisitive about what they got up to or where they did so.) Fifteen of us gathered amongst the dusty tomes, Richard Maton, the college dean, presiding over matters in the way that sports referees operate best—almost unnoticed. I was not entirely alone in my excitement of what we had just witnessed, but neither was the sensation unanimous. Richard noted my especial enthusiasm, and he knew of my fiscal predicament. After we had been dispersed for the night, he went back to the meeting hall to find a solitary book left on the display table. He bought it and gave it to me as a Christmas present a few weeks later: *Portraits of Christ in the Tabernacle.*

Forty years later, I continue to treasure the gift as I cherished the giver. I thumbed through Epp's book again recently, still inspired by its contents, but now aware also of a distinct dearth that had previously passed undetected. The key, I believe, belongs to a distinction between three crucial words: knowledge, understanding, and wisdom. To my mind, knowledge is the acquiring of knowable facts, whereas understanding is concerned with the assimilation, systematization, and presenting of those facts. To deliver this knowledge and understanding in a way that is life-changing to the recipient, however, requires wisdom. This, in my view, is where Epp and others fall short.[1] Not that they necessarily lack wisdom, but that they too often fail to apply it adequately or accurately.

It is one thing, for example, to become privy to the meaning and significance of the color of the priests' robes on any given day of the Jewish calendar,[2] but how does this affect the way I relate to my next-door neighbor, the happiness of whom seems annexed to how many times the Amazon delivery van stops at her door each week? Likewise, what functional purpose for today is there in knowing the exact measurements of the various curtains, veils, and linings other than that such facts unveil a God of precision and design? To be similarly disposed may well be a token of the retention of God's image in us, but those without such knowledge are still inclined to think of others who are so attentive to be autistic.

The reader needs to be aware that this introduction is written before any intensive research has begun. It is meant to be a kind of roadmap, if you will, outlining where I intend to go, as much for my benefit as anyone else's. Even at this preliminary stage, however, it has become clear that there are debates associated with the tabernacle with which I have no intention to engage. For example, I shall touch only briefly upon the so-called two-tabernacle theory, evoked by the writer to the Hebrews in the New Testament (see Heb 2:9, 6, 8). This is not because I consider it to be unimportant or the truth of it to be without value, but because it forms only a minor part of the mandate I believe I have received. Moreover,

1. See also Childs, *Exodus*; Horton, *Tabernacle of Moses.*

2. E.g., Soltau, *Tabernacle.*

others more qualified than I have given a far better account of what I would wish to express, most notably Ray Stedman.[3]

So, what shall I be tackling? In the main, this will be limited to the tabernacle furnishings, especially as types of which Christ is the antitype. Of course, my use of the word *antitype* is in the sense of that which is represented by something else as a symbol, not as that which represents the opposite of its type. As such, I trust that Christ will be seen not only to have been typified by each article of tabernacle furniture under consideration, but to have fulfilled the type, that is, filled it out to its fullest potential.

A widely recognized principle of hermeneutics is to garner as much information as possible regarding what the text(s) under consideration meant to its/their original audience or readership. For a western Christian three and a half millennia hence, this is perhaps more difficult than might be imagined. In order to remove as many of the obstacles as possible, therefore, I propose taking a sideways step by looking at how current Judaism regards the understanding of its own forbears. Already I am learning of criticism to such an approach. My response is that perhaps if Christian leaders and teachers down the centuries had not shied away from taking similar steps, then our paucity of understanding in such matters might have been somewhat diminished.

For many Christians of my acquaintance, texts like the ones we are about to consider don't even make their nice-to-know list, never mind the need-to-know. They fall into the same category as the seemingly endless genealogical records or prescribed ceremonial cleansing rituals, and help form the opinion that the Old Testament is as uninteresting as it is unnecessary. I would contend that such an attitude is cultivated largely by poor teaching. "New covenant people belong to the New Testament age," they are told, and so they arrive at church each Sunday with half a Bible. Fed an exclusive diet of Jesus turning water into wine, raising the dead, and Paul's espionage-like encounters, why would they want to snack on the contents of a haberdashery catalogue or butchery manual?

This is where we take the step from knowledge towards wisdom. I don't claim to have all the answers; I wouldn't even dare to suggest that I have more than a crumb of wisdom. But as much as some does reside in me by God's Spirit, I'm prepared to follow his leading to discover more. Why don't you join me on the journey? It will do you good (Num 10:29)!

3. Stedman, *Hebrews*, 92–94.

1

The Tabernacle of Worship

THIS CHAPTER SERVES AS an overview for all that follows. It provides—I hope—a contextual background by which to understand everything from chapter 2 onward. I realize, of course, that there will be some readers who have a specific interest in only one item of furniture at a time. They will treat this work as a reference tool for a pet subject or current project. I trust they will not be disappointed, but I fear that their understanding will not be as enhanced as it might have been by looking here first. Sadly, they will not have read this warning either. For others, I trust you will allow what you discover in this opening chapter to shape how you receive the information in subsequent chapters. My desire that this should prove to be the case is true of the whole chapter, though it becomes no more intense than in relation to the opening section . . .

ACCORDING TO THE PATTERN

> See that you make [the tabernacle furnishings] according to the pattern shown you on the mountain.[1]

A quarter of a century ago, I belonged to a charismatic church that used the title of this section for their beginners' guide to Christianity course. It

1. Exod 25:40.

was good intentioned, well put together, and expertly delivered. But none of the weekly lessons contained anything that was more than loosely related to what you are about to read. Were they wrong to lift the title from its context? Not necessarily! Whatever we do, as far as we are able to discern it, we can do no better than to adopt God's design for our actions. In fact, we can only do worse. But the phrase "according to the pattern" appears in Scripture only within the framework of the building of God's tabernacle in the wilderness, here in its original setting (see also Exod 26:30), and later by the writers of the New Testament when citing it in the context of Christ's giving substance to the shadow (Acts 7:44; Heb 8:5).

In over forty years as a Christian, I must have heard it employed dozens of times, but can only recall a handful of occasions when it wasn't divorced from its rightful setting. I don't want to put a downer on proceedings before we even get going, but that information should sober us. At the same time, we are able to discern the principle in operation even where the verbal declaration of it is absent. Creation is perhaps the obvious example of this, with Noah's ark a close second. But there are others, most notably the unfolding plan of salvation for humanity in Christ Jesus. This, too, is linked to the tabernacle, at least in shadow form, though I believe that certain aspects of it remain outside its remit, as we shall see.

No Modification Required

The pattern in question, of course, is not just any old pattern. Nor does our understanding of it reach its full extent by knowing that it was the one shown to Moses by God on the mountain. What was revealed to Moses already existed in the creative mind of God. He both designed and devised it. The pattern in and of itself was flaw proof. But the guarantee for remaining so in its practical outworking was conditional upon being adhered to without the slightest deviation. In other words, it was a model requiring no re-envisaging or helpful Mosaic emendations.

My wife makes many of her own clothes. She is not a trained seamstress, but belongs to a generation that was taught how to thread a needle at about the same time as they learned that *a* is for apple. She is also very patient, keen to learn new techniques, and her attention to detail is second only to that of her husband. Her expression when something doesn't quite work out is often more of consternation than disappointment: "How could this be!" Occasionally it can be a design fault or even a typo in the printing of the pattern. More often than not, however, the resultant debacle has arisen because of Barbara's reluctance to believe the designer's instructions or insistence that she knows better. Sound familiar?

Objectivity Rules

A significant, yet oft-overlooked, aspect of the divine pattern is that it is theocentric, not anthropocentric; that is, it is as viewed from God's perspective, not from ours. Of course, that perspective is presented to us in language that we can understand and with terminology that is familiar to us, but the origin is exclusively divine. This is vastly important, but I must warn the reader of a number of tensions involved before I explain why. A great difficulty we all face as Christians when reading the Bible is to do so from within anything other than a subjective milieu. This is perfectly understandable and not always inappropriate. We will see later that many of the features of the tabernacle were for the benefit of the Israelites and that advantage is transferred to New Testament believers by virtue of Christ's fulfilment of the type. But here, at the very beginning, we must acknowledge that humanity played no part in its design except as a recipient of the architectural blueprint.

Why does such information create tension? Well, I've already alluded to one reason: ensuring that we understand that it is to be viewed objectively rather than subjectively, but that it is not without subjective application. Another reason is closely allied to this. When we regard things as subjectively, it is often—some might say without exception—with personal benefit in mind. There is no benefit to God in viewing the design of the tabernacle—or its purpose, for that matter—objectively. It adds nothing of value to his essence, nor would its absence diminish him in any way. The only conceivable way I can think that anything related to the tabernacle might be said to change God is the Fatherly delight it brings him in seeing the obedience of his children in following his instruction or the displeasure he finds in our rebellion. This is alien territory for many of us, but it is territory with which we will need to come to terms if we are to add understanding to our knowledge, and wisdom to them both.

This is not to say that we find nothing subjective in the pattern. The purpose of the pattern is to ensure that we follow its directives to the letter, which attracts a certain reward that may be described in terms of their benefit toward us. The original Hebrew employed is *tabneeth*, which is closely related to form (*tenuma*), image (*selem*), and likeness (*demut*), but with an inherent precision factor. Often when we speak of likeness it is with reference to a vague similarity or passing resemblance. The Greek equivalent of *tabneeth* is *tupos*, used both in the Septuagint version of the Old Testament and in the New Testament. It is employed by both Luke and the writer to the Hebrews in the texts cited above (i.e., Acts 7:44; Heb 8:5). Vine has this to say of it:

> [*Tupos*] primarily denoted a blow . . . hence an impression, the mark of a blow, the impress of a seal, the stamp made by a die.[2]

That *tupos* is used of both the original and its copy is not without significance. In appearance they are identical. However, this apparent indistinguishability does not extend to their respective characters. We will look at this in more detail later when we consider each specific item of tabernacle furniture, but it is important that we establish now that design is annexed to purpose. When we consider type and antitype, we will see that foremost among their differences is that the type was perishable and corruptible, whereas the antitype is not, and yet both function according to the same divine pattern. Moreover, in so doing they each accomplish the purpose for which they were designed. For example, the rings and carrying poles were designed to effect the portability of those pieces of furniture to which they related; the richly ornamented, lavishly dyed, jewel-encrusted fabrics demonstrated the splendor of God's presence.

Cogs in the Machine

Therein lay another tension. We can discuss the purpose of each component within the tabernacle and how this was inextricably linked to its design, but the parts must not be divorced from the whole, except insofar as our analysis of them contributes to an enhanced understanding of the purpose and design of the tabernacle in its entirety. This remains true even when we must concede that there are factors associated with it that are forever beyond our comprehension. For ancient Israel, the tabernacle was the temporary dwelling place of Almighty God. How can you possibly localize the omnipresent? Its features were to be treated with respect and attended in a dignified manner, but it was not to be so venerated that

2. Vine, *Expository Dictionary*, 363.

God's glorification was thereby diminished in its favor, or those responsible for its realization were afforded more honor than was appropriate.

This is what I like to call "the little Jack Horner syndrome." It is where pride begins to raise its ugly head in the midst of communal prayer groups or times of testimony, even in the preaching of God's word, where the closing "Amen!" may well have been replaced by "Oh, what a good boy/girl am I!" I don't think I'm alone in such experiences. In fact, I doubt whether there is a reader out there who has not had to endure the prayers of those who seem to imagine that God is lucky to have them fighting his corner. If only they had been around sooner, then it is surely questionable whether the church would have found itself in such a mess. We would then have been able to wrap up early and go home.

I would even go so far as to say that my overriding concern with much current church polity is not so much to do with the practice and proclamation, as it is with the parenthetical self: "Lord, we really want to see your kingdom values being ushered forth in our day (and could you please arrange for it to be seen that I played my part in doing some of the ushering in)." Or, "Father, will you please send revival/a mighty outpouring of your Spirit/a sense of your very real presence in our meetings (and allow those so touched/blessed to recognize how instrumental I was to the unfolding of your purpose in this way)." Perhaps, "Jesus, help me to keep my gaze focused only on you (and remind everyone else that they must hang on my every word if they are to enjoy the same privilege)."

This is not a new phenomenon. It was certainly one with which Jesus was familiar. He addressed it in the form of a parable, contrasting the different approaches of two men who came to the temple to pray (Luke 18:9–14). One man was a member of the Pharisees, legalistic separatists whose proud traditions owed more to their ancestral interpretations of the law than the law itself. The other man was a tax collector, hated as a traitor to his people by serving the ruling Roman power. The major difference between the two men, however, lay not in their social status, but in the acknowledgment or otherwise of their true standing before a holy God. The Pharisee even cloaked his pride in pseudo-religious garb: "God, I thank you that I am not like other men—robbers, evildoers, adulterers—or even like this tax collector" (v. 11).

Now, I must confess that I have never heard these exact words prayed, but the sentiment behind them has oft been replicated. This is nowhere more obvious than in the Pharisee's choice of comparisons. William Hendriksen elucidates further:

> He begins by comparing himself with other people. Not, however, with truly devout men like Samuel . . . or Simeon . . . but with those of bad reputation. He says that he is not a robber . . . as if he were not at that very moment robbing God of the honor due to him. He is not a cheat or a dishonest person . . . as if he were not cheating himself out of a blessing. And he is not an adulterer. Well, probably not literally, but was not this proud Pharisee departing from the true God, and thereby making himself guilty of the worst adultery of all?[3]

True Spirit for Worship

I don't want to jump the gun too much, but suffice to say here that there are clear steps to coming into God's presence. Of the two, the tax collector came closest to doing so according to God's predetermined pattern. The purpose of the pattern was that it might produce the object of its design—the tabernacle—as the appointed means to a desired end: worship. But the direction of that worship was not left to the proclivities or sensibilities of fallen creatures; it, too, was to be according to design. That reminder of Christ having given substance to the shadow I mentioned earlier formed part of Stephen's defense before the Sanhedrin (Acts 7:1—8:1). Collectively, Stephen's accusers were no different from the proud Pharisee in Jesus' parable. Martyn Lloyd-Jones identifies the primary trait of their religiosity as hypocrisy, before adding:

> Then the second characteristic of this false religion is that it is always very keen on what we must call "institutionalism." I mean something like this: these people in the Sanhedrin actually worship the temple—and here Stephen really comes to the point. They are putting up temple worship against Christianity. Stephen says, in effect, "You accuse me of saying that the temple is no longer necessary, that this Jesus has done away with it, that he has finished with all the sacrifices and the burnt offerings, and that now it is all in him." To these leaders the temple is everything, that is their whole trouble. The temple has become an idol. And that is always a characteristic of false religion.[4]

Lloyd-Jones's concluding remarks were true of Stephen's day concerning the temple, it was true of Israel's wilderness experience under

3. Hendriksen, *Luke*, 819.

4. Lloyd-Jones, *Authentic Christianity*, 251.

Moses in relation to the tabernacle, and it is true of our own day. True worship is wholly objective. And yet, much that currently passes for Christian worship has a tendency toward subjectivism. How it makes us feel, how uplifted we are by the experience, the tingly sensation of being part of a large number of the redeemed who are all enjoying God together, and "imagine how much more ecstatic will be the sense of God's presence in eternity." In and of themselves, of course, there is nothing inherently wrong with any of these thoughts, except insofar that they detract from both the object and objectivity of worship.

Following the divine blueprint to the letter is only the first part of the challenge. It is a vital component, but the journey does not end there. Moses' generation constructed the tabernacle "according to the pattern." Having come out of Egypt, been delivered in the Red Sea miracle, been supernaturally provided for in the desert, the apostle Paul gives this warning concerning them to the church at Corinth:

> Nevertheless, God was not pleased with most of them; their bodies were scattered over the desert.[5]

Why was this? Well, any number of reasons could be cited, and have been. But I am of the opinion that the root lies in a failure to identify the object of the pattern with its purpose. The objective purpose of the tabernacle is revealed by its Hebrew name *mishkan*, meaning "dwelling place." Subjectively, however, it was to be a place of worship. In conversation with the Samaritan woman at the well, Jesus said:

> A time is coming and has now come when the true worshippers will worship the Father in spirit and in truth, for they are the kind of worshippers the Father seeks. God is spirit, and his worshippers must worship in spirit and in truth.[6]

A New Testament teaching? Yes! But one that unveils an eternally valid truth, giving rise to a constant premise: God has always been essentially spirit and the requirements of those who would worship him remain unchangeable.

5. 1 Cor 10:1–5.
6. John 4:23–24.

PORTABLE AND TEMPORARY

The tent-like structure of the tabernacle meant that it was portable. It needed to be. Israel as a people group were never intended to settle for long in the desert. Conservative estimates suggest that their forty-year journey was around thirty-eight years too long, which about accounts for the time they spent in the region of Mount Sinai (ten months) and settled at Kadesh Barnea (almost thirty-eight years). This is not to imply that their sojourn at Sinai was spent in idleness. During the first three months or so, Moses was receiving the law and other instructions from God regarding the tabernacle. Israel then had to assemble supplies and construct the constituent parts of the tabernacle. The rest of the time, they were setting up camp and moving off again in response to the pillar of cloud by day and the pillar of fire by night.

Not a Sell-by Date in Sight

It would be convenient to imagine that the portability of the tabernacle was an accommodation on the part of God to the situation in which his people found themselves. Certainly, the parallels between type and antitype cannot be overlooked. But I prefer to think of it as God making provision for Israel's obedience to his own will. If there is any hint of accommodation to be gleaned, then I believe we do better to focus our attention rather on the durability of the tabernacle than its portability.

Now I don't do camping. That is not to say that I have never been camping. In fact, one of the main reasons why I don't do camping is because I *have* been camping. To my mind, a holiday in a tent or caravan is a blessing only in the sense that it enables you to appreciate home comforts all the more when the vacation is over. Please don't think of me as a snob: I'm not particularly fond of hotels either. Give me a good old-fashioned bed and breakfast or self-catering cottage and I'm in my element. In this, at least, some of my closest friends think I'm mad; we have a kind of reciprocal agreement. These same friends think nothing of replacing their all-singing, all-dancing mobile holiday home every five years or so and, to be perfectly frank, I don't think much of it either. However, I'm not talking about the kind of people who feel an obligation to keep up with the Joneses, in the same way that some people are with their cars. Five years of gas stove accidents, the compound effects of inclement weather, and the natural wear and tear of three runaround preschool kids renders further investment something of a necessity.

Therein lies the point. When we think of portability, it is easy to do so with the same kind of reference that we attach to a portable television, radio, or refrigerator, as if the whole thing was conveyed from place to place *in situ*. Perhaps that image is reinforced by the fact that there are online retailers who specialize in the production and sale of portable tabernacles, which are really a scaled-down facsimile of the original. This was no such thing. Each time the Israelites left one location, the tabernacle had to be deconstructed in order to render it portable and re-sited when they set up camp elsewhere. This happened forty-two times. When it was standing, it was in constant use. Some of us can be overly enthusiastic at the mega-church phenomenon, whereby there are in excess of two thousand regular weekly attendees. The tabernacle was the spiritual home for around fifteen hundred times as many. The vast majority of them got no further than the first piece of furniture in the entrance, but the offerings that took place there were made on their behalf, all three million of them. Nothing wore out or needed replacing; the people provided and God preserved.

A great deal is made in Scripture of God's people being witnesses, with the emphasis on the being rather than what we would nowadays understand as witnessing. In their wilderness experience, God's old covenant people witnessed to those who fell outside their ranks just by being the people of God. Imagine being a nomadic tribesperson during those years. You and half a dozen others of your clan are settling by the door of your tent when, in the distance, there seems to be a murmur in the air and a faint light in the night sky. As both draw nearer, they grow in volume and intensity. An hour or so later, it passes you and you realize this is what your cousins said they had seen. This is the group who are going to put the clothiers and cobblers out of business at the Rephidim branch of Walmart. They don't speak much to outsiders, but can be heard muttering "*Toda raba, Yahweh!*" each morning as they gather their daily portion of angel food, baked in the ovens of heaven. What were they? They were God's witnesses. What were they doing? They were being God's people.

A Fixed Usefulness . . .

You might think that the tabernacle's portability points in the direction of its non-permanence. But is this an anachronistic viewing of the facts from what we also know of later history? For the sake of clarity, I am not commenting here on the shadowy temporariness of the tabernacle in relation to the permanent substance by which it was fulfilled in the New Testament. Rather, I wish to address the tabernacle's proven temporary state in contrast to the temple built under Solomon's governance.

The reader will remember that it was David who proposed the building of a temple after the ark had been recaptured from its abductors and eventually brought back to Jerusalem:

> After David was settled in his palace, he said to Nathan the prophet, "Here I am, living in a palace of cedar, while the ark of the covenant of the Lord is under a tent." Nathan replied to David, "Whatever you have in mind, do it, for God is with you."[7]

Before we proceed with the narrative, it might prove helpful to backtrack a little to David's initial decision to bring back the ark. Four chapters earlier, we are told that David, having already discussed the matter with his army commanders, put it to the people:

> "If it seems good to you and if it is the will of God . . . [l]et us bring the ark of our God back to us, for we did not enquire of it during the reign of Saul." The whole assembly agreed because it seemed right to all the people.[8]

It may well have seemed right to all the people, but what about the directive also to determine God's will? At least David's motives seem to have been pure: to enquire of the ark in state affairs. But then we come back to chapter 17, with the ark now securely returned, and there is absolutely no mention of either David or Nathan enquiring of it (that is, the dwelling place of God's Presence) concerning the proposal to build something in which to house the tabernacle furnishings, which was to give the appearance of being as lavish and extravagant externally as it was on the inside. God had to take the initiative to intervene. He allowed the venture to proceed, but only in adherence to his strict terms and conditions and, even then, there seems to be a note of reluctance in the permission being granted:

7. 1 Chr 17:1–2.
8. 1 Chr 13:2–4.

> Go and tell my servant David, "This is what the Lord says: You are not the one to build me a house to dwell in. I have not dwelt in a house from the day I brought Israel up out of Egypt to this day. I have moved from one tent site to another, from one dwelling-place to another. Wherever I have moved with all the Israelites, did I ever say to any of their leaders whom I commanded to shepherd my people, "Why have you not built me a house of cedar?"'[9]

I'm not sure what David or Nathan might have anticipated, but this does not fall into the "Good idea; I wish I'd thought of it myself" category. Martin Selman has little to say on the matter, though I do think he pretty much hits the nail on the head:

> David's desire to build a temple . . . is typical of many ancient kings who sought an appropriate expression for their piety and at the same time a public testimony to their achievements.[10]

As someone with a keen interest in English Tudor history, I must resist the temptation to substitute David's name with that of Henry (VIII) and replace the word "temple" with "cathedral." It might be argued that what follows, in this context at least, is a befitting appraisal of the primary motivation of both men. Thankfully, the similarity ends there.

. . . or a Permanent Temporariness?

But there is further evidence, before we even arrive at David's reign, regarding the status of the tabernacle. Throughout God's instructions to Moses concerning the piecing together of the tabernacle and its component parts, a common theme emerges: perpetuity. This is expressed in a number of ways, though each one points in the same direction: "This is to be a lasting ordinance for the generations to come" (Exod 27:21); "This is to be a lasting ordinance for Aaron and his descendants" (28:43); "For the generations to come this burnt offering is to be made regularly" (29:42); "Aaron [and his descendants] must burn incense on the altar every morning . . . [and] at twilight so that incense will burn regularly before the Lord for the generations to come" (30:8); "It will be a [continuing] memorial for the Israelites before the Lord" (v. 16); "This is to be a lasting ordinance for Aaron and his descendants for the generations to

9. 1 Chr 17:4–6.

10. Selman, *1 Chronicles*, 184.

come" (v. 21); "Say to the Israelites, 'This is to be my sacred anointing oil for the generations to come'" (v. 31).

I realize, of course, that all of the above remains valid despite the later building of Solomon's Temple. Indeed, there are those who maintain that the whole tabernacle was housed within the temple,[11] which thereby effectively became a permanent outer shell. I remain unconvinced that this idea of perpetuity was what was intended when the words were first spoken, and even less so that this was how they were initially understood.

Passing through toward the Promise

Now, if you will forgive the familiarity, we must deal with "the elephant in the room." As alluded to earlier, in the context of its shadowy relationship to Christ giving substance both to it as a whole and to its component features, the tabernacle was both temporary and temporal. The writer to the Hebrews could hardly be more forthright:

> When Christ came as high priest of the good things that are already here, he went through the greater and more perfect tabernacle that is not man-made, that is to say, not a part of this creation. He did not enter by means of the blood of goats and calves; but he entered the Most Holy Place once and for all by his own blood, having obtained eternal redemption.[12]

The placement of the headings in the NIV is perhaps a little unhelpful in this regard. The impression is given that a completely new subject is begun at verse 11. But verse 11 follows on from verse 10 and what precedes it in this chapter, including verse 8. My apologies for stating the obvious, but the point I am seeking to address really does seem to be similarly lacking in obscurity. If the mention of a "first tabernacle" implies a subsequent second tabernacle, then surely it is that "greater and more perfect tabernacle" through which Christ went to obtain "eternal redemption." Whereas the first tabernacle was temporal and earthly, this second tabernacle is spiritual and heavenly. The essence of both is to be found in their function as a dwelling-place: it is the presence of God. Jesus had already been "God with us" by virtue of the incarnation; he had now made it possible for us to be with God in him by whatever it was that took place in the spiritual realm while he hung on the cross.

11. E.g., Friedman, "Tabernacle in the Temple," 241–48.

12. Heb 9:11–12.

It is perhaps not without significance that Christ is described as having gone "*through* the greater and more perfect tabernacle" to reach his goal. This is also the appropriate preposition to use in relation to Israel's desert wanderings: they came *out of* Egypt; they went *through* the wilderness; they were to go *into* the land of promise. Passing through is vital. It was for Christ in his appointed mission, it is for us in accomplishing our God-given tasks, and it was for Israel, too. The danger for us as Christians is that our experience of coming through can be so much more pleasant and pleasurable than what we came out of that we either think we've arrived at our destination or settle for it anyway, because we've heard that the place where we are heading has giants in the land. In this sense, the good can become the enemy of the great, the better given preference over the as-yet-unattained best that God has in store for us.

The generation of Israelites who came out of Egypt failed to set foot in Canaan; thank God that Jesus went through what he had to in order to achieve the Father's desired objective. There was no back-up plan. It was the only way.

NOT FOR THE UNCONVERTED

For anyone who is old enough to remember the days before the advent of the internet, I wonder if you can also bring to mind a phenomenon that my circle of friends would describe as "the preachers' library." Notice where the apostrophe is placed. This was not any individual's collection, but one to which all church ministers seemed to have access, comprising pithy one-liners, "personal" anecdotes to which anyone could lay claim, and even whole sermons in some cases. One perceived pearl of wisdom doing the rounds in the 1980s, with neither qualm nor qualification, was: "The church is the only institution that exists exclusively for the benefit of its non-members." I wasn't entirely convinced of its veracity back then and am even less so today. I continue to be of the opinion that the church exists primarily for the glory of God. While a little sympathetic to the intentions of those who promoted the original idea, all it seemed to produce was a mentality that Sunday meetings were not so much an opportunity for communal worship as one in which to showcase the best in local Christian entertainment.

Israel Saved in Egypt

We shall see this perhaps a little more clearly when we come to the next chapter, but it is important that we establish here that, though the tabernacle was designed as a dwelling-place for God's localized presence, and the worship that took place therein was to be directed exclusively toward him, the sole beneficiaries were his covenant people. It was not a place for the alien, the guest visitor, or the ultra-inquisitive, but for the people of God.

This may come as a surprise to some readers. I know I have heard it preached that the offerings made at the tabernacle were symbolic/typical of the Christian believer's conversion. However, the conversion experience for the people of Israel took place, not in the wilderness, but in Egypt. This is why the apostle Paul could remind his Corinthian readership that their forebears had all been "baptized into Moses in the cloud and in the sea" (1 Cor 10:2).

What such "baptism" meant or what implications it might have would make an interesting study, but that is not our concern here. What I can say is that it, too, was post-conversion. Collectively, Israel at this time was the redeemed community of believers. Now, I know that the context of Paul's argument was that those at Corinth should learn from the bad example set by Israel of old and not fall into the same trap of rebellion, but that does not invalidate the incidentals. Indeed, the peripheral information Paul provides is like feathers giving flight and direction to the point he wishes to make. It is also what gives thrust to his "Nevertheless . . ." of verse 5. The lesson, as Alan Johnson correctly points out, is that "great spiritual blessings are no guarantee of continuing divine favor."[13]

So, what was it that constituted Israel's mass conversion experience? It took place during the last of the plagues upon Egypt and was such a momentous occasion that it heralded the inauguration of the religious calendar in Israel (Exod 12:1–2). It was, of course, the Passover, an event never to be forgotten:

> This is a day you are to commemorate; for the generations to come you shall celebrate it as a festival to the Lord—a lasting ordinance.[14]

13. Johnson, *1 Corinthians*, 155.

14. Exod 12:14.

Oh, to Be Passed Over!

The Passover continues to be celebrated on (or around) the fifteenth day of Nisan (i.e., March/April in the Western calendar). It marks the beginning of Israel's covenant nationhood. The overarching theme of Passover is not atonement per se (this belongs to Yom Kippur), but redemption: God redeemed Israel by freeing them from their bondage to Egyptian slavery. The story is well known to many of us from an early age, being a particular Sunday school favorite. As representative of his own people, Moses had requested that Pharaoh allow them to leave and thus be rid of his oppression and tyranny. This was not just a plea evoked by sympathy, but in direct obedience to his Lord's command (see Exod 6:2–8).

A series of plagues unfolded, each more terrible than the last, yet God's people were miraculously preserved from the immediate effects of any of them. Although there were occasions when it seemed that Pharaoh would relent, he remained obdurate to the last, until God's final plague, the tenth, came upon the land of Egypt. The Israelites were to be spared this time, too, but only by availing themselves of the prescribed precautions. On the chosen day, at around midnight, the Lord would smite every firstborn son in Egypt, of both men and animals (Exod 11:5; 12:12). The only households to be exempt were those that had slaughtered a lamb and smeared some of its blood on their doorframes:

> The blood will be a sign for you on the houses where you are; and when I see the blood, I will pass over you. No destructive plague will touch you when I strike Egypt.[15]

Because of the severity of the punitive measures involved, it would be easy to think that only the Egyptians came under judgment, but that is not strictly true. The Israelites were subject to the same judgment, and were adjudged to have met its conditions whereby they would escape death on this night (providing they did so, of course). But what do we make of that opening phrase: "The blood will be a sign for you"? More specifically, in what context are we to understand the word "for"? Is it "as representative of" or "on behalf of"? It certainly proved to be both, but could there also be an element of the blood being a sign *to* them? I think this is more likely as it retains the same sense as that of the previous plagues being signs *to* the Egyptians. A sign always points to something of greater significance than itself, whether it is a road sign, a sign

15. Exod 12:13.

directing us toward the exit from an auditorium, or signs of the times. Some of Jesus' miracles were described as signs; so much so that some of those who came to hear him were rebuked for being so obsessed in their clamor for signs that they failed to see what they pointed to (Luke 11:29). It is not without some irony that Jesus' refusal to give the Pharisees the sign they demanded (Mark 8:11–13) began with a sign of sorts, had they been sufficiently observant to recognize it: "He sighed deeply" (v. 12a; Greek *anastenaxas*—literally "with a groan of exasperation").

The sign of the Passover blood might be said to consist in many features, both immediate and long term. For the people of that time, it pointed them in the direction of a greater awareness of God's authority, his grace, his redeeming power, his preservation, and his protection. It was also a sign in the sense of a guarantee of the pledge that God would be merciful to them, lest they imagine that he be given to bouts of sudden asperity, on the one hand, or sullen insouciance, on the other. Christ, as God's Passover Lamb, effected all of this by the shedding of his blood on Calvary's cross.

Privilege and Responsibility

I shall digress no further; we must return to the tabernacle. To say that the tabernacle was only for the people of God is but one side of the truth. It is not merely that they alone were allowed to enter its precincts, nor that they could do so as the fancy took them. Unlike the contributions to be made toward its construction (Exod 25:2), or the burnt (Lev 1; 6:8–13; 8:18–21; 16:24), grain (2; 6:14–23), or peace offerings (3; 7:11–37), which were voluntary, the sin offerings (4:1—5:13; 6:24–30; 8:14–17; 16:3–22) and guilt offerings (5:14—6:7; 7:1–6) were mandatory for all of them. They formed part of their cultic obligations, which were to be met in accordance with a divinely prescribed timetable. Whereas the burnt offerings and grain offerings were for consecration, and the fellowship offering, as you might expect, was for communion, the sin and guilt offerings were for propitiation. Moreover, with regards to sin and guilt, levels of intentionality and ignorance were not to be regarded as mitigating circumstances (see 4:13). Nor were they permitted to place their consciences into witness protection.

Although the priest was to act as intermediary on behalf of the people before their God, he too was culpable for his own transgression:

> If the anointed priest sins, bringing guilt on all the people, he must bring to the Lord a young bull without defect as a sin offering for the sin he has committed.[16]

Notice the priest's extra burden of responsibility. If the individual sins, that person is guilty; if the community sins, each person shares in their collective guilt; but if the anointed priest sins, he is guilty *and* brings guilt on the people. Jay Sklar paints the picture for us:

> Because of his elevated status, his sin's consequences are more serious, and the Lord could withhold his favour from the entire nation, (which they might experience in terms of defeat before enemies [see Josh 7:3–5] or lack of blessing on crops [2 Sam 21:1]). This would, in turn, prompt the priest (and the Israelites) to discover whether a wrong had been committed.[17]

Now, before we run away with the idea that the new covenant equivalent to the Old Testament priest is the pastor or elders, let us remind ourselves of Peter's counsel. Having established that Christ is God's chosen and precious living stone, he adds:

> You also, like living stones, are being built into a spiritual house to be a holy priesthood, offering spiritual sacrifices acceptable to God through Jesus Christ . . . you are a chosen people, a royal priesthood, a holy nation, a people belonging to God that you might declare the praises of him who called you out of darkness into his wonderful light. Once you were not a people, but now you are the people of God; once you had not received mercy, but now you have received mercy.[18]

This concept of the priesthood of all believers has been much debated down the years. I think Ernest Best gets as close as anyone to the hub of the matter when he argues that all members of the church are priests engaged in priestly service, though they do so not as individuals, but within the context of the corporate existence of the church.[19] I would go even further by saying that it is only our status in Christ that affords us that privilege; it is his Name alone by which we may claim the right of attendance in the presence of God. I know there is a tendency in some circles to preach that we may come boldly before the throne of grace

16. Lev 4:3.
17. Sklar, *Leviticus*, 111.
18. 1 Pet 2:5, 9–10.
19. Best, "1 Peter II 4–10," 270–93.

because of what Christ has now given us access to, and that is perfectly true; but it is still his Name by which we must claim that authority.

Relationship versus Fellowship

Sin that is unaccounted for mars our relationship with the Father; or does it? It certainly has an adverse effect on our capacity to express ourselves within the broadest parameters of that relationship, but this has more to do with fellowship. If I offend my wife, I do not thereby cease to be her husband until such a time as reparation is made. Fellowship may well be strained, the degree of which is often commensurate with the level of offense, but I continue to be related to her by marriage in precisely the same way as before the incident took place. Moreover, our measure of happiness is identifiably related to the absence of anything that would impinge upon that joy.

This same quality (or lack thereof) is applicable in our relationship with God. Objectively, only divorce can separate us. Subjectively, happiness is inextricably linked to holiness. Before we consider the biblical support for such a premise, please take a moment to consider the evidence of your own experience. Who has not known the sensation of being in God's presence and feeling as if you could almost touch him? And was not that intimacy of enjoyment possible for the simple reason that there was nothing by which it might be hindered? What about the other extreme: those times when you were in the company of others who were in harmony with God's Spirit, but for you heaven seemed as far away as it is possible to be? Was not your inability to enter in caused by a barrier on your part? An impure thought? A harsh word? A failure to behave in a way befitting a child of the Almighty?

Happy Are the Holy

We may well all be priests, but Christ is our high priest. This is what the writer to the Hebrews says of him at the very beginning of that letter, citing the psalmist:

> About the Son [the Father] says . . . "You have loved righteousness and hated wickedness; therefore God, your God, has set

> you above your companions by anointing you with the oil of joy."[20]

The man, Christ Jesus, was the happiest person there has ever been. Why? Because he was the holiest; he loved righteousness with the same intensity that he hated wickedness. It is not without significance that a more accurate reflection of the original Greek here translates "wickedness" as lawlessness. I am once again indebted to the scholarly erudition of Vine for the following:

> *Anomia* . . . is most frequently translated "iniquity" [and] "lawlessness" . . . In 1 John 3:4, the RV adheres to the real meaning of the word, "every one that doeth sin (a practice, not the committal of an act) doeth also lawlessness." This definition of sin sets forth its essential character as the rejection of the law, or will, of God and the substitution of the will of self.[21]

Little wonder that Christ hates it so. It militates against everything within him to be otherwise, for his righteous nature dictates that he must be righteous in character and conduct. We must persist to ensure that this basic spiritual dynamic is and remains true also of us.

PREPARATION ESSENTIAL

We shall see in subsequent chapters that each piece of furniture in the tabernacle represented a step toward worship in the presence of God, between the cherubim, in the Most Holy Place. We shall also see the furnishings as shadows of which Christ is the substance. But they are also types of the Christian experience in how we relate to his fulfilment. As such, it is important to remind ourselves that the freedoms we now have in God by the Holy Spirit do not permit us to dismiss as unnecessary the requirement to come before the Father's presence as a people prepared.

Remembering Where You Are

I don't get around as much as I used to. Gone are the days when I would see almost as many different church settings in a year as there are weeks. This doesn't disappoint me in the slightest; I point it out only to make

20. Heb 1:8–9; Ps 45:6–7.
21. Vine, *Expository Dictionary*, 647.

the reader aware that my current experience is somewhat restricted. Be that as it may, however, a long-held concern has been the lack of due reverence in the presence of God. It would be easy to fall into the trap of generalization by insisting that it seems to be a generational issue, and I must confess that the younger folk do appear to be particularly prone, but not exclusively so—not by a long chalk.

I have never belonged to what might be described as a traditional church. I say that with neither pride nor regret; it is merely a statement of fact. However, my wife and I do enjoy visiting traditional church buildings while on vacation. The attraction is partly the architecture, a little to do with the history, but in more recent times it has been an appreciation of the respect shown to the house of God. It is given because it is expected; some might even go so far as to say that it is demanded. In this respect, at least, I think those of us from less formal backgrounds could learn much that would aid us in our pursuit of Christian worship.

Alarm bells first began to ring for me around twenty years ago in a home group setting (almost quite literally). The church we were attending at the time operated the cell system for midweek groups, each gathering modeled on the three Ws: welcome, worship, and word. The welcome part was usually very low key, more often than not in the form of an icebreaker, whereby a short game would be played. If new additions were in attendance, everyone would be invited, in turn, to introduce themselves, including the visitors. This first part was intended to blow away the cobwebs, but usually contributed too much of a relaxed atmosphere for the rest of the evening. I remember one particular visitor being so traumatized by her experience of "the welcome" that we never saw her again.

Then came the worship, which was a loose term to include also praise and prayer. As a prelude to prayer, we would often be advised of things that were in need of such attention, some of which we might otherwise be blissfully unaware. Too often we would spend so much time discussing the specific requirement and its vagaries, or how one of the members remembered the one in need as a small boy coming to church with his mother, whose niece was married to the greengrocer, who lived on such-and-such a street . . . I think you get the picture. There was often not much time given over to actual prayer. The word part is as self-explanatory as it sounds. It usually consisted of the group leader recapping the major points from the previous Sunday's evening sermon and inviting questions from those who were in need of further clarity.

The incident to which I refer took place during one of those rare occasions when we actually got around to praying. In those days, we tended to get things back to front: we presented our shopping list of requests to God, as if he was some hired hand in a grocery store, before we considered acknowledging his worthiness for worship. We had just eased from one to the other when a mobile phone buzzed into life. Now, you could argue that the rest of us should have been so tuned into God that our attention was not so easily diverted. Well, we weren't and it was! So much so that the group leader had to announce an early benediction, while the phone user continued to chat by text for the next ten minutes or so, more oblivious to her surroundings than the rest of us had been. On such occasions, my body invariably goes into one of two auto-modes: I either give off an involuntary sardonic smirk, before shuffling away in nervous embarrassment or, more frequently, I become agitated to the point that my face resembles the surface of Mars, which is a clear signal for my wife gently but firmly to lead me away by the elbow, thus narrowly avoiding self-combustion.

While resisting most urges to jump on the bandwagon of blame, I think some lessons can—indeed must—be learned. Why is it that such occasions are now more commonplace? Why do many church gatherings so often fail to get beyond the bland and mediocre? What is it that conspires to make us believe that it is acceptable to blunder into God's presence as if he was a workmate on sick leave? And then we blame him for not turning up! What is it that is missing?

I believe two key ingredients are generally absent in our coming before God, both bred by familiarity, and the lack of each contemptible: reverence and respect. Like unruly and wayward parents, they produce after their own kind, and it is their firstborn offspring to which I wish to direct the reader's attention: unpreparedness. It is often said that procrastination is the thief of time. On some occasions, that may well have proved true. But lack of or inadequate preparation is the enemy of a fruitful outcome. I'm not referring here primarily to putting in the necessary hours for a forthcoming preaching engagement or insufficient practice for a solo performance at next weekend's evangelistic endeavor, though they may well be included. Rather, it is about making effective groundwork to come into God's presence for no other reason than simply to be there.

Working Things Out Requires Forward Planning

John the Baptist had but one mission in life. His removal from the scene having completed that mission was divinely orchestrated. Matthew identifies it by quoting from Isaiah:

> A voice of one calling in the desert, "Prepare the way for the Lord, make straight paths for him."[22]

In modern parlance, John was something of a one-trick pony. He had only a single message: "Repent, for the kingdom of heaven is near" (Matt 3:2). This was the sole weapon in his armory to prepare the way for the imminent coming of Messiah. Repentance has become so identified with initial conversion as a prerequisite for baptism that it is often not regarded as an ongoing requirement for the Christian. There can be no denying that repentance is the first step we take in coming under God's kingdom authority. It not only marks the commencement of our transitional journey from autonomy to God's government, but it also heralds the acceptance of his judgment on our condition before him, and the acknowledgment of our desperate need for his solution to the problem in which we find ourselves because of sin.

In its more restricted sense, salvation is a once-only experience. But it is also a continuing development, otherwise known as the process of sanctification, in which we engage synergetically with the Holy Spirit. In my early days as a Christian, I was exposed to the idea of repentance only in its limited application. From the very beginning, I was also a very keen Bible reader. For years, I was puzzled by what Paul meant by advising the saints at Philippi to "continue to work out [their] own salvation" (Phil 2:12). How could this possibly be? Salvation is not by works; it is by faith in what Jesus has done. We don't earn it; we simply receive it. Then it finally dawned on me. The recipients of Paul's letter were already Christians. They had come into salvation by the prescribed way. They were now being instructed to work out the daily practicalities of what they had previously laid hold.

Some years ago, an acquaintance related to me an experience of his while visiting a friend in California. Toward the end of his stay, he was shown a fertile valley, richly cultivated, and filled with an abundance of flora, fruit, and fauna. "You would barely believe it," began his guide, "but less than ten years ago this whole valley was a barren wilderness, with

22. Matt 3:3b; Isa 40:3.

only a handful of hardy shrubs punctuating the sandy hillsides. What you see before you is the product of one man's vision. He saw not what was but what might be. He bought the land, brought water to it, purchased just the right seeds for the terrain, and hired a small group of agriculturalists. He gave them only a brief outline of his plans and said, 'Here is the seed, here is the water, there is the soil: now, work out my purpose.'"

Fear without Favor

But notice also that I stopped short in the above citation. Not only were the Philippians to "continue to work out [their] own salvation," but they were to do so "with fear [Gk. *phobos*] and trembling [*tromos*]." I am not for one moment suggesting that such "fear and trembling" are products of anxiety or doubt regarding the assurance of salvation, but I do think the apostle is counseling his readers to treat the matter of their ongoing conduct with a certain measure of sobriety and a reverential response to God's grace. As far as the New Testament is concerned, this phrase is exclusively Pauline (see also 1 Cor 2:3; 2 Cor 7:15; Eph 6:5). Although his use of it is not without variety, its target is always Christian believers. However, the essence Paul seeks to convey is borrowed from the Old Testament, where the terms are applied chiefly in relation to unbelievers' experience of God's presence (Exod 15:16; Isa 19:16), and, by extension, the dread of facing those upon whom his favor rests (Deut 2:25; 11:25).

The absence of such "fear and trembling," if not checked, can pave the way for disdain and disrespect to gain a foothold. I can think of two notable examples, one from each Testament, with a common tie linking them as a pair. Let us deal with the New Testament first. The book of Acts is rightly renowned for its previously unprecedented demonstration of God's power on the earth. It could hardly be described as a revival, but it did provide the basis by which all subsequent revivals would be judged. Mass conversions, miraculous healings, supernatural transportation, speaking in unlearned tongues, and territorial advancement of the gospel are just some of its highlights. We can just about cope with the odd martyrdom and imprisonment, because these can also be viewed positively in the context of the furtherance of God's kingdom rule and Jesus' name being exalted. But what about that little incident tucked away in the fifth chapter?

The context may be alien to many of us, but in a spirit of common purpose, the believers were ensuring that the needs of the many poor among them were met from the purses of the relatively rich few. For no other reason than ease of administration, funds were brought to the apostles to distribute according to their perception of urgency. There is no suggestion of obligation except insofar as it was stirred in the heart by the Holy Spirit. A couple, named Ananias and Sapphira, sold a piece of land and brought part of the proceeds to the apostles for reallocation, but they kept back part of it for their own use (Acts 5:1–2). Now see what Peter said:

> Ananias, how is it that Satan has so filled your heart that you have lied to the Holy Spirit and have kept for yourself some of the money you received for the land? Didn't it belong to you before it was sold? And after it was sold, wasn't the money at your disposal? What made you think of doing such a thing? You have not lied to men but to God.[23]

Ananias was struck down dead and, three hours later, his wife joined him (Acts 5:5–10). Why was this so? We are not explicitly told, but given that the text makes clear that they were free to keep back as much or as little of the sum received implies that their sin may have been in claiming to give all when this was not the case. The phrases "kept back" in verse 2 and "kept for yourself" in verse 3 translate different Greek words in the original (*enosphisato* and *nosphisasthai*), though both are derived from the same root. To keep back obscures the fact that it was to do so deceptively. A more accurate reflection might be to appropriate or to purloin. What is particularly striking is the effect this had on those who were witness to it:

> And great fear seized all who heard what had happened . . . . Great fear seized the whole church and all who heard about these events.[24]

This, too, is *phobos*. In the context of the believer's relation to God, there may well be an element of being fearful lest we displease him, but the overriding theme is one of awe in his presence.

The other incident I mentioned takes us back to the tabernacle. I mention it only briefly here, as we shall consider it in more detail in due

23. Acts 5:3–4.

24. Acts 5:5b, 11.

course. It concerns the sons of Aaron. The Scripture says of Nadab and Abihu that "they offered unauthorized fire before the Lord, contrary to his command" and they died for it (see Lev 10:1–2). Moses wasted no time in drawing Aaron's attention to the gravity of his sons' misdemeanor:

> This is what the Lord spoke of when he said: "Among those who approach me I will show myself holy; in the sight of all people I will be honored."[25]

God's presence is first and foremost a holy presence, and we do well to remember that when we prepare to enter into it.

NO PARTIAL SACRIFICE

Immediately prior to giving more detailed instructions about the construction of the tabernacle, God had Moses relay the terms and conditions of his covenant to the people of Israel. Quite a sizeable delegation ascended the mountain: Moses, Aaron, Nadab, Abihu, and seventy elders of Israel (Exod 24:1). However, only Moses was permitted to come into God's presence (v. 2). Aaron and his sons may have been Israel's anointed priests, but Moses was God's chosen mediator of the covenant. This is how Scripture records Israel's response to his words:

> When Moses went and told the people all the Lord's words and laws, they responded with one voice, "Everything the Lord has said we will do."[26]

Unanimous Agreement

We must concern ourselves for the moment only with the facts as they are revealed to us in this text and any reasonable inference that may be drawn. Whether they meant what they said, or came to regret what they had said, or failed to live by the implications of what they said belongs to another time. It is who said what, and what they said it in relation to, that we must first establish. Those reasonable inferences I mentioned amount to the introduction of the word "all" in two other places: immediately prior to both "the people" and "responded." Thus, we have:

25. Lev 10:3.
26. Exod 24:3.

> When Moses went and told [all] the people all the Lord's words and laws, they [all] responded with one voice, "Everything the Lord has said we will do."

Allow me to be more explicit still: All Israel accepted all that Moses said regarding all that God had commanded about everything. I don't think this is taking too much of a liberty or investing the word of God with more than is legitimately implied. At that moment, they were entirely and utterly committed. This was not only true of them as a community of God's people; it was equally true of each of them as individuals within that community. Neither was it some happy accident or stroke of luck on their part (much less God's). Nothing less was demanded of them (see Exod 23:32–33).

As if to reinforce the point even further, and at the same time draw attention to precisely what was involved, we are told just a few verses later that, having had the Book of the Covenant read to them: "They responded, 'We will do everything the Lord has said; we will obey'" (Exod 24:7). I have absolutely no doubts concerning the sincerity of the words with which they voiced their commitment. I say this even with my hindsight of what were then future events. There is nothing in the text to suggest that God disputed their genuineness, even allowing for his foresight of those same episodes to come. But just in case, let us take a look at the back-up plan in verse 8: "Moses then took the blood [of the burnt offering], sprinkled it on the people and said, 'This is the blood of the covenant that the Lord has made with you in accordance with all these words.'" The humor of the occasion is not lost on Alec Motyer:

> So the Law of God was read to them, and they gave their assent . . . . Henceforth they will be wholly people of the revealed word. But—and how significant this is—no sooner had they made this enormous commitment than the shed blood was sprinkled over them like a huge covering of mercy. They were committed to obedience, that was their prime concern, but God knows that the best intentions fall constantly short and provided the blood of sacrifice to be ready to cater for each and every lapse from his revealed way.[27]

One of the dangers associated with looking back at history is that we know how things worked out from that point, because we are aware—or, at least, we are able to become aware—of more recent developments.

27. Motyer, *Message of Exodus*, 249.

Similarly, as Christian believers we are partakers of the new covenant in Christ and, therefore, look to episodes like those under consideration as those belonging to the old covenant. To the Israelites, however, this was *their* new covenant. So new was it, in fact, that they did not have the luxury of an old one with which to compare it. Of course, throughout the rest of the period covered by what we now know as the Old Testament, the Israelites had the prophets to remind them of their covenantal obligations. What they did not have was an apostle Paul figure pointing to the failures of a previous generation of God's people and saying things like: "These things happened as examples and were written down as warnings for us" (1 Cor 10:11a).

The Shedding of Blood Was Not Optional

The basis of Israel's covenanthood was blood. It was shed blood that had saved them in Egypt, and it would be the continuing shedding of blood in the tabernacle that would maintain their fellowship with God throughout the coming generations. We have looked at this briefly already and will consider it in more detail as the work progresses. But for now, I would like to draw the reader's attention to that phrase used by Moses and cited above: "the blood of the covenant" (Exod 24:8). As if to provide a clue as to the journey we are about to take, this is what Alan Cole has to say about it:

> This phrase reappears in the solemn phraseology of the Last Supper (Matt 26:28). Christ himself would be, at the cross, not only the mediator of a covenant (like Moses), but also the sacrifice that initiated that covenant.[28]

All the divine covenants were essentially covenants initiated by blood. This is how Palmer Robertson defines such covenants: "A covenant is a bond in blood sovereignly administered," before adding: "When God enters into a covenantal relationship with men, he sovereignly institutes a life-and-death bond."[29] I have written extensively on this subject elsewhere.[30] What concerns us primarily here, however, is not the covenants of which Moses and Christ were mediators per se, but specifically the blood relating to those covenants.

28. Cole, *Exodus*, 194.
29. Robertson, *Christ of the Covenants*, 4.
30. See Woodall, *Covenant*.

William Gilders identifies Moses' "sprinkling" of the blood on the community of Israel as "a striking ritual act."[31] It was certainly that. The context suggests that Gilders's use of the word "striking" is both in the sense that it was at the time unprecedented and remained unique in Israel's recorded history thereafter. Nowhere else do we read of the entire community being subject to being so literally covered ("dashed" NRSV) in covenant blood. But we must also consider what we understand by Gilders's use of the word "ritual." We are somewhat hampered in our application of the word to Old Testament practices, as there is no direct Hebrew word of the period for which it might be an accurate translation.

This is not to say that there are no occasions where the primary features normally associated with ritual do not appear. There are plenty, but we must be careful that we do not see ritual where it does not exist. A ritual may also be symbolic, but there is a distinction between the two and they should not be used interchangeably. A ritual is essentially a communicative activity that actually achieves something in its own right (or rite). For example, the application of blood to the right ear lobe, right thumb, and big toe of the right foot for candidates to the priesthood is rich in symbolism (Exod 29:19–20), but there is evidence also that it effected actual change in those so presented (v. 21).

Similar caution must be applied when attaching symbolism to an event or episode. We have already established that a sign is something that always points to something of more significance than itself, but is the symbol in question univalent—as we seem to have a tendency to assume—or is this one of those occasions when it might reasonably be regarded as multivalent? Many prophecies of the Old Testament fall into this latter category where they often find multiple fulfilment or outworking by degrees.

A Better Covenant to Come?

As far as the sacrificial aspect of the Old Testament offerings is concerned, only one contrast is worthy of our attention here. It falls to our faithful anonymous friend, the author of the epistle to the Hebrews, to be our guide once more. Both the symbolism and the ritualistic aspects of the first covenant are identified, along with its inherent inadequacy:

31. Gilders, *Blood Ritual*, 39.

> The blood of goats and bulls and the ashes of a heifer sprinkled on those who are ceremonially unclean sanctify them so that they are outwardly clean. How much more, then, will the blood of Christ, who through the eternal Spirit offered himself unblemished to God, cleanse our consciences from acts that lead to death, so that we may serve the living God.[32]

So far, so good! But, so far, the "much more" is only hinted at. Is it "much more of the same," which still leaves us only "outwardly clean" and in need of an annual top-up? We must read on before we look back:

> For this reason Christ is the mediator of a new covenant, that those who are called may receive the promised eternal inheritance—now that he has died as a ransom to set them free from the sins committed under the first covenant.[33]

What "promised eternal inheritance" is this? This is where we need to look back, ostensibly to the words of Jeremiah, but the writer to the Hebrews eases our burden by citing him in the previous chapter:

> The time is coming, declares the Lord, when I will make a new covenant with the house of Israel and with the house of Judah. It will not be like the covenant I made with their forefathers when I took them by the hand to lead them out of Egypt, because they did not remain faithful to my covenant, and I turned away from them. This is the covenant I will make with the house of Israel after that time, declares the Lord. I will put my laws in their minds and write them on their hearts. I will be their God and they will be my people. No longer will a man teach his neighbour, or a man his brother, saying, "Know the Lord," because they will all know me, from the least of them to the greatest. For I will forgive their wickedness and will remember their sins no more.[34]

A Much Better Covenant!

What a promise! What an inheritance! Let us take a closer look at some of the benefits of this new covenant:

32. Heb 9:13–14.
33. Heb 9:15.
34. Heb 8:8b–12; Jer 31:31–34.

No longer merely outwardly clean

To help us to understand this a little more clearly, we need to avoid the temptation to separate Jeremiah's words from their immediate context. Israel's recurring obstacle under the terms of the old covenant was that their hearts of flesh remained largely unchallenged and unchanged by God's Spirit. They could hardly accuse God of leaving them to their own devices to figure out the problem for themselves (see also Jer 32:40; Ezek 37:14, 23). But the solution was always beyond their grasp. It was meant to be. In order for a remedy to be welcomed, a crisis must first be precipitated. Who among us has not discovered, along with Israel of old, that a stubborn heart requires the most invasive operation and the most skilled of surgeons? The question we must ask ourselves is: Do we possess a heart of ice or one of clay? They each respond differently to the application of heat: one will melt, the other harden.

Intimate fellowship with the Father

The relationship between this and the previous point should not be underestimated. Indeed, intimacy with the Father is dependent upon an unpolluted heart, the level of one being governed by the measure of the other. To put it more simply: pure hearts allow us to see God (Matt 5:8). What did Jesus mean by this? I used to think it was the promise of future blessing as a reward for having met a present condition. This may well be included, but I'm unconvinced that it is the full extent of what was intended. To see God in the present is not so much akin to intimacy of fellowship with him, but develops from it: it is to cultivate a spiritual perception of his actions and to nurture a sacred pleasure in his Being. Though I doubt whether it could be scientifically defined, there does seem to be a direct correlation between pleasure and desire.

A universal awareness of God's dealings with humanity?

This is not an easy passage to understand, though it is apparently not difficult to misunderstand. The above subheading (without the closing question mark) is, in my opinion, a gross misrepresentation of the text, which fails to take due cognizance of the context. Both Jeremiah and the writer to the Hebrews were writing for the illumination of God's covenant people of their respective generations. This "know[ing] the Lord" was to be a product of him putting his "laws in their minds" and writing "them on their hearts." Thus, those of whom this proved to be true would not need another person, his neighbor, fellow citizen, or brother, to convey such basic information. Evangelistic effort is still required for the furtherance of the gospel message, pastors are still vital under shepherds providing care for God's flock, and godly teachers are indispensable tools for equipping the saints with instruction on how to bring practical application to the revelation they have received. These ministries, along with those of apostles and prophets, will cease to be necessary one day: when "we all reach unity in the faith and in the knowledge of the Son of God and become mature, attaining to the whole measure of the fulness of Christ" (see Eph 4:7–13). We ain't there yet, folks!

Everlasting forgiveness of sins

An interesting concept arises here in relation to God's omniscience: as an attribute, it is always subject to his divine will. Thus, his knowledge of something—in this case, our sins—can be terminated if he wills it so. The development of the English verb *will* masks this somewhat, but this is precisely what is meant by the text in both the original Hebrew and the Greek: "I *will* forgive their wickedness and *will* remember their sins no more" (Jer 31:34; Heb 9:12). Moreover, once God's will has been exerted in that direction, any subsequent lapse on our part cannot bring back into play that which he has previously willed to forgive and forget. They are gone forever, never to be recalled. That is not to say, of course, that such incidents are obliterated from the historical record; they took place. But they are no longer held against us and never can be.

SUMMARY

The eagle-eyed among you may have noticed that for a chapter entitled "The Tabernacle of Worship," there has been precious little mention of worship throughout. Much depends upon how we define worship and what our perception is of the purpose of the tabernacle in the wilderness. Whatever else it might have been, the tabernacle was only ever intended to be a shadow of which Christ would be the substance. In their own way, each was designed to equip a sin-cursed people to engage in a process of purification by which they might come into the presence of their God. The basis of the relationship between the two was always covenant, that he might be *their* God and they would be *his* people. Reflecting something of his nature, such a people must be a spiritual people and a people of integrity, a combination forming the essence of true worship (John 4:23–24).

2

The Brazen Altar

As Christian believers of all persuasions and denominational allegiances, we need to understand that God has set aside the first sacrificial system in order to establish the validity and veracity of the second. Perhaps it is time for some of us to follow his lead in this regard. That said, however, our task of working toward a fuller recognition of the precepts attached to the second is greatly enhanced by absorbing the lessons to be learned from the picture of the first. This, of course, is a principle that is always true of type and antitype, but it seems especially so here. To that end, and in preparation for what is to come, I must ask you to read the following Scriptures, which are too lengthy to cite in full:

Lev 1:1–13; Heb 10:1–12.

CONSTANT ACTIVITY

One of the first things that even a casual observer must notice about the tabernacle in general is the absence of anywhere to sit. Even the mercy seat was devoid of that characteristic. More specifically, there were no seating arrangements in the courtyard area, which housed the brazen (i.e., bronze, which speaks of judgment when used in conjunction with fire) items. Non-Levites within Israel were only permitted to enter as far as the brazen altar, to which they brought their sacrifices to the priest on duty. The priests themselves officiated at this altar and at the brazen laver in the courtyard, and as far as the veil inside the Holy Place (aka Tent of Meeting). Only the high priest was allowed beyond the second veil into the Holy of Holies (or Most Holy Place), and he wasn't inclined to linger in God's presence longer than necessary in case the sacrifice offered proved unacceptable. The tabernacle was not a place of rest.

Always on the Go, Until . . .

What is perhaps not so clear from the Old Testament narratives is just how constantly active were the priests in the tabernacle. Apart from those occasions when everything was being packed away to be transported elsewhere, actually in transit, or being set up again on arrival at their destination, the tabernacle was in continual daily use for over forty years. That amounts to well in excess of fourteen thousand days of virtually ceaseless sacrifice in the tabernacle alone, which was then continued when it was replaced by the temple. We have the writer to the Hebrews to thank for clarifying the picture for us:

> Day after day every priest stands and performs his religious duties; again and again he offers the same sacrifices, which can never take away sins.[1]

Perhaps not entirely meaningless, but certainly ineffective and presumably exhausting. Now look at the contrast:

> But when this priest [i.e., Christ Jesus] had offered for all time one sacrifice for sins, he sat down at the right hand of God. Since that time he waits for his enemies to be made his footstool, because by one sacrifice he has made perfect for ever those who are being made holy.[2]

Now, I wouldn't want to be guilty of investing the idea of Jesus with a sinful nature, nor even an air of effeminacy. However, I cannot help but think of him as he sat down delicately rubbing his partly clenched hand against the left lapel of his tunic, before inspecting his finger ends to see if his exertions had caused him to damage a nail. My immediate and most profound apologies if this damages your sensitivities regarding the Holy One of God, but that phrase, "he sat down," tickles me. It reminds me of one of my very first tasks as an apprentice at the local colliery, having only

1. Heb 10:11.
2. Heb 10:12–14.

recently left school. I soon discovered from others of my ilk that the way to prosper was to work very hard at doing very little, at which I became very good.

On the day in question, I had been left alone in the workshop, awaiting the arrival of someone to assign my daily duties, when I noticed the office floor was becoming increasingly wet. I was soon standing in almost an inch of water, when I noticed in the corner a mop and bucket. Even as I began frantically attacking the deluge, I saw myself as others might if they were viewing the scene from a distance: an object of laughter and ridicule. But somebody had to do something practical; the thing was that what I was doing seemed to bring no visible solution to the problem. Then the foreman arrived; with a knowing smile, he calmly and confidently waded over to the same corner from which I had extracted the mop and bucket, and nonchalantly switched off the tap. He, too, sat down, before asking that I put the kettle on for a cuppa.

Seated, Until . . .

The reasons given for Jesus sitting down are perhaps as illuminating as the fact of it. There are two and, though both have yet to come to fruition, the unfolding of each is guaranteed by Christ's achievement on the cross. Ray Stedman[3] is correct to draw our attention to the allusion between the first and the psalmist's glimpse into heaven:

> The Lord says to my Lord: "Sit at my right hand until I make your enemies a footstool for your feet."[4]

It was common practice in ancient times for the victor to be seen standing upon the neck of the vanquished as a demonstration of their conquest (see also Josh 10:24). In the most humiliating way, it presented the defeated foe as utterly impotent. But I think the reference harks back even further than David. Cast your minds, if you will, to the fall of Adam in the garden, specifically the part dealing with God's curse upon the serpent:

> Cursed are you above all livestock and all the wild animals! You will crawl on your belly and you will eat dust all the days of your life. And I will put enmity between you and the woman, and

3. Stedman, *Hebrews*, 105.

4. Ps 110:1.

> between your offspring and hers; he will crush your head, and you will strike his heel.[5]

In theological terms, this is known as the *protevangelium*, a compound of two Greek words, *protos* and *euangelion*, which together refer to the Bible's first mention of the gospel of salvation. (Some commentators refer to it as "the maternal promise."[6]) Thus, the verse is said to have exclusively prophetic soteriological implications. Kent Hughes puts it this way:

> What we have here is an astounding gospel prophecy because God's curse upon the serpent turned into a word of grace, giving what has been recognized from the second century AD as the "first gospel," the protevangelium, when the post-apostolic fathers, Justin Martyr and Irenaeus, preached the woman's offspring (literally "seed") here referred to Christ, who would crush Satan's head.[7]

It would be foolish even to begin to challenge the idea that it has prophetic significance that relates especially to soteriology. However, my doubts are concerned with the notion that it is exclusively so; or, at least, that it relates only to the initiation phase of salvation and not also to the sanctification process that follows: the being saved and the becoming saved.

Sharing the Spoils of Victory

John Calvin makes a point worthy of consideration when he posits as fact that the Hebrew word translated "seed/offspring" (i.e., *zerah*) is not singular but a collective noun. He then draws attention to what the apostle Paul has to say in his closing remarks to the believers at Rome: "The God of peace will soon crush Satan under your [i.e., corporate] feet" (Rom 16:20).[8] While it is true that *zerah* is often used literally of a harvest and metaphorically of descendants in the plural, it is not unusual to find the emphasis being placed on a single seed producing such bounty. The use of the personal pronoun "he" suggests this to be the case in the Genesis account.

5. Gen 3:14b–15.
6. E.g., Berkhof, *Systematic Theology*, 279.
7. Hughes, *Genesis*, 85.
8. Calvin, *Genesis*, 170–71.

Moreover, the link to Paul's reference is not misplaced. But it must be seen in the context of those Paul had earlier described as "co-heirs" (Rom 8:17), who thereby become also co-victors in the conquest over Satan and his emissaries, perhaps most notably those whose aim is to cause division, obstruction, and deceit (16:17–18). Did not Jesus himself say in anticipation of his imminent crucifixion: "Unless a grain of wheat falls to the ground and dies, it remains only a single seed. But if it dies, it produces many seeds" (John 12:24)?

In terms of God's kingdom, there is a constant tension in the New Testament between the now and the not yet. Even much of the not yet has already been achieved, but has yet to find practical application or expression. Nowhere is this more evident than in the letter to the Romans (see especially chapter 8). Satan was dealt a death blow at the cross; his end is inevitable, but still he continues. He wins some skirmishes and loses others. His wins will not change the outcome, yet each loss is a further crushing blow, leading to his final binding (Rev 20:3) and being cast into the lake of fire (v. 10). Figuratively speaking, he will thus be beneath Jesus' feet.

But the enemies forming Christ's footstool are plural. What might these enemies be? They are not identified and there is insufficient evidence elsewhere to piece together an accurate picture without trespassing into the realm of conjecture. Could it be the hordes of Satan? It could be, but we are not told. Might it be those who obstinately remain opposed to the gospel and, thereby, stubbornly refuse to yield to the Lord's authority? It might be, but we don't know for sure. Again, I am reminded of a dear college lecturer who, when presented with such occasions, would gently rest his hands palm-side down on his ample Welsh tummy and simply sing in his lilt of the valleys: "Where Scripture is silent, it is sagacious not to speculate." At the time, I didn't even know what the word "sagacious" meant; you could say my sagacity did not extend that far. As soon as the college library opened after lunch, I made it my business to discover its meaning and immediately concurred with the lecturer. I should like to say that I have succeeded in emulating Ieuan Jones in more ways than I have. Sadly for me, coming close to the number of Sunday roasts he must have put away is of no spiritual benefit. Let us, therefore, hold unswervingly to those things of which Scripture gives us confidence to be certain: it is better to be a friend than an enemy, and the last enemy to be defeated will be death (1 Cor 15:25–26). When death is no more, Christ's wait for all his enemies to be made his footstool will be over, whoever or whatever they are.

Still We Come to the Altar

Although coincidental, it is no accident that death's end and the sanctification process of the saints will be coterminous. Both are inextricably linked, not just to each other, but also to the one sacrifice of Christ. Christian believers are holy because of our standing in Christ; we are progressively becoming holy as our standards of interrelational conduct increasingly become more Christlike. Once again, I am indebted to Ray Stedman:

> It is both an accomplished fact (Heb 10:10) and a continuing process (v. 14), a phenomenon found frequently in Scripture. We may not understand such a mystery, but we can revel in its reality, as the writer intends us to do. All progress in the spiritual life comes from personally apprehending a fact that is already true. To put it simply, we must see what we already are by God's grace, in order to manifest that by godly behavior.[9]

All this would have been unimaginable to the tabernacle priests. It is not so much that they would have thought it impossible, they simply would not have thought about it at all. As far as they were concerned, the deleterious stench of sacrificial death would always be necessary as long as the people continued in sinful disobedience, and that wasn't going away any time soon. They were right, of course. It is not as if we, having the advantage of coming to God via the perfect sacrifice, no longer need daily to approach Jesus in his role of the brazen altar's antitype and plead the blood to cleanse us again, life for life, the innocent for the penitent. Only then may we take the next step toward the now more widely accessible presence of God.

The correlation between type and antitype is often viewed exclusively in respect of their similar traits. But we must not be too hasty to dismiss obvious contrasts. Christ's sacrificial act of atonement at Calvary was essentially God's gift to humanity to effect the reconciliation of relationship between the two. Under no condition or circumstance could the sacrifices offered under the terms of the old covenant be described as humanity's gift to God: they were necessary obligations. Are we then free from any such responsibilities? Let the writer to the Hebrews continue to be our guide:

9. Stedman, *Hebrews*, 106.

> We have an altar from which those who minister at the tabernacle have no right to eat. The high priest carries the blood of animals into the Most Holy Place as a sin offering, but the bodies are burned outside the camp. And so Jesus also suffered outside the city gate to make the people holy through his own blood. Let us, then go to him outside the camp, bearing the disgrace he bore . . . . Through Jesus, therefore, let us continually offer to God a sacrifice of praise—the fruit of lips that confess his name. And do not forget to do good and to share with others, for with such sacrifices God is well pleased.[10]

With what do we imagine God to be well pleased: empty ritual or righteous expressions of faith; seeking to earn divine favor by lavish donations of material splendor at the expense and exploitation of the poor and impoverished, or genuine heart-triggered praise toward God and compassion toward humankind? This is not a trick question. The only "trick" involved is to be led by the Spirit and not by the flesh, or, at least, not by flesh that has yet to be presented on the altar of burnt offering.

THE SHEDDING OF BLOOD

> Any Israelite or any alien living among them who eats any blood—I will set my face against that person who eats blood and will cut him off from his people. For the life of a creature is in the blood, and I have given it to you to make atonement for yourselves on the altar; it is the blood that makes atonement for one's life.[11]

> [Moses] said, "This is the blood of the covenant, which God has required you to keep." In the same way, he sprinkled with the blood both the tabernacle and everything used in its ceremonies. In fact, the law requires that nearly everything be cleansed with blood, and without the shedding of blood there is no forgiveness.[12]

10. Heb 13:10–16.
11. Lev 17:10–11.
12. Heb 9:20–22.

Would You Be Free?

The first thing I can remember from my introduction to Christianity was the emphasis given to blood. Of course, this wasn't just any blood, but specifically the blood of Jesus, though this wasn't so easily identifiable to a recent convert. Being peppered with questions like "Have you been washed in the blood?" "Has the blood cleansed you?" and "Don't you think it's about time you allowed the blood to set you free?" might not have sounded out of place at the local branch gathering of the Bram Stoker Appreciation Society. So, what is it about blood? Why must blood be shed? And what is so uniquely effective about Jesus' blood? Is it only symbolic or is there truly power in the blood?

Let us deal with that last question first. And let me begin by removing the implied antithetical premise: symbolism does not necessarily negate potency. There are several accounts, both in the Old Testament and some of the related halakic midrashim (e.g., Sipra[13]), where the blood of slain animals is said to have been tossed, daubed, smeared, and sprinkled with tangible effects. Purification, consecration, and protection may well be attributed to some kind of pre-medical placebo effect by the cynic, but there is also evidence of recognizable transformation in the form of empowerment for tasks previously deemed beyond the scope of the recipient. Symbolism, yes; but hardly impotent.

The primary principle we must establish and explore is the Bible's identification of blood with life. Much of what Scripture has to say on the matter is in the context of the prohibition of blood consumption (Deut 12:16, 23–25; 15:19–23). Although each occasion cited is with reference to the non-cultic slaughter of domestic animals for food, the principle attached to them is more far reaching: "the blood is the life" (12:23b). It is interesting that it is clearly not the flesh that is identified with the life of the animal, as this was subject to no such injunction. You might even think, given from what we know of the creation account (Gen 2:7), that the breath might somehow equate to life, but breath might be said to be rather life-giving or life-sustaining than life itself.

Although no mention is made of any penalties for disobedience, the fact that conformity attracts certain benefits would seem to suggest that the converse is equally true. If not eating blood results in things going well for the compliants and their children, because such conduct will be regarded as "doing right in the eyes of the Lord" (Deut 12:25), then

13. Nebada 4:10.

we may reasonably infer that defiance would be considered as doing wrong in the eyes of the Lord and, thereby, bring about its own negative consequences. The prohibition is further reinforced by the introductory admonition, which may be lost in some English translations. "Take care," "Beware," and "Be sure" appear as *hazaq* in the original, which is often used of a severe prevailing attitude, even if in conjunction with a positive outcome.

Well, that answers the question about the importance of blood. Or does it? I think the best we may say is that it resolves as much as Scripture makes clear without us resorting to trespass beyond acceptable limitations of interpretation. Blood is important because it is equated with life, but we do not know why this is so. We might hazard a guess that life/blood must not be consumed for the same reason that we are commanded not to murder: all life belongs to God and it must be returned to him and his pleasure. But there is no explicit biblical reference to this effect and any implications require considerable hypothetical leaps of everything but faith. This is yet another of those occasions where we must consign our query to the "I don't know" folder, and leave it at that. What we can know we do know, and that is sufficient for our study here.

Cleansing Properties Released

Why the blood had to be shed almost falls into the same category. The difference here, however, is that any guesswork may be considered more educated. That having been said, my conscience still requires me to make clear that what follows is only my opinion, and I posit it without any demands that it be regarded as anything more. I believe that the reason that blood must be shed in relation to sin is linked to what we have already discussed about the equation of blood with life. Life—any life—is God's most precious gift. Sin is the most serious affront to his righteous Being. For the moment, cast aside the idea of specific sinful acts, though they obviously carry the same taintedness and are particularly relevant in relation to the brazen altar, as we shall see.

Rather, I am thinking here about sin as a principle that governs our deeds, thoughts, motivation, life choices, even those things that might otherwise be regarded as noble. Again, it is not the things themselves but of what they are products, what is it that tarnishes them, and why the prophet Isaiah was forced to concede that "all our righteous acts are like filthy rags" (Isa 64:6). It is that for which we have our first father, Adam, to thank, and that for which a second Adam was required to come and die; it is original sin.

I realize there is a tendency, even within the ranks of those who lay claim to evangelicalism, to avoid the use of the phrase "original sin," and for a variety of reasons. If you prefer, let me put it this way: I am referring to the origin of sin as it relates to the human condition thereafter of unavoidable strayfulness from God's holy standard. I find it impossible to reconcile in my mind that anyone who accepts the authority of Scripture could at the same time deny the concept of original sin. It relates both to an insistence on the historicity of Adam and Eve as real persons, the truthfulness of the Bible's narrative regarding their fall in the garden, and the New Testament account of both those things and God's remedy. Paul could hardly be more emphatic: "sin came into the world through one man . . . [and] the judgment following this one trespass brought condemnation" (Rom 5:12–16).

What concerns us here is not my view of sin or that of the reader, but the seriousness with which Scripture reveals God to regard it. Therein lies the key to our understanding of why blood had to be shed. The extent of the atrocity demanded the highest measure of atonement (if, indeed, atonement can be measured). The highest price had to be paid, such is the intensity of God's distaste for sin. And we must remember that it is God who is affronted here. This is why such atonement is rightly spoken of as a propitiation (1 John 4:10 NASB) rather than merely an expiation (though expiation is inevitably included). Expiation deals with an object, whereas propitiation has to do with a person. It is not so much God's holiness as an attribute that is offended, but God in his holiness.

Perhaps it is because of an overemphasis of the love of God, the kindness of God, the meekness and tenderness of Jesus, and the gentleness of the Holy Spirit that many of us find the idea of God's wrath so uncomfortable and discomfiting. Well, if the Bible truly is to be the basis of our understanding of God—as much as we are able to understand anything at all—then we need to acknowledge what it has to say about the wrath of God, what attracts it, and how it is to be averted. It is impossible to overemphasize God's love or kindness, but we commit great disservice to both when we fail to view them in the context of his justice and his holiness. Bizarrely, in so doing we fail to grasp the full extent of his love and kindness, because of which he took the initiative to ensure that appropriate propitiation was made that his wrath might thereby be averted.

It is in this broad context that we must view the sacrificial offerings that were required to be carried out at the brazen altar in the tabernacle. They were effective in the following ways:

- they demonstrated the Israelites' obedience to the command;
- they instructed the Israelites concerning the nature of God;
- they were a reminder of the utter sinfulness of sin;
- though each member of the Israelite community was personally responsible for their own actions, they each became aware of the commonality of their shared sinful experience before a holy God; and
- they proved their own inadequacy to deal with anything other than external issues and, thereby, the need for the shadow ultimately to give way to the substance typified by them.

Temporary Purification Only

On this last point, you find no finer apologist than the writer to the Hebrews:

> The blood of goats and bulls and the ashes of a heifer sprinkled on those who are ceremonially unclean sanctify them so that they are outwardly clean . . . But those sacrifices are an annual reminder of sins, because it is impossible for the blood of bulls and goats to take away sins.[14]

The sanctification in view here is not what we might understand as the inner working of the Holy Spirit to make us progressively more Christlike. A couple of clues to its true identity may be gleaned from the subjects' condition prior to such "sanctification" taking effect (they were "ceremonially unclean"), and the modifier attached to the act of sanctification: "so that they [become] outwardly clean." This being the case, perhaps a better translation might be to substitute "sanctify" for "purify."

Similarly, at first glance, the final clause seems to be at odds with some of the language of Leviticus in this regard where the idea of forgiveness appears repeatedly (e.g., Lev 4:20–35; 5:10–18). The Hebrew verb used throughout is *salach*, which means "to become favorably disposed towards," where this was previously not the case. While this may well be attendant upon the removal of guilt associated with moral violation, it is

14. Heb 9:13; 10:3–4.

not necessarily so. Again, purification is at least as likely to be implied; following a period of ritual uncleanness after a bodily discharge might be one example (see Lev 15). The design was not absolution, but acceptance for attendance in the sight of God.

A Better Sacrifice

The blood of Jesus achieved what the animal blood of the sacrificial system could not. It is not as if any blame could necessarily be attached to the Israelites' level of commitment to the cause, certainly not initially. It reminds me of my report book from high school. At the end of each year, the subject teachers would give an overall grade based on a combination of course work, attendance, and conduct in class. The form master would also write a comment by way of appraisal. The first year evoked just one word from Mr. Thurlow: "Trying!" It doubled at the end of the second year to "Still trying!" Year three also had an extra word added, though it also gave a slightly different perspective to the previous two: "Still very trying!"

This just about sums up Israel's Old Testament history: they both tried and were trying. Indeed, a case could be made that this might equally be applied to the people of God under both covenants. The irony is that it now need not be so. This is not to suggest that Christians should not make every effort to live in accordance with their calling as representatives of Christ on earth, but we do so from a position of strength that was unavailable to our spiritual forefathers.

Remember me mentioning earlier that the brazen altar in the tabernacle was representative of Israel's persistent attempts to deal with the problem of their sins *post*-conversion? This continued to be necessary because the blood of the Passover lamb was precisely that: a symbol of their evasion of God's judgment in Egypt. It was effective in that and that alone. With us, however, it is quite different. The blood that rescued us from the prospect of hell at Calvary avails for us still. How are we free from sin? There is power in the blood of Jesus! How might we live as those who have been freed from the burden of sin? There is power in the blood of Jesus! At the risk of offending some readers, it is a nonsense to suggest that the cross was unnecessary. God considered it to be vitally necessary, and I think we can trust his judgment here—quite literally.

GETTING RID OF GUILT

What is this burden of sin from which Christians have been freed? Is it sin itself, which might easily be described as burdensome? Or is it another "quality" that attaches itself to sin and remains even when the sin has been dealt with? I believe it can be both, but it is this latter aspect that concerns us here: guilt. One of the five principal sacrificial offerings of the Old Testament was the guilt offering. It would be misleading for me to suggest that it was *the* most important, but it takes its place near the top as one of only two mandatory offerings (the other being the sin offering).

Guilt Detached from Awareness

I should also make clear at the outset that the guilt in question may well include an inner conviction of wrongdoing, but the absence of such an assault on an individual's personal conscience did not remove the requirement to make the offering. What do I mean by that? Allow me to explain. Primarily, the guilt offering (or trespass offering) was similar to the sin offering: neither was to be the object of a voluntary decision, both were made in respect of violations committed without malice aforethought, and each brought cleansing from defilement.

There were, however, a couple of notable differences between the two. First of all, though the Lord's honor had been challenged by the specific sin associated with each offering (see Lev 4:1–2; 5:14–15), the guilt offering was particularly annexed to transgressions against a third party, for which restitution was required to be made. Such compensation was never like for like, but always included a multiplication factor (for example, 20 percent) added to the value of the stolen property or that upon which a wrongful claim had been made (v. 16).

Secondly, and just as significantly, not only was past ignorance no defense, but also continuing unawareness in the present was no obstacle to the impartation of guilt:

> If a person sins and does what is forbidden in any of the Lord's commands, even though he does not know it, he is guilty and will be held responsible. He is to bring to the priest as a guilt offering a ram from the flock, one without defect and of the proper value. In this way the priest will make atonement for him for the wrong he has committed unintentionally, and he will be

> forgiven. It is a guilt offering; he has been guilty of wrongdoing against the Lord.[15]

This, in turn raises a couple of questions (or, at least, two that I wish to address here). First of all, to what precisely does the individual's ignorance pertain? Is it the act itself, which incidentally just happens also to be a forbidden one? Or are they fully aware of having committed the act, but failed to realize that this extended beyond the parameters of God's tolerance? The text is unclear, and the context is inconclusive. Even what we are able to glean elsewhere from Scripture does not help us to determine which is the most likely. In such cases, I often find that one of two paths remain open to us. Either we must accept our present incapacity and hold the two in tension until such a time as our understanding is improved, or acknowledge the probability that both options are equally viable unless specified otherwise.

My second question in relation to this is more easily and immediately resolved: if an individual commits an unintentional sin, and is unaware of having done so, what provokes the need to make a sacrificial guilt offering? Again, there appear to be two alternative views. The first is that initial ignorance becomes subsequent awareness, at which point appropriate action is taken (see ESV). The more commonly prevailing view, especially in the rabbinic tradition, is that the individual remains in the dark concerning the specific nature of the sinful act having been committed. They thence either bring a guilt offering on a balance of probabilities, that is, it is likely that they will have sinned, or suspect this to be the case by other means. The obvious challenge to either option is that if the act committed (or omitted) was one that would otherwise have required compensatory reparation to be made, then ignorance of what and toward whom would render this impossible.

But what could feasibly arouse suspicion in the first place? If there are injured third parties involved, then they might take it upon themselves to make their woundedness known. Even if they lacked the confidence to be forthright, a few subtle hints dropped here and there might do the trick. This is something with which those involved in a long-term personal relationship would identify. It is certainly something to which I can relate as a husband, and I guess my wife would say the same thing. Dare I suggest that we are not alone? Need convincing? Here goes, then . . .

15. Lev 5:17–19.

Cavalier or Careless?

I am approaching my mid-sixties and my memory for more recent events is becoming increasingly frayed. The distant past, on the other hand, seems to lurk around every corner, its lingering hope to draw me out into a battlefield of as yet undetonated recollections. My wife is a little older and marginally more given to bouts of forgetfulness. So far, there have been no serious consequences, but time will tell if this remains so. Nevertheless, our developing condition has produced irritating little niggles. For example, during the course of this last week Barbara had a booked hair appointment in town. It is less than four miles away and, therefore, only a short bus ride, but the local public transport is such that we only have one bus per hour in either direction. The next one was due in around ten minutes and the pots needed washing from lunch. "Don't worry," I said, "leave them to me and you get off. Don't hurry back; it will all be done when you return." So, off she toddled.

You can probably guess what is coming next. You may even have played exactly the same scene out in your own life. It's not as if my inaction was motivated by deliberate malice. I just thought, "I know; I've plenty of time, I'll just check out that website while it's fresh in my memory." Except by the time I'd got through with that, there was nothing else even remotely fresh in my memory, so I decided to pour myself a wee dram and listen to some music through the headphones—and fell asleep. In my dream, Andy Latimer had been taken ill at the last minute and I had to step in to take his place, fronting the seventies prog-rock band Camel. Everything was going well until we had to take to the stage for the final encore. The screaming fans seemed to be joining in one voice to make a song request, but I could barely make it out: "What about . . ." something or other. "The Box"? "The Fox"? I also began to feel an annoying tugging at my sleeve from backstage.

As slumber gave way to wakefulness, my still gormless expression slowly adjusting to one of cautious indifference, I heard such dulcet tones from my baffled and battle-wearied number one fan: "What about those pots?" Hardly a criminal offense, I protested. Nor one for which the consequences should be particularly dire. Wherever your sympathies may lie—and I can guess where—you must surely agree with that. But measures of guilt seem to bear trivial relation to rational thought. And I paid; boy, did I pay!

The point here, however, is not so much the seriousness of the misdemeanor or the gravity of its effects, but the fact that, had Barbara not brought it to my attention, I would have continued in blissful ignorance, with not a trace of remorse. But would that have made me any less guilty? Here is where we must draw the distinction between guilt and feelings associated with such guilt (or lack thereof). According to the *Concise Oxford English Dictionary*, guilt is "the fact of having committed a specified or implied offence."[16] It is synonymous with blameworthiness. Guilty feelings are an inner sense of conviction relating to such blameworthiness and a potential product of it. Their absence, however, does not necessarily negate the existence of guilt.

Sin Is Seldom without Effect

Another means by which suspicion of guilt might be aroused is sin's consequences. For the Israelites of this period, the simple withholding of divine favor would probably have remained sufficient. The only difficulty with this was that its observance by others became so depended upon that the merest hint of suffering was thence equated with sin having been committed. Third party imposition of guilt is not recommended; examples of it in Scripture are often by way of highlighting its inadvisability (e.g., Job 4–23), or drawing attention to a paucity of understanding concerning God's grace (see John 9:1–3).

There are essentially two Hebrew words translated "guilt" in our Old Testament: *asham* and *chata*. There continues to be much critical debate regarding the difference between them. The apparent weight of evidence has led Girdlestone to say that:

> An examination of all the passages in which the word occurs leads to the conclusion that *asham* is used where a sin, moral or ceremonial, has been committed through error, negligence, or ignorance. A loose code of morality might permit such offenses to pass by, but not so the law of Moses. An offense against the person of another is an offense, whether it be known or found out at the time or not. When it comes to our knowledge we are liable . . . . When the matter is brought to a man's cognizance he is not to content himself with the excuse that he acted in error. Rather, he is to acknowledge himself as *asham*.[17]

16. Allen, *COED*, 525.

17. Girdlestone, *Synonyms*, 99.

Apart from the obvious, notice also that a clear distinction is implied between actual guilt and the acknowledgment of guilt, where the existence of the former is not dependent upon that of the latter.

Under the terms and stipulations of the old covenant sacrificial system, the guilt offering was designed to make atonement on that day on behalf of the offerer, in respect of the offense(s) in relation to which the offering was being made. There was no attending guarantee of any removal either of the capacity to repeat the offense or feelings of blameworthiness associated with it. Despite experiential evidence to the contrary, this need not be so for beneficiaries of the atoning sacrifice of the new covenant.

Freedom from Censure

We'll leave our anonymous friend to his letter to the Hebrews for the time being, and instead consult the apostle Paul on the matter. Here is what he had to say to the believers at Rome:

> Therefore, there is now no condemnation for those who are in Christ Jesus, because through Christ Jesus the law of the Spirit of life set me free from the law of sin and death. For what the law was powerless to do in that it was weakened by the sinful nature, God did by sending his own Son in the likeness of sinful man to be a sin offering. And so he condemned sin in sinful man, in order that the righteous requirements of the law might be fully met in us, who do not live according to the sinful nature but according to the Spirit.[18]

"But Paul is talking about a sin offering being made, not a guilt offering." Yes, but guilt is the product of sin. If the law's requirements have been fully met in regard to the one, the other becomes obsolete *ipso facto*. By lateral extension, there can be no condemnation because there is no guilt to which it might reasonably be attached. That word "therefore" at the beginning is a conjunctive, linking what follows with that which precedes it. Moreover, it does so in a special way: what follows is a consequence of what precedes it. Indeed, the word "consequently" might just as readily be used. One of the very first things I remember being taught as a would-be Bible student is that whenever you encounter the word *therefore*, look to see what it is there for. Let us follow that advice.

18. Rom 8:1–4.

In cases like the one before us, we would almost always look to the last few verses of chapter 7 for clues. But there is nothing there that would help us greatly, without resorting to a good deal of interpretive gymnastics, even if we retraced our steps to take in the whole chapter. This is because chapters 6 and 7 are mostly a parenthetical fleshing out of a principle identified in chapter 5, to which we must turn our attention if we are to see the proper context of the verses cited from the beginning of chapter 8.

Chapter 5 also begins with a "therefore," but this time we have both the premise and its consequence spelled out for us:

> . . . since we have been justified through faith, we have peace with God through our Lord Jesus Christ, through whom we have gained access by faith into this grace in which we now stand. And we rejoice in the hope of the glory of God.[19]

Hence, there can be no condemnation; justification has negated its validity and thereby disempowered it. Its condition is faith in Christ's achievement to affect our standing thus, but its consequence is that those of us so affected thereafter conduct ourselves in accordance with God's Spirit, rather than the demands of our previous sinful nature (Rom 8:4). This is our covenantal responsibility.

A REMINDER OF COVENANTAL RESPONSIBILITIES

I now want to take you back to the first of our two readings that introduced this chapter and ask that you read it again:

Lev 1:1–13

Disobedience Necessitates the Prescribed Sacrifice

Leaving aside the ornithological alternative that follows (i.e., vv. 14–17), God here offers the Israelites, through Moses, one of three sacrificial options to deal with their sin: a young male bull from the herd (vv. 3–9), or a male sheep or goat from the flock (vv. 10–13). Whichever is chosen must be without defect (vv. 3, 10) and follow a divinely prescribed process of slaughter, preparation, and presentation. But the phrase to which I want to draw particular attention occurs twice, once in each section:

19. Rom 5:1–2.

> He is to wash the inner parts and the legs with water, and the priest is to burn all of it [i.e., the young male bull] on the altar.[20]

> He is to wash the inner parts and the legs with water, and the priest is to bring all of it [i.e., the male sheep or goat] and burn it on the altar.[21]

I guess I shouldn't need to define what is meant by the word "all," but I have learned to take nothing for granted. Whether we are considering the English masculine noun *all*, the Hebrew *hakkol*, or the Greek *pas*, the meaning is the same; we might even say that they *all* agree: the whole of or every part of that to which it is appended as a qualifying prefix, without exception or exemption, unless otherwise specified. Have I taken leave of my senses to labor the point so? My point, which must be established before we may go any further, is that the sacrifice was total and complete.

The main reason that obedience is better than sacrifice—at least, in this context—is that the one negates the need for the other. Or, to put it another way, sacrifice only becomes necessary because of disobedience (1 Sam 15:22). Such disobedience constituted behaving in any way—or measure—that was contrary to God's revealed will. Indeed, many of the divine promises—if they may so be called—were dependent upon obedience to a precondition: "I will . . . if you will . . . " But notice also that there was provision in God's will for disobedience: "I will . . . if you will not . . . "

There was no tolerance or allowance for what might be called partial obedience; anything less than full compliance was disobedience. Similarly, sin was sin full stop, with no range by degrees from whopper to minor. This is why James could say that "whoever keeps the whole law and yet stumbles at just one point is guilty of breaking it all" (Jas 2:10). He possibly had in mind his own brother's words:

> Do not think that I have come to abolish the Law and the Prophets; I have not come to abolish them but to fulfil them. I tell you the truth, until heaven and earth disappear, not the smallest letter, not the least stroke of a pen, will by any means disappear from the Law until everything is accomplished. Anyone who breaks one of the least of these commandments and teaches others to do the same will be called least in the kingdom

20. Lev 1:9a.

21. Lev 1:13a.

> of heaven, but whoever practises and teaches these commands will be called great in the kingdom of heaven.[22]

"Well, at least they will be numbered among those who get to inhabit God's kingdom." Some of them will, but apparently not all. He goes on:

> For I tell you that unless your righteousness surpasses that of the Pharisees and the teachers of the law, you will certainly not enter the kingdom of heaven.[23]

No License for Ingratitude

How can this be? Isn't one of the prime benefits for a child of the new covenant that we are no longer under the law but under grace? As you might imagine, I have heard this argument being posited countless times over the years. I don't wish to be intentionally rude, but its perpetrators have usually been either those genuinely lacking in understanding or those of devious intelligence, with a clandestine agenda of antinomian self-interest (and, in many cases, not particularly well hidden). Either way, the premise they promote should be eyed with a replete and indolent malevolence. It is an edifice of speculative nonsense erected by imaginative propagandists, the most creditable feature of whom seems to be an overt lack of substantive evidence. But neither is it a phenomenon with which Paul was unfamiliar. Indeed, he may even be said to have been the father of the not-under-the-law brigade (see Rom 6:14b). But a closer look at the context alters the common perspective considerably, even the immediate context, and it need not be all that close an inspection:

> In the same way [that Christ died to sin once for all and lives to God], count yourselves dead to sin and alive to God in Christ Jesus. Therefore do not let sin reign in your mortal body so that you obey its evil desires. Do not offer the parts of your body to sin, as instruments of wickedness, but rather offer yourselves to God, as those who have been brought from death to life; and offer the parts of your body to him as instruments of righteousness. For sin shall not be your master, because you are not under law, but under grace.[24]

22. Matt 5:17–19.
23. Matt 5:20.
24. Rom 6:11–14.

Without yet delving deeper into what may be meant by the phrase "not under law," we are able to deduce from this citation alone that it is not a license for libertine conduct or the liberty to pursue licentious behavior. So, what is it? Before we press on to seek answers to that question, I would like to ask the reader to pause for a few moments to reflect on some more: In the light of what you know already, what sort of person do you imagine you ought to be as a Christian believer? In what ways does this differ from the kind of person you were before coming to Christ? Is there any difference at all? Now, how would you presently differentiate between a life that is under grace and one that is lived under law?

One of the difficulties we often face in arriving at a correct understanding can be a failure to realize that some words shift meaning dependent upon the context. Thus, to apply universal definition to some words can hinder our cause rather than help us. A linguistic grasp of the original tongue can sometimes help, but this is not always the case. One such word is *righteousness*. Outside of Christ, righteousness is beyond every one of us; and yet, it is a requirement demanded of us if we are to stand before God, lest we be so judged (i.e., as unrighteous). Hence, the cross of Christ, where the righteous died for the sake of the unrighteous that they might thereby stand righteously in God's presence. This righteousness is called imputed righteousness and lies at the center of what theologians describe as the great exchange.

Thereafter, it is expected of us that we live accordingly, as those befitting their newfound status. It is our covenantal responsibility to live righteously. Remember, the context of Paul's counsel is not an evangelistic street sermon, but an apostolic letter to Christian believers. Like those who brought their sacrificial offerings to the tabernacle in the wilderness under the old covenant, his recipients, too, were the covenant people of God. He presented before them not many options, but two, one the direct negative consequence of failing to adhere to the other: either present "the parts of [their] bodies" (literally, their whole bodies) to God as "instruments of righteousness" or they would thereby be offering "the parts of [their] bodies" (again, whole bodies) as "instruments of wickedness." The choice was theirs, as was the responsibility. And both are ours.

Why Bother?

But what is our motivation? If we are saved now, come what may, why should I care how I live? Surely, the more we continue to sin, it only really serves further to demonstrate God's grace. Strangely enough, Paul had already dismissed the idea of any legitimacy being attached to this way of thinking at the very beginning of the same chapter (see Rom 6:1–7). He resolved it by expertly outlining the lack of validity in such an approach, but he did so without really answering the question before us. What, then, should be our motivation?

Allow me for a moment to continue along Paul's path by suggesting what it should not be. There seems to be a direct correlation between happiness and holiness, though it might be to our advantage to modify each with the same adjective, *true*. It would be both improper and unnecessary to give too much detail, but I wonder how many readers would be able to identify with my experience when I say that my happiest as a Christian coincided with those all too brief moments when I was at my holiest. Again, I mean truly happy and truly holy, rather than just tolerably satisfied and smug in my own self-righteousness. In the midst of his teaching on the Beatitudes, Jesus said: "Blessed are those who hunger and thirst for righteousness, for they will be filled" (Matt 5:6). But the object of the recipients' desire was not the happiness that came their way; the happiness was a by-product of receiving that for which they yearned. We pursue righteousness for better reasons than to be happy. Otherwise, its absence might cause us to cease our quest.

What about the horrors associated with evil? Surely they should play a part in directing us toward paths of righteousness. Yes, they should, and yes, they do; but I am seeking to address the primary motivation for doing so, not lesser contributory factors. Neither should the road to righteousness be regarded solely as a means of escaping hell, simply because it stretches out in the opposite direction. I have encountered all of these theories at one time or another, but there is one that is equally erroneous and worryingly far more commonplace than any: a striving to earn one's salvation.

This was essentially the Galatian problem. Having begun their Christian journey by accepting the gospel terms of a faith-based salvation, they were thence influenced by Judaistic infiltrators, who insisted that the largely Gentile converts were obliged to keep certain Jewish rites, such as circumcision. It was essentially a justification by faith, sanctification by works philosophy. Paul would have none of it:

> We [Christians] who are Jews by birth and not "Gentile sinners" know that a man is not justified by observing the law, but by faith in Jesus Christ. So we, too, have put our faith in Christ Jesus that we may be justified by faith in Christ and not observing the law, because by observing the law no one will be justified.[25]

Living Sacrifices

No arguments from anyone so far, least of all a certain Mr. Luther: justification is by faith alone. But Paul goes on to say that the same is true also of the Christian walk thereafter:

> For through the law I died to the law so that I might live for God. I have been crucified with Christ and I no longer live, but Christ lives in me. The life I live in the body, I live by faith in the Son of God, who loved me and gave himself for me. I do not set aside the grace of God, for if righteousness could be gained through the law, Christ died for nothing![26]

Herein lies our motivation for offering our bodies as "instruments of righteousness" (Rom 6:13). The life we live in them is under new ownership, the sole purpose of whom, in his earthly body, was to do the will of the Father (John 6:38). I would contend that he retains precisely the same purpose as he lives through his new covenant people by the Holy Spirit. It is our covenantal responsibility to facilitate that as much as it resides within us to do so.

"But doesn't what Paul said to the Galatians take us right back to not being under law, but under grace?" Much depends on what we understand by the phrase "not being under law." Certainly, Christian believers are no longer subject to the ultimate penalty demanded by the law for its contravention, or as an instrument by which sin is more readily identified (see Rom 3:20; 4:15; 5:20; 7:7–12). But that is not to say that the law is thereby rendered utterly ineffective or impotent in other ways.

In the first of his extant pastoral epistles, Paul acknowledged to Timothy that "the law is good if one uses it properly" (1 Tim 1:8). Older

25. Gal 2:15–16.

26. Gal 2:19–21.

translations have: "the law is good if a man use it lawfully" (e.g., KJV). Two negative premises are immediately suggested: it is possible to use the law unlawfully, and to do so would not be good. The law is essentially a tangible revelation of God's ethical standard for human conduct. John Calvin described it as a prism (i.e., a mirror), a prison (a cage), and a pedagogue (a teacher).[27] That standard of expectation has not been abolished or minimized, nor has a divinely appointed blind eye been turned to it post-Calvary. Moreover, it must be regarded as the law, the whole law, and nothing but the law. No part of it need be obscured or suspended in order to promote or more clearly see another. To do so would be to use the law unlawfully.

Elsewhere, Paul takes us back to where we began by linking the life of a Christian with the sacrificial offerings first made in the tabernacle under the old covenant:

> Therefore, I urge you, brothers, in view of God's mercy, to offer your bodies as living sacrifices, holy and pleasing to God—this is your spiritual act of worship.[28]

It should also be our corporate response; it is our covenantal responsibility.

THE PRIEST'S ROLE

An easy way to narrow down the priest's role in the tabernacle is to remember that the only function of non-Levites was to bring the offerings to them at the entrance. Israelites who belonged to any other tribe had no further business in the tabernacle and went no further than the brazen altar. Nothing about this venture could be described as pleasant. It was worse than an abattoir, for the slaughtering of animals was only part of what went on there. After the presentation and preparation would come the burning; the smell of that was incessant, the attendant incense barely managing to disguise its repugnant pungency, combined with the foul odor of fecal ordure.

27. Calvin, *Institutes II*, vii.6–12.

28. Rom 12:1.

Servants under Contract

We must tackle a common misapprehension at the outset. The legitimate Old Testament priests were exclusively of the house of Levi but, contrary to popular misconception, not all Levites were priests. The right to priesthood was reserved for the sons of Aaron, brother of Moses and Miriam, and eldest son of Amram, of the Levitical line of Kohath (see Exod 6:16–20). Levites who could not trace their ancestry back to Aaron were permitted to minister in the tabernacle (and later temple) under Aaronic supervision. It was they who were responsible for disassembling, transporting, and constructing the tabernacle from one site to another (see Exod 38:21; Num 1:47–54).

These were not the Levites' only responsibilities in relation to the tabernacle service (see Num 3–8). Nor should it be forgotten why such duties befell them. They were "set aside" in lieu of the firstborn son of every family throughout Israel, in recognition of God having spared them during the Passover in Egypt (Exod 13:1–13).[29] The Levites thus became God's ministers by entitlement on the grounds of substitutionary redemption. We might even say that they were indentured servants on the basis that, unless otherwise prohibited (Lev 21:16–23), there was effectively a contractual requirement for them to give twenty-five years' service, until retirement at the age of fifty brought reduced responsibilities (Num 8:24–26).

Priestly Requirements Do Not Negate Personal Responsibilities

The priests proper, however, had considerably more entrusted to their care, both in the standing tabernacle and in its transportation. Only the priests, for example, were authorized (by God, through Moses) to carry the ark of the covenant (Num 4:5, 15). This was a particularly solemn task, which demanded appropriate responsibility, as it symbolized God himself leading his people toward their promised reward. David Hubbard speaks of it thus: "God . . . was marching forth conquering and to conquer."[30] A more cynical eye might not take such a triumphalistic view.

But it was in the functioning tabernacle where the priest's role came to the fore (or should that be priests' roles). The priests were accountable

29. See also Num 8:13–19.

30. In Douglas, *New Bible Dictionary*, 967.

for the maintenance and upkeep of everything within the tabernacle confines, even if such responsibility extended little further than the delegated supervision of tasks to the remaining Levites. We have seen—and will continue to see—that the new covenant application of the old covenant priest belongs to everyone who can lay claim to Christ Jesus as high priest. That is not to say, however, that there are no lessons to be learned from the priests in the tabernacle for those currently enjoying leadership status in their local church. The forsaking of God-focused holy days for self-gratifying holidays may prove to be the least of their concerns.

The first is perhaps not as obvious as it should be. Maybe our gaze is so trained in seeking the obscure and the overt that it evades us. There is no escaping the fact that the Levites were a chosen tribe within Israel. Nor can we easily miss the fact that the sons of Aaron were especially chosen from within them to serve as priests. But they were not only also, but first and foremost, fellow Israelites. Their elevation to priesthood did not negate this, nor did it diminish their covenantal obligations attendant upon it. If anything, their newfound status served only to increase their accountability as members of the covenant people of God. It was not within their gift to neglect their duties as children of Israel in order the more fully to direct their attention toward their responsibilities as sons of Aaron.

I should not need to unpack that any further by way of modern example, but I have a feeling that I must. Those who fall under a cloud of conviction have a propensity to find any excuse imaginable in their quest to unburden themselves of guilt. The auditor's account book tends to be the preferred option: "In the balance sheet of heaven [whatever that is], surely the credit and debit columns still favor the former." And the biblical evidence to support such a theory? None is proffered; and, believe me, I have asked. I've even tried to locate a verse or two on their behalf, and have failed, just as I suspect they have. Even any experiential evidence is thin on the ground. How many pastors and elders (or overseas missionaries) have sacrificed the spiritual welfare of their children on the altar of a "my ministry" syndrome, "trusting" God to take care of that with which he has entrusted them? And then wonder why rebellion ensues.

The tabernacle priests knew that their capacity to function in their God-appointed tasks was dependent upon them fulfilling their personal obligations as individuals within the covenant community. Only then could they give themselves to their vocational duties. Though each could be divided further, these comprised essentially two:

- to ensure that the sacrificial offerings were made in accordance with God's prescription; and
- to make intercession with God on behalf of his people.

If anyone needed any convincing that the old covenant mode of priesthood is now redundant, then surely it is that these two functions have been rendered obsolete by Christ's once-for-all atoning sacrifice and his continuing intercessory role at the right hand of the Father. It must also be observed that the finality of Christ's work in these regards is not to be fully appreciated in their similarities, but in the contrasts that exist between the priests of the old covenant and the high priest of the new:

- they offered sacrifices continually, day after day; Jesus made one sacrifice for sins, for ever; and
- they first of all had to make an offering in relation to their own sins; Jesus was entirely sinless.

Blood Again

The priests' primary concern in the tabernacle was to deal with the sacrificial offerings; first their own, then those of all Israel. It was a task that left little room for meditative contemplation. Of the five offering types made at the brazen altar, two were compulsory: the sin offering and the guilt offering. But the first set of comprehensive instructions given are for the voluntary burnt offering. As the regulations for all the offerings were set out according to the same basic structure, we will focus on what spiritual lessons may be learned from the burnt offering.

To speak of the burnt offering as voluntary can be misleading; it was incumbent upon the gift-bearer's conscience to determine whether such an offering was necessary. Its purpose was nominally that petitions might be brought before the Almighty (or thanksgiving for the favorable receipt of previous pleas), but atonement was required before these would be deemed acceptable. Animals brought from the herd or the flock had to be male, without defect, and brought to the entrance to the outer court. Non-Levites were permitted no further.

Once the animal was handed over to the priest, the offerer having identified himself with the offering by way of a simple hand-laying rite to the animal's head, the rest of the ceremonial duty in respect of that offering became that of the priest who had received it. A priest had to officiate from this point on because only a priest was authorized to do so, on pain of death. His first duty was to ensure—as far as he was able—that the animal being presented met the qualifying criteria.

This being acknowledged beyond any reasonable doubt, the offering was then slaughtered on the altar, its blood being liberally dispersed against the altar sides. A point of translation is worth noting here. It is a minor point, but an important one. The Hebrew verb here is *zaraq*, which means "to throw in copious amounts" or "to splash." If the action being conveyed was sprinkling, as some translations suggest (e.g., NASB, KJV, YLT), the correct verb would be *naza*, which relates to smaller amounts of liquid being scattered. A similar mistranslation occurs in respect of the consecration blood finding its way on to the garments of Aaron and his sons (Exod 29:21).

Another—minor, but important—point before we press on: if this splashing/throwing was ritualistic in its own right, then its identification was not with atonement per se, but in celebratory demonstration of the fact that atonement had been attained. Whence came its attainment? At the moment the blood was shed. But the symbolism did not end there:

> [The priest] is to skin the burnt offering and cut it into pieces. The sons of Aaron the priest are to put fire on the altar and arrange the wood on the fire. Then [they] shall arrange the pieces, including the head and the fat, on the burning wood that is on the altar. He is to wash the inner parts and the legs with water, and the priest is to burn all of it on the altar. It is a burnt offering, an offering made by fire, an aroma pleasing to the Lord.[31]

God Is in the Detail

If the skin represents anything, it is that which is on public display. To all intents and purposes, prior to the animal being skinned, only its outward appearance can have provided the basis for its earlier assessment as one without defect. Once the external has been removed, the hidden is thereby exposed. This is not the first time, of course, that the removal of skin had been associated with atonement. Although not mentioned directly, that "accolade" belongs to God's provision for Adam and Eve

31. Lev 1:6–9.

in the garden following the fall, their own attempt to cover their shame proving wholly inadequate (see Gen 2:25; 3:7, 21).

Having been cut into pieces and arranged on a pre-prepared fire, Moses seems at pains to bring to our attention that—unlike the skin—the head and fat of the animal were not excluded from being burnt up (Lev 1:8). Elsewhere in Scripture, the head often symbolizes human intellect or wisdom (e.g., 1 Sam 9:2 NIV, NLT, NET). The fat speaks to us not of vigor and health, but of material excess, all that we treasure that is surplus to our need. These may include those things that are not necessarily dangerous in themselves, but our abuse and exploitation of them renders them so, such as wanting tomorrow's manna today. Our gratuitous boasting of what we have and are, especially when displayed against a backdrop of others' lack, is a particular example of such spiritual obesity.

The washing of "the inner parts [or entrails] and the legs" betrays another interesting concept (Lev 1:9, 13a). Why wash them before burning? And why specifically these anatomical parts? I find it difficult to venture an opinion with more than a modicum of conviction, but I do think some commentators take too sudden a leap when they speak of the perfect purity of the emotions and actions without having the courage to fill in the gaps. If "the legs" in question are the hind legs, which may be inferred by the primitive root of the original *kara*, meaning "to bow down" (as in a kneeling position), then I can understand the reluctance of some to make the connection. Jay Sklar proves not to be quite so squeamish, though he prefers to attribute the theory to an anonymous third party:

> It has been suggested that the internal organs would include the intestines, which might contain fecal matter, and the legs—or at least the hind legs—could have come into contact with fecal matter as well. Such filth had to be removed from presenting these things to the Lord.[32]

I will leave the reader to decide of what this might be symbolic.

Again, save the already removed skin and splattered blood, the sacrifice is total; everything else was burned up. And it was the priest's responsibility to ensure that it was. The fallenness of humanity has nothing of value with which to come before God, except in recognition of its utter lostness. This idea of totality is reinforced at the end of the citation (see also v. 13b), though it is not so obvious in all translations: "a burnt offering" is *olah* in the Hebrew (from which our English word *holocaust*

32. Sklar, *Leviticus*, 93.

is derived; see Douay), meaning literally "a whole burnt offering" (see GNT, LXX).

At the very end, we are reminded of the purpose of the sacrifice: it is "an aroma pleasing to the Lord" (see also v. 13c). We are not given any further detail or clues as to why it meets with such divine favor, other than what may be identified elsewhere. Indeed, it is only when this old covenant shadow is fulfilled by its New Testament substance that the mist begins to clear. In the context of giving instructions on how to live as children of the light, Paul cites Christ's example, who "loved us and gave himself up for us as a fragrant offering and sacrifice to God" (Eph 5:2). He uses the same phrase to describe the gifts he received from Philippi by Epaphroditus: "a fragrant offering, an acceptable sacrifice, pleasing to God" (Phil 4:18). Herein lies the essence of what constitutes "a sweetsmelling savour" (KJV): acceptance to God.

SUMMARY

A brazen altar is not the place for a brass-necked people. The carefree are often careless in the carrying out of their obligations. The busyness surrounding the tabernacle's slaughter area suggests that Israel was not slack in this regard. In the early days, their immediate context would have played no small part in this. The recent exodus from Egypt's clutches would have brought with it a great sense of relief and gratitude. The lessons learned in their experiences toward the end of their bondage would have also stood them in good stead. Not least among these would have been the idea of blood sacrifice. Whether or not they fully grasped the associated implications is neither here nor there; they recognized both the divine requirement and the power of obedience. That was sufficient for them. Such information would continue to shape Israel's destiny thereafter. Disinhibited they may have been; they were now free to honor their God as he saw fit.

3

The Brazen Laver

We now continue our journey through the tabernacle courtyard to consider its other item of furniture: the brazen laver. To that end, the following reading will provide the basis for all that follows in this chapter:

> Then the Lord said to Moses, "Make a bronze basin, with its bronze stand, for washing. Place it between the Tent of Meeting and the altar, and put water in it. Aaron and his sons are to wash their hands and feet with water from it. Whenever they enter the Tent of Meeting, they shall wash with water so that they will not die. Also, when they approach the altar to minister by presenting an offering made to the Lord by fire, they shall wash their hands and feet so that they will not die. This is to be a lasting ordinance for Aaron and his descendants for the generations to come."[1]

THE DESIGN AND CONSTRUCTION OF THE LAVER

. . . and this is relevant only here:

> They made the bronze basin and its bronze stand from the mirrors of the women who served at the entrance to the Tent of Meeting.[2]

1. Exod 30:17–21.
2. Exod 38:8.

Overcoming a Conditioned Mindset

I have seen some quite obscure theses posited in relation to the above citation, many of which fail to quicken the pulse, even with indignation. The most obvious lesson, however, seems to be that God requires nothing of us that is beyond our capacity to begin to meet from the resources he has placed at our disposal. A wave offering had already been taken to provide materials for the tabernacle's construction (Exod 25:22–29). Included among these were gold, silver, bronze, different colored yarns, fine linen, goat hair, skin and hide, and acacia wood. So responsive was the community, that the skilled craftsmen responsible for the work had to ask Moses to say that they had enough to complete their tasks (36:4–7).

Western minds tend to think of chronological order as strictly linear. This, then, causes us to beg the question: if a first offering had already been taken, and it was deemed that more than sufficient had been mustered to complete the task, then why this subsequent need to supplement the earlier giving? Without pausing to question our own methodology, we then proceed to consider plausible reasons on the basis of false premises. Had the craftsmen miscalculated? Was the treasury subject to pilfering? Had they originally underestimated the size of the basin and now decided to go for a deluxe model instead?

Now remove the linear chronology angle and see what other possibilities emerge. The most likely explanation now seems all too clear. In typically Hebraic style, what we are presented with in chapter 30 outlines the general overview of what is brought as an offering. Only when we arrive at each specific item do we find more particulars, but those details, found in the later chapter, still relate to the one original offering. Moreover, the bringing of the items for use still required work if they were to become usable. Alec Motyer makes a valid observation. Although not posited in the context of the brazen laver per se, the principle he unearths is just as applicable:

> The order within the lists arises from the purpose for which that list is designed. For example, the first list concentrates on doctrinal priorities, and therefore the ark comes first of all . . . . On the other hand, the second list (chs 36–39) is much more like a builder's specification and is written in the order in which a practical craftsman would approach his multiplex task.[3]

3. Motyer, *Message of Exodus*, 322.

A Positional Priority

The laver (or washstand) was located in the outer court between the altar and the entrance to the Tent of Meeting (or tabernacle proper). Its placement can hardly be divorced from its purpose, the former giving a hint to the latter. Having fulfilled their sacrificial responsibilities, the priests were required to wash before they could enter the Holy Place. In modern parlance, they quite literally had blood on their hands, and this must be remedied before venturing any further. Thus, the laver was simply a necessary means of cleansing from outer physical defilement. (Notice also that the return journey required the same attention.)

Ritual cleansing of Aaron and his sons had already taken place at their inauguration (see Exod 29:1–4). Although a vastly different exercise to that which would thereafter take place within the constructed tabernacle (and later temple), there are certain principles attached to it that remain consistent. Chief among these was the elimination of ceremonial uncleanness, symbolic of the purity and propriety of character and conduct that was demanded of them. But there appears to be a kind of *ordo consecratio* implied here. Aaron and his sons are not only proclaimed as priests, but their line is declared a dynastic priesthood (v. 9b). This follows immediately after them being dressed in priestly garments (vv. 5–9a). But their robing could not take place until their bodies had been prepared to be dressed thus by such cleansing (v. 4).

As mentioned previously, my first job after leaving school was at the local colliery as an apprentice mechanic. I spent three years there before deciding that weekend work, involuntary overtime, and awkward shift patterns were not for me. The final eighteen months of my time were spent almost exclusively underground. It was a dirty place. Even if you spent only one hour of your shift "downstairs" checking an oil level, you would re-emerge on the surface looking as if you were auditioning for the part of Larry Parks's understudy in *Jolson Sings Again*. No end of scrubbing with carbolic soap could remove the permanent mascara line of coal dust. Communal shower time at the end of each shift was compulsory and engaged without complaint.

At the end of one particularly hectic day shift, I was running late for a date. I needed to be clean, but I hadn't time to wait for a shower cubicle to become available. So, as soon as I reached the colliery surface, I handed in my authorization disc, cap lamp, and resuscitator mask, and ran home, no doubt giving the appearance of an asylum abscondee to passing motorists, in my mucky orange overalls. I was planning to take a bath, change to clothes more suitable, and go on my romantic way; my grandmother was not planning on allowing me beyond the front door in such a state. Guess whose strategy prevailed. I'll give you a clue: by the time I re-entered the colliery shower room, I didn't have to worry about queuing for a cubicle. When I arrived home for the second time, I was deemed sufficiently undespoiled to enter the premises.

Symbolism Revisited

Consistent with its placement, the material used in the construction of the laver is similar to those of the altar. The outer court was a place of judgment. Only inside the Tent of Meeting do we find gold. It might be argued that this, too, speaks of judgment, but it is judgment that has been exacted to bring about a new condition after every impurity has been removed; it is a refined metal. Outside there is only wood and bronze; the laver was made entirely of the latter. And it was bronze, not brass. Despite the insistence of some translations (e.g., KJV, ASV, Webster), brass is a relatively modern compound of copper and zinc, whereas bronze—as an alloy of copper and tin—was not unknown at this time.[4]

The cleansing that took place at the laver was not an all-over body wash, but one of the hands and feet only. It would be an easy inference to regard these as representative of our works and our walk, though a washing of the face might be said to deal with these as a symbol of purified thoughts, which govern both. This is not the only time that hands and feet are placed together in Scripture, though their collaborative emphasis is not as common as you might imagine. The most striking example comes to us in nail-pierced cruciform. Although this is not explicit in any of the crucifixion accounts, the nailing of the wrists and ankle bones is known from archaeological evidence of the period. Moreover, when the resurrected Christ appeared to his doubting disciples, Luke's account is most illuminating:

> They were startled and frightened, thinking they saw a ghost. He said to them, "Why are you troubled, and why do doubts rise in your mind? Look at my hands and my feet. It is I myself! Touch me and see; a ghost does not have flesh and bones, as you

4. See Epp, *Portraits of Christ*, 72.

see I have." When he had said this, he showed them his hands and feet.[5]

The stigmata revealed Christ's identity as the resurrected Son of God (see also Ps 22:16), just as the washed hands and feet exposed something of the priests' identity as servants of Yahweh in the tabernacle. Perhaps lessons of more relevant value may be gleaned from those occasions when hands and feet appear, but not together. This is particularly true of the psalmist:

> Who may ascend the hill of the Lord? Who may stand in his holy place? He who has clean hands and a pure heart, who does not lift up his soul to an idol or swear by what is false. He will receive blessing from the Lord and vindication from God his Savior.[6]

> For you have delivered me from death and my feet from stumbling, that I may walk before God in the light of life.[7]

> . . . he has preserved our lives and kept our feet from slipping.[8]

How is all this possible?

> Your word is a lamp to my feet and a light for my path.[9]

In the first of these citations, clean hands are linked with a pure heart. One is not a natural consequence of the other, though both are required. What can this mean? Our outward profession must be a legitimate expression of our inner condition if the criteria upon which the promised blessings may flow are deemed to have been met. For each case, an example follows of what might constitute unclean hands and an impure heart. The way they are presented in the NIV gives the impression that they amount to the same idolatrous issue, but I find myself in agreement here with Tremper Longman, who reminds us that the original Hebrew for the latter clause (i.e., "swear by what is false") "is not used

5. Luke 24:37–40.
6. Ps 24:3–5.
7. Ps 56:13.
8. Ps 66:9.
9. Ps 119:105.

anywhere else to refer to false gods, which thus strengthens the case for the type of translation offered by the NET Bible":[10]

> The one whose deeds are blameless and whose motives are pure, who does not lie, or make promises with no intention of keeping them.[11]

The accompanying blessing for such solemn approval is the right to sanctuary attendance: that they may stand in God's presence. In this respect, the psalmist identifies the outcome of the condition. There is an element of this regarding the attention we pay to our feet: that they might not stumble or slip. But the emphasis is on how we may attain and maintain a state of sure-footedness: by virtue of the illuminating guidance of God's word.

A (*Rhema*) Word to the Wise

There are, of course, those who have not found God's word to be so. Scripture is not—nor was it ever intended to be—a magical promise box of tricks, whereby we might be instructed in just the right kind of inflection or word combinations for our most urgently uttered prayers to receive a favorable response. Nor was it designed to be read by the light of self-interest. Rather, Scripture is a light and a lamp to those who have taken preparatory steps to ensure that it becomes so to them. The psalm from which the above text is taken is the longest of all the psalms. The context, as ever, is all important. The kind of person who finds God's word to be "a lamp to [their] feet and a light for [their] path" is also able to say:

> Oh, how I love your law! I meditate on it all day long. Your commands make me wiser than my enemies, for they are ever with me. I have more insight than all my teachers, for I meditate on your statutes. I have more understanding than the elders, for I obey your precepts. I have kept my feet from every evil path so that I might obey your word. I have not departed from your laws, for you yourself have taught me. How sweet are your words to my taste, sweeter than honey to my mouth! I gain understanding from your precepts; therefore I hate every wrong path.[12]

10. Longman, *Psalms*, 139.
11. See also KJV, NASB, GNT, NLT.
12. Ps 119:97–104.

Quite a commitment! Well, the prize is worth the price, the hill of truth meriting the climb. As a mental exercise only, I often like to take cause and effect texts like this and invert them in an attempt more fully to appreciate their value and veracity. For example, ignorance of God's commands diminishes my wisdom when compared with that of my enemies; neglect in meditating upon his statutes weakens my insight; lack of obedience to divine precepts brings with it a commensurate deficiency of understanding; and a stubborn refusal to apply myself to the word of God can end only in a meaningless meandering in the darkness. Like David, I have found all of these to be true, and not just when I have set my imagination to work.

It is not without significance that this cleansing quality is attributed to "the word" by Paul in his letter to the believers at Ephesus (Eph 5:26). There can be no question that sanctification is the aim of such cleansing. There can equally be little doubt that, though the specific instance of husbands loving their wives as Christ loved the church is important, it is nonetheless incidental to the underlying doctrine being established. I remain unconvinced that "the washing with water" is here to be identified with baptism, though similar uses of the same phrase elsewhere are admittedly beyond dispute (e.g., John 3:5; Titus 3:5; 1 Pet 3:21).

What concerns us most here, however, is what precisely is meant by "the word." The Greek is *rhemati*, which the apostle employs also in the following chapter in relation to the word of God being the sword of the Spirit in the Christian armory (Eph 6:17). The root *rhema* denotes an utterance, either spoken or written down as recorded evidence of that which has been spoken. Vine clarifies further:

> The reference is not to the whole Bible as such, but to the individual scripture which the Spirit brings to our remembrance for use in time of need, a prerequisite being the regular storing of the mind with Scripture.[13]

Thus: "Man does not live on bread alone, but on every word [that is, *rhema*] that comes from the mouth of God" (Matt 4:4); it is for our cleansing.

13. Vine, *Expository Dictionary*, 1,242.

THE LAVER IS FOR PRIESTS

The bronze laver was out of bounds as far as non-Levitical Israelites were concerned. Sharing the vast space of the outer courtyard with the bronze altar, it was certainly not out of view. Whether anyone actually saw it or not is an entirely different matter, though I would guess that its forbidden nature would have served only to increase its curiosity value. Once this had been satisfied, however, I doubt whether much attention would have been diverted beyond the important matters to be attended at the altar. Aaron, his sons, and their male descendants (Exod 30:19, 21b), on the other hand, would have found their duties at the laver to have brought welcome relief.

Divinely Ordained

Remember, the priests had already undergone a bathing for consecration (Exod 29:4); it had been—and remained for successive generations—a once-for-all occasion. The requirement here was a bathing for continuation, that their right of access into the Tent of Meeting might be uninterrupted and unhindered. In the light of what we now know of Christ's fulfilment of the type, it is easy to fall into the trap of viewing the old covenant priesthood with a somewhat jaundiced eye. However, we must not fail to recognize that the tabernacle priesthood was God's gracious—and, therefore, glorious—provision for his covenant people, and a fitting response to what he deemed to be necessary at the time.

I mentioned earlier that the priest's role was essentially two-fold: to represent the people before their God and to make intercession for them in his presence. Preparatory to this was the need for them to ensure that they themselves were without defilement. They sacrificed at the altar on behalf of their fellow Israelites and washed at the laver to remove the stain of uncleanness by association; but they also made sacrifices in respect of their own shortcomings, and the requirement to be thence unsullied was no less urgent.

Regal Intercessors Are Righteously Integrated

It would be a mistake to imagine that the New Testament fulfilment of the Old Testament type means that there are now no priests. Just as Aaron was the high priest and his sons accompanying priests, so Christ is now high priest, with those in whom his seed resides being priests also. Let us consult the writer to the Hebrews once more:

> Therefore, brothers, since we have confidence to enter the Most Holy Place by the blood of Jesus, by a new and living way opened for us through the curtain, that is, his body, and since we have a great priest over the house of God, let us draw near to God with a sincere heart in full assurance of faith, having our hearts sprinkled to cleanse us from a guilty conscience and having our bodies washed with pure water.[14]

The imagery is unmistakable. We do not know who wrote this, but we do know a little about the intended readership. They were primarily Jewish converts to Christianity, who were under some pressure to Judaize the gospel or revert to Judaism (see also Gal 2:14). Some may even have been priests under the old order (Acts 5:7), though these were most likely in the minority. They would all have been familiar with the Hebraic heritage. How is it, then, that the writer of the Hebrews could write this of what amounted to ordinary Christian believers?

By comparison, Peter's first letter is short, though it does touch upon some important doctrines, including this one: the priesthood of all believers. His intended readership was both mixed and scattered, comprising both Jewish and Gentile Christians dispersed throughout Asia Minor (see 1 Pet 1:1). In chapter 2, Peter provides the basis for what has become known as the doctrine of a universal priesthood:

> But you are a chosen people, a royal priesthood, a holy nation, a people belonging to God, that you may declare the praises of him who called you out of darkness into his wonderful light.[15]

In the first instance, "you" refers to the recipients of Peter's letter. The fact that he chooses to be no more specific suggests that the declaration that follows is not restricted to a special class of super-Christian. But the communal relationship that provides the necessary framework for such a priesthood to flourish should not be ignored or underestimated. The priesthood of believers is not a disparate group of individuals doing their own thing in isolation under the guise of priestly service, much less a loose confederation of warring tribes. Rather, it speaks of those

14. Heb 10:19–22.

15. 1 Pet 2:9.

expressing that divinely appointed ministry within the corporate auspices of the local church environment.

Availing Ourselves of the Prerequisites

This is implied by the writer to the Hebrews, particularly in his use of pronouns: "we," "us," and "our." But neither is it completely absent in the five conditions by which we might draw near to God in such service:

- "a sincere heart";
- "full assurance of faith";
- "hearts sprinkled to cleanse us from a guilty conscience"; and
- "bodies washed with pure water."

"Wait a minute! That makes four conditions, not five." Ah, yes! These are the four over which we have a measure of input. The fifth actually comes first, by which all of these are possible: "the blood of Jesus." Yes, I know; it can hardly be described as a condition, given that it has already been met. But it is the basis upon which the rest become of any value. Is that not a condition? And beyond justification, there is a measure of responsibility attached to our receptiveness. His blood does, indeed, avail for me, but the full benefits annexed to it require that I avail myself of the opportunities afforded by it.

A former colleague on the ambulance service was grossly overweight (the technical term at the time was morbidly obese.) For the sake of anonymity, let us call him Benny. Benny was a true cockney, born within the sound of Bow Bells, in London. From what I knew of him privately, Benny was heir only to his father's maladroitness and his mother's foibles. He had two main weaknesses, each of which led to his stomach: food and drink. Around three hours into every shift (including nights), the mess room air would be filled with the aroma of the frying pan. Bacon, eggs, sausage, tomatoes, mushrooms, baked beans, and fried bread sizzled on the hob and jostled for position on the plate to find their way first onto Benny's fork. And woe betide any patient whose emergency interrupted his lard-drenched cuisine. On one occasion, Benny's wife was so concerned about his health that she put him on a banana diet she had seen being promoted in one of her subscripted magazines. What she forgot to tell her dearly beloved was that it was supposed to be a substitute for the norm, not a supplement to it.

Benny was also a heavy drinker. So much so, in fact, that to include the word "very" as an adverb hardly does justice to how heavy a drinker he was. His normal capacity for a session was ten pints of beer, irrespective of his working shift pattern. If he finished an afternoon shift at ten o'clock at night, he would race to the nearest working men's club, order his full quota, and have them all lined up at the bar in nursery rhyme fashion, to be guzzled before closing time at eleven.

Desperate times call for drastic measures, so Benny's wife made an appointment for him to see their doctor. She, in turn, arranged for Benny to visit a dietary consultant specialist, who advised him to buy an exercise bike. So he did! It was a top of the range model and the best make available to the man in the street. Six weeks later, he placed an advertisement in the local newspaper, making the exercise bike available for sale. It had not been a successful purchase. At the time, my wife was looking for just such an addition to her growing gamut of implements with which to fill the garage, so I decided to buy it for her. As you might expect, when I arrived to collect the bike, it was as new; what you might not anticipate is that it had never been taken out of the box.

Up Close and Personal

Simply buying the bike was not enough; storing it in the attic was never going to see its objective realized. Just as Benny needed to avail himself of the bike's possibilities, so we, too, must take steps to ensure that our path to God's presence remains clear and uncluttered. Let us take a closer look at them:

A sincere heart

Our understanding of the biblical use of the word *sincere* is somewhat diminished by its current use. After all, sincere motives can be misplaced, an opinion may be sincerely held, yet error-strewn, and letters ending "yours sincerely" can be designed to lead the recipient into a false sense of security. The original is helpful here, as *alethinos* derives from a root meaning "true" (see KJV, ESV), the ideal of which is absolute and found only in God (e.g., John 7:28). The Vulgate translates *alethinos* with the Latin *verus* (hence Nicene Creed: "very God of very God").

Interestingly, the same writer employs the same Greek word in the previous chapter when contrasting the true tabernacle with its type (Heb 8:2). This raises an observation that the true is not always seen in antithesis to the untrue (though that is frequently the case), but also as set in juxtaposition to the imperfect or shadowy. Thus, a sincere heart is a heart without a trace of falsehood, pretense, or guile and—as far as is possible for the redeemed fallen nature—it is a heart that accurately reflects the inner working of the Holy Spirit to make us progressively more Christlike: "For the law was given through Moses; grace and truth [that is, *alethinos*] came through Jesus Christ" (John 1:17).

Full assurance of faith

The faith of which Scripture speaks knows of no other kind than this: full assurance. But we must be clear in our own minds that we know the basis for such confidence. The guarantee resides not in ourselves as worthy vessels or effective channels, nor even so much in faith itself as an efficient instrument. "So then, faith cometh by hearing, and hearing by the word of God" (Rom 10:17 KJV). Newer versions that substitute the final part with "the message about Christ" do so in an attempt to link the "faith" of which Paul speaks here exclusively to saving faith and, thereby, rob it of its more universal application.

Moreover, to my mind, debates on whether the assurance of faith is an element attached to faith or a separate gift that comes by divine revelation seem to be missing a more obvious approach. The assurance we have by faith is because we have heard from God, or more precisely, because God has spoken. God's word is reliable because he is trustworthy; it leaves no room for doubt because he is utterly dependable; we can have full assurance because he is absolutely faithful. Thus, the Christian believer's assurance is not so much in faith's object per se, but in faith's source. This is how Paul speaks of it in relation to Abraham:

> Yet he did not waver through unbelief regarding the promise of God, but was strengthened in his faith and gave glory to God, being fully persuaded that God had power to do what he had promised.[16]

16. Rom 4:20–21.

Hearts sprinkled to cleanse us from a guilty conscience

This is really the first of a two-part sub-plot, which combine to bring about full purification. In line with the old covenant ritual, the sprinkling of blood on the altar symbolized God's acceptance of the offering being made and, therewith, his forgiveness ratified; the sprinkling of blood on the people of Israel confirmed their commitment to the covenant offered to them (see Exod 24:1–8). The blood of the covenant served also to generate an expectation and yearning for God's especial immediacy. The presence of God was restricted to the high priest, but God was not his God alone; the high priest may well have represented the people, but he alone did not constitute the whole of the people of God.

But what has this to do with having "hearts sprinkled to cleanse us from a guilty conscience"? We must first note that our hearts are not sprinkled to prevent us from having a conscience or, indeed, a guilty one should the occasion arise. A guilty conscience is (usually) the product of having committed a prohibited deed (or deeds). For the Christian, we may think of it as God's red-light warning on the dashboard of the soul. How do we rid ourselves of a guilty conscience? All we can do, all we are expected to do is, again, avail ourselves of God's gracious provision and allow our hearts to be sprinkled by his Son's new (and better) covenant blood (1 John 1:7, 9).

Bodies washed with pure water

This is part two of the procedure begun above. Where that dealt with the internal, this is concerned with the external. What they each share is an apparent passivity on the part of the subject: "having our hearts sprinkled . . . having our bodies washed." Any activity on our part is limited to our submission to the process. The word "washed" here is the past and/or present continuous participle of the Greek verb *louo* (i.e., "to bathe"). Also, "pure water" translates *hudor katheron*, which was employed in the Septuagint version of the Old Testament to refer to the water used in ritual purification, with which the Hebrew readership of the epistle addressed to them would no doubt have been familiar.

The order is also vastly important. Just as ordination followed consecration under the old regime, so what we do must emanate from who we are. This is diametrically opposite to the world's philosophy and how it operates. If you doubt this, try to remember the most recent conversation you had with an unbelieving stranger. My guess is that their preoccupations found their place somewhere in the range of the trivial or the transitory, and included among their questions were things like what you do for a living, what you get up to in your spare time, and where you went on vacation last year. These may well give clues as to the type of person you are, but I doubt whether this was their reason for asking.

CLEANSING THROUGH JUDGMENT

Given the material used in the construction of the laver, the question might well be asked why there remains the need for judgment beyond the altar. After all, wasn't all the sacrifice burned up? Answering that question in relation to the tabernacle sacrifice is relatively trouble free. Remember, the offerings were presented by the people and God's judgment fell upon the sacrificial animal at the altar in respect of their sins. The sins of the priests were dealt with in the same way, but as members of the community. The judgment that took place at the brazen laver was concerned with the priests' contamination, having handled the sacrificial offering at the brazen altar.

To Be Holy Is to Be Set Apart

It would be easy to discredit the idea of uncleanness by association, especially perceived external impurity, on the basis of New Testament evidence. We shall look at Jesus' rebuke of the Pharisaical approach in due course. For the time being, however, we must remind ourselves that the priests on tabernacle duty were observing divine instructions. Indeed, contamination of this sort was a serious matter for the old covenant people of God. At its most basic, the distinction is between what is clean and what is unclean. But it is not a distinction that you and I are left to adjudicate.

Cleanness—and, indeed, uncleanness—can be subjective, even relative. Do we determine what belongs to one or the other solely upon hygienic criteria, are we arbiters of what is more or less so according to culture or custom, can it be governed by circumstances largely beyond our control, and can it be measured by an absolute standard? References to uncleanness occur well in excess of one hundred times in the Old Testament, more than half of which are to be found in the book of Leviticus in the form of some sort of prohibition. The word "clean" occurs over two hundred times, with a third of that total coming also in Leviticus. It seems a good place to start.

From chapter 11 onward, we are treated to a catalogue of regulations about clean and unclean foods, required purification rites after childbirth, protocols surrounding infectious skin diseases and mildew in the home, and bodily discharges and their range of contamination. These are not the rants and ravings of some reclusive mountain prophet, but what God conveyed to Moses and Aaron to relay to the people of Israel (see Lev 11:1–2a). The key, however, I believe belongs to the preceding chapter:

> You must distinguish between the holy and the common, between the unclean and the clean.[17]

This is God's appraisal, no one else's. At first glance, it seems like a reverse couplet, typical of Jewish idiom, where the clean is to be equated with the holy, the unclean with everything that falls short of that standard. But is it a standard or a calling? I believe it is neither to the exclusion of the other, because it is both. Before we consider that, we need a more accurate understanding of this verse as it stands before us. Let us consider it in another translation:

> . . . so as to make a separation between the holy and the common, and between the unclean and the pure.[18]

A Pedant's Playground

As Jay Sklar points out in the introduction to his commentary, Israel knew of not two but three ritual distinctions: the holy, the pure (or clean), and the impure (or unclean). Everything that was not categorized as holy was labeled as common, which included both the pure and the impure. The analogy Sklar uses is one with which I am familiar, so we'll stay with it:

> A person with the flu may not go into a hospital to hold a newborn baby, while a person who is healthy may. A person who is healthy and sterilized may go into an operating room, but a person who is simply healthy may not. Just as your physical health and cleanness determine what you can do and where you

17. Lev 10:10.

18. Lev 10:10 YLT.

> can go in a hospital, the Israelites' ritual state determined what they could do and where they could go in terms of ritual actions, places and times.[19]

To be absolutely pedantic, the healthy and sterilized individual needs also to be authorized before being allowed into the operating theater, but the analogy serves well to get the point across. As you might expect, the context is not without relevance. Let us glean from it what we can together. We are not told precisely what constituted Nadab and Abihu's sinfulness other than that they somehow acted outside of their appointed jurisdiction. Whatever it was, they were doubly guilty in that they were personally responsible for their own act of disobedience and complicit in each other's. There may have been rivalry between them, or it may have been provoked by a sense of sibling oneupmanship against the other two brothers. We do not know.

What we do know is that the occasion of the priests' inauguration prior to that seemed to be observing due respect and decorum, everything being carried out in accordance with the Lord's command. Scripture is clear on this: the offering of unauthorized fire by Nadab and Abihu was "contrary to his command" (Lev 10:1). The outcome also teaches us something about God's holiness, especially his dispensation of justice in relation to its breach: irrelevant circumstantial excuses provide no justifiable grounds for mitigation.

Separateness Is Not Optional

In the relative absence of anything bar the usual festive repeats, my wife and I opted to watch a new three-part drama on TV last Christmas. We soon discovered that it was described as a "Christmas drama" only by virtue of the fact that it was scheduled to appear on our screens during the final week of December. It was called *Black Narcissus*, a loose adaptation of the mid-twentieth-century film of the same name, and even further removed from the book on which both lay claim for inspiration.

The gist of the plot is that five nuns are sent to a remote Himalayan outpost to establish a mountainside convent school. The building to which they are assigned has a dark history, bordering on the demonic, of which the local villagers are all too aware. The main problem to be faced by the nuns, however, comes from within their own number, one

19. Sklar, *Leviticus*, 45.

whose outspokenness and desire for all things worldly threatens both their witness and their ministry. But the fact that there are only five of them, including the headstrong would-be superior sister, and that possible replacements are several days' journey away, mean they must make allowances. After all, let she who is without sin, etc.

Coincidentally, there were five priests in the tabernacle at its induction, including Aaron, the high priest. But God was not in the business of making similar allowances where his honor was being called into disrepute. Many hands do not make light work if some of those hands are unclean and the work requires that they be holy. This idea of holiness has taken on a meaning that, while not altogether removed from its biblical use, often places the emphasis on human attainment rather than divine calling. The Hebrew *qados* is thought to derive from a root meaning objectively to separate or subjectively to be set apart, not only *by* God, but also *for* him.

By (super)natural extension, the notion of separateness, or set apartness, for divine use or service is often expressed adjectivally to the noun to which it finds itself so attached. Thus, in the book of Exodus, we come across "holy ground" (Exod 3:5), "holy dwelling" (15:13), "holy Sabbath" (16:23), "holy nation" (19:6), and "holy people" (22:31). The word *holy* appears many times outside of Exodus, but only once before it, and that in relation to the seventh day in the week of creation (Gen 2:3). What all of these—and others not cited—have in common is that the holiness attributed to them is not inherent, but comes their way by virtue of divine investment. To put it another way, in the first instance, sanctification is attendant upon and with separation.

Distinctiveness the Only Distance

Let us look briefly at those last two features in the list. Though there is a connection between them, they are not synonymous terms. The difference between them is in tense: Israel was called out, separated, and set apart from others to be a holy people, the purpose of which was that they might become a holy nation. This becoming signifies transition from one thing to another, but it was not in terms of holiness, for that was consistent throughout (remember, we are still dealing with holiness in the sense of being set apart by God). The change was to be by means of process, but with an end product in view: from a peoplehood (or non-nationhood) to nationhood.

In relation to each, however, Israel's holiness remained both a calling and a code of conduct. They were called to be set apart from others and they were required to maintain a standard of ethical purity befitting such a calling. Roderick Finlayson describes the relationship between them in the following fashion:

> These two aspects of holiness are generally present, since it was understood that being holy meant not only living a separate life, but bearing a character different from that of the ordinary man. Thus the word attained a distinct ethical implication. Holiness is therefore recognized as belonging to what has been chosen and set apart by God and given a character that conforms to God's law.[20]

God's choice in the matter remains precisely that: his choice. Our understanding of his reason for making such a choice cannot—indeed, must not—be extended any further than an acknowledgment of the divine prerogative. Beyond that, the tide of familiarity begins to recede. The choice having been made, however, we are thence treated to a little more by way of the terminology employed to describe the object of that choice. This, in turn, helps us to understand something of the seriousness with which pollutant effects upon the object are regarded.

Alongside that earlier reference to Israel being described as becoming a "holy nation," and perhaps of far greater moment, is another more intimate phrase: "my treasured possession" (Exod 19:5). It is a term oft-repeated thereafter throughout the Old Testament (see also Deut 7:6; 14:2; 26:18; Mal 3:17). It translates the Hebrew *segullah*, which essentially means the most prized of personal possessions. I am grateful to Eugene Carpenter for the following:

> In the theological usage of the term its most important referent is Israel, whom God makes into his *segullah*, his own unique possession. Although all nations are his, Israel will become the "crown jewel" among all the nations. Her unique quality lies in her position/function/character as his kingdom of priests and a holy nation.[21]

The question naturally arises whether Israel was called to be a holy nation because they had first been nominated as a treasured possession or vice versa. It must be noted that the term *segullah* is never applied

20. In Douglas, *New Bible Dictionary*, 487.

21. In VanGemeren, *Old Testament Theology & Exegesis*, 3:224.

to Israel solely on the basis of their relational standing before God, but only at such times as they were being faithful to their covenantal obligations. Even when this is not the case, however, the emphasis is not so much on the contamination, but on what is being contaminated, why it is considered to be a contamination and, therefore, worthy to be purged of corruption and pollution.

A Responsibility to Be Relevant to God's Command Only

Note also that, in its technical sense of being set apart, holiness can be compounded. The most obvious example of this is to be found in the tabernacle itself, where the outer court was distinguished from the Holy Place by the latter's designation. Beyond the second veil, however, was a locus separated further still: the Holy of Holies (or the Most Holy Place). This is further reflected in the permitted attendees of each site. Everyone allowed to enter the outer court belonged to the people called out from among other people groups, from which were reserved those of the tribe of Levi for tabernacle duties; the priests were set aside for a particular task from within that group, and the high priest was separated from his fellows as having exclusive entry into the divine presence.

With privilege comes responsibility. At each step of separation, the one grows commensurately with the other, the purification demands becoming progressively more intense. There are two points I want to make in relation to this. The first is that the requirements of the people of Israel as a holy people were not thereby diminished, as if there was scope for abrogation. They were set apart and were expected to conduct themselves in a manner befitting of such a calling. In other words, holiness demands righteousness. But secondly, we should not imagine that just because the high priest's calling required him to function within the Holy of Holies only once a year that this formed the extent of his especial separateness, as if a lower standard might be acceptable for the rest of the year.

An oft-overlooked aspect of separation is that it works in both directions. What we are separated from becomes also separated from us by virtue of our being set apart. One of my major concerns in recent years is how many Christian churches have their agenda dictated by outside agencies in the guise of being more relevant to a needy society. And so, times of corporate worship more resemble the *X-Factor* audition room, conversations between believers leave little room for spiritual content, and so-called secular morality has the upper hand when determining the apparent rightness or wrongness of a situation.

As you might guess, I tend to blow more cold than hot regarding the somewhat undue diligence afforded popular opinion. Moreover, it remains my contention that the people of God have no business conducting their affairs in a manner that satisfies the philosophies and/or ideologies of those from whom God has set us apart. The gospel is not enriched by such an attitude, nor is its advancement any more rapid in real terms. Let us rather be cleansed from any approach that would undermine the integrity of our calling before God. He has prescribed a means to that end . . .

DEALING WITH DEFILEMENT

So, what is the divine prescription for dealing with defilement? We have already looked briefly at the cleansing properties of the word of God for Christian believers; it is now appropriate to delve a little more deeply. Before we do, let us first take a glimpse at the causes and effects of defilement.

If in Doubt, Steer Clear

In some ways, defilement is associated with guilt but not exactly synonymous with it. As a verb, to defile and to befoul are the same thing, though neither requires an outside agency to complete the action. Even when this is so, the accountability is usually ours in some measure for the corruption having taken place. The defilement of inanimate objects or treasured precepts suggests a perceived sanctity, which has the potential for being subject to desecration or profanity. When it comes to any of these taking place within a religious context, the resultant defilement is often seen as one of ceremonial uncleanness.

However it may be applied, it should be obvious that to defile is to bring about a condition that is inferior to that prior to the defilement having taken place. It has only negative associations. Interestingly, its most common use in Scripture sees this negativity compounded by warning against defilement (e.g., Lev 11:43; 18:20; Num 35:34), and lauding those who take steps to ensure that they do not become befouled (see Dan 1:8; Rev 14:4).

The Hebrew *yitga'al* is translated by the Greek *alisgeo* in the Septuagint version of the Old Testament, which means literally "to pollute." A derivative of this verb occurs only once in the New Testament, in connection with James's pronouncement that the newly converted Gentile brothers should "abstain from food polluted by idols" (Acts 15:20). Although this is the only one of the four recommendations to be specifically marked by pollution, it is hardly a stretch to see the corrupting influence also of sexual immorality, eating the meat of strangled animals, and blood consumption, all expressly forbidden under Jewish law (Lev 17:10–14; 18:6–24).

This last point is particularly important, especially so for successive generations. That which God considered to have a defiling effect was listed as such in what constituted his word to his covenant people. They were catalogued as prohibitions. But divine counsel did not end there. There were penalties for disobedience, but provision was also made for deliverance. This is pretty much how it went: "Here is a list of things you should do, and here is another one outlining the kind of things you should avoid. Fail to comply with any of it and there will be consequences, which may or may not be immediate. In order to restore fellowship (note, not relationship), I will accept an offering." This was one provision. But God also provided a means of negating the potential effects of ignorance by making Israel aware of what was and what was not acceptable. If followed, this would cleanse his people before they became defiled. It was God's written word.

God's Word Carries the Weight of His Authority

This is what the apostle Paul had to say of it to Timothy, his "true son in the faith" (1 Tim 1:2):

> All Scripture is God-breathed and is useful for teaching, rebuking, correcting and training in righteousness, so that the man of God may be thoroughly equipped for every good work.[22]

Quite an intense cleansing process! If it was to achieve its objective of so dealing with defilement that the end product would be "thoroughly equipped for every good work," then it needed to be. "But that's a New Testament directive. I thought we were looking at lessons from the tabernacle?" Well, yes we are, but in such a way as they teach us as those upon whom has come "the fulfilment of the ages," in and through Christ (1 Cor

22. 2 Tim 3:16–17.

10:11). Even if that were not the case, we must bear in mind that, at the time of writing to Timothy, Paul's primary reference would have been the Old Testament, as much of what we now know as the New Testament had not been written.

My first inclination was to take Paul's counsel and delve a little deeper into his proposed benefits of Scripture. On reflection, however, the terminology used—even without any understanding of the original Greek—is reasonably self-explanatory. What seems more necessary to me is a proper appreciation of what it is that lends itself to such usefulness: God-breathed Scripture.

As an evangelical Christian—as traditionally defined—I hold to the authority of Scripture. I make no apology for that, nor do I feel under any compulsion to waste time defending my position, especially to those whose opinions are fixed and impervious to argument. Neither is it worthy of any effort to reiterate what is meant by the word *all*. But it is worthwhile considering precisely what constitutes Scripture in a biblical context, for it is that and that alone which has the power to bring about all that the apostle claims of it.

One of the major contentions when I first became a Christian was that the Bible did not contain the word of God, but comprised the word of God in its entirety. I got the point, but the premise was somewhat undermined by the inclusion of concordances, maps, introductory overviews, and commentary footnotes that were often denominationally vetted for constitutional allegiance.

This was almost fifty years ago. The New International Version was only three years old, and I knew of only two others at the time. The Revised Standard Version was what we were given at school and I had been taught that anything that was free wasn't really worth having. My rejection of the King James Version owed more to the escapades of a fictional thirteenth-century folk hero. When I was about eight years old, my mother spent some time with an old school friend on the south coast of England, taking my sister with her, but leaving me with my grandparents. When she returned, my mother had bought me a book as a gift: *The Adventures of Robin Hood*. It was written in English, but not as I knew it. An acclaimed literary masterpiece it may have been, but I could understand only one word in three. The "thees," "thous," "didsts," and "inasmuch as wheretofores" scared me to death and scarred me for life. So, I adopted the NIV.

Over the years, I have remained faithful to it, though in more recent times I have discovered that fidelity to have been more of a one-way street than I might have imagined. More of that later. For now, please allow me to give one or two pointers on how to choose and how to use a good Bible:

How to Choose a Bible Version That Will Serve You Well

How to choose a good Bible might suggest that there is such a thing as a bad Bible. That is not really for me to say, but there are some that are better than others, in my opinion. So, how do we ensure that our choice is based on criteria other than personal preference or one that is available in an aesthetically pleasant maroon Moroccan leather? The availability of several versions online is a useful tool, especially for interlinear comparison, but I would still opt for a hard copy edition for personal devotional or study use. It is also good from time to time to look in versions with which you may not otherwise be acquainted, to breathe new life into texts with which you are all too familiar.

A good starting point is to narrow your search to an up-to-date translation. My earlier antipathy toward the KJV may have been largely unfounded but, like it or not, language does change over time, often to mean the exact opposite of its original. There were at least two of my fellow Bible college students who found themselves there on the basis of Paul's advice to the young Timothy: "Study to show thyself approved unto God" (2 Tim 2:15). Their seventeenth-century counterparts would not have understood it that way, nor do I imagine Timothy would have been immediately enrolling in the local theological seminary.

Some versions, however, are so up to date that they pay scant regard to the original ancient texts. Modern paraphrases are often just a recent revision of a slightly older English version. At one time, these were easy to spot, as they made no attempt to disguise exactly what they were. Nowadays, even the most recent edition of the NIV has taken a translation route that, to my mind, seems beyond its remit, the results of which could have catastrophic theological significance (e.g., Isa 9:7; Rom 10:17). Similarly, translations that are subject to political correctness or the spirit of the age may or may not deserve to retain the title "Holy" Bible.

With apologies to Messrs Moffatt, Taylor, and Peterson (though with perhaps slightly less sincerity toward the latter), I would say that, on the whole, the work of a translation group is more reliable than a sole contributor. The most obvious reason for this is that it minimizes the risk of personal bias, though this may still be present if the body of contributors are of the same denominational allegiance. Some cults are particularly prone to this, the translations of which should be treated with more than a whiff of suspicion.

How to Get the Best from Your Version of Choice

Anyone who has read more than half a chapter of anything I have written will have come across the word "context" in relation to Bible study. When I was involved in directing university degree studies, one of my students once challenged me that anyone would think to hear me that understanding Scripture was all about the context. I smiled, laid what must have seemed like a patronizing hand on his left shoulder, and said: "Now you're getting the picture!"

The context for a text will include the verses in its immediate vicinity, but it will not be restricted to these alone. The passage to which it belongs, the chapter, even the whole book can provide contextual clues that will prove invaluable. One way I find helpful to extract this information is to ask questions: "What was Paul's purpose in writing this letter to this particular church group or individual?" "What cultural differences of their respective target audiences prompted the approaches of Matthew and Luke in presenting their gospel accounts?" "How do historical factors affect the apparent contradiction of two messages to the same national recipient of God's prophetic word in the Old Testament?" And be careful to whom you address such questions; the author in prayer would be a safe strategy.

A recognition that some hermeneutical principles are not universally applicable—or, at least, in exactly the same way—can help in our understanding of Scripture. Is the genre of the text under consideration easily identifiable? For example, you would not treat narrative in the same way as you would a portion rich in composite symbolism, nor must parabolic illustrations be interpreted as if they were allegories. The books of Psalms and Proverbs are awash with stylistic expressions, such as couplet parallelisms, and are reasonably straightforward to detect, because they belong to the poetic works of the Old Testament. But similar traits appear elsewhere also, as this way of representing truth is typical of Hebrew idiom.

Biblical numerology is an area of which it is good to be aware, but must also be treated with a hefty dose of caution. Some numbers do reflect a certain amount of symbolism, such as the number eight is often representative of a new beginning (circumcision on the eighth day, eight human adults in the ark, etc). Complex systems, however, are best avoided. I once heard a senior lecturer give a detailed thesis on the formula to be expatiated from the number of fish caught at Jesus' post-resurrection command (John 21:1–14). It went something like this: (12 + 5) x (3 x 3) = 153. The numerical equation went: Government plus grace multiplied by a compound (i.e., utter) completeness. It is certainly complete and utter something, but I was thinking more along the lines of nonsense.

Imagery can similarly be beset with pitfalls. Some features are represented by different symbols and some symbols have multiple applications. Yeast is a case in point. It is used to represent both the teaching of the Pharisees (Matt 16:6) and the kingdom of God (13:33), though the underlying referent for each is surely their influence upon those things with which they come into contact. Likewise, oil can be representative of gladness of heart (Ps 45:7; Isa 61:3), but it is not consistently so (see Deut 33:24; Job 29:6). Again, the context will usually provide its own clues.

I recognize that some readers may regard this section as something of a departure from the essence of our study together. However, if the laver of God's word is to cleanse us from defilement, then we need to know that it truly is God's word, without inherent pollution, and how properly to apply it. This has been precisely the most appropriate place to discuss that. My apologies for ending on a dogmatic note, but it remains my conviction that any Bible study that fails to take due cognizance of the core principles annexed to its interpretation is doomed to fall short of its primary objective.

SANCTION FOR NEGLECT

From one solemn warning to another, and please remember, these are not my words, or ultimately those of Moses; they are God's words:

> Whenever [Aaron and his sons] enter the Tent of Meeting, they shall wash with water so that they will not die. Also, when they approach the altar to minister by presenting an offering made to

> the Lord by fire, they shall wash their hands and feet so that they will not die. This is to be a lasting ordinance for Aaron and his descendants for generations to come.[23]

More Than a Slap on the Wrist

By the time this work finds itself in print, twenty-five years will have elapsed since I worked my last shift as an ambulance paramedic. One of the few things I miss is the camaraderie between staff colleagues. Our station worked a twenty-two-week rota, which included just about every shift pattern imaginable and a regular change of crew mates. Occasionally, we would be assigned to work with one in particular, largely because others who were scheduled to do so arranged their vacations around such times.

John was difficult to befriend; just when you thought you might have cracked the ice, a chill wind blew to freeze it over again. I once worked seven successive night shifts with him and quickly learned that he was in the habit of picking up the conversation at the beginning of one shift where it had been cut short at the end of the previous one. Without warning, he would begin: "But then again . . ." as I tried frantically to unscramble what had provoked his current thought process from sixteen hours earlier. By the end of the week, I thought I had made some progress, but the next time our shifts collided I was crewed with someone else and just another target if I stepped so much as a millimeter out of line.

One of John's few pleasures in life was to deduct pay from those who arrived late for work. If the alarm clock failed to ring you from your slumber for the early morning shift—or, more likely, you failed to hear its attempts to do so—the first thought on your mind was not "Where did I leave my uniform trousers?" or "Can I get away without brushing my teeth until later?" but "Which sub-officer is on duty today?" Once the large hand on the station clock ticked over to one minute past six, that was half an hour's pay docked. John took these things seriously.

Failure on the part of Aaron's sons to comply with God's commands would not result in the loss of earnings, or the requirement to make up for not meeting their obligations by staying over at the end of their shift of duty. It was more severe than that—much more severe. Nor was it an idle threat. Although related to another matter entirely, we have already

23. Exod 30:20–21.

seen that God was not averse to bringing about the premature demise of those who forsook their priestly responsibilities (Lev 10:1–3).

Pure Worship Requires Pure Hearts

It should be obvious by now, but just in case it is not, the command for the priests to perpetuate the ceremonial rite of washing was not a means to reconsecration; that had been a once-only event, which required no repetition. This was at least a daily event to cleanse from contracted defilement, as we have seen. Just to turn the situation around for a moment, the priests' earlier consecration did not thereafter absolve them of the responsibility to observe this command for ritual purification. When Cyrus of Persia allowed the released captives to take with them the temple articles purloined by his predecessor, Nebuchadnezzar, God issued this simple directive to the returning priests and Levites: "Depart, depart. Go out from there! Come out from it and be pure, you who carry the vessel of the Lord" (Isa 52:11). The sanction for neglect was so solemn because the measure of purity required was so absolute.

Why this was so in this case and not in others has been the cause of much speculation. Perhaps because the means of addressing the situation was made so easy and, therefore, its abandonment was deemed all the more disrespectful is one possible reason. Matters concerned with worship always seem to demand a more sober approach than we might otherwise imagine. Although confined to worship as an act of corporate Christian praise, Wayne Grudem attributes a more broadly applicable definition of worship as "the activity of glorifying God in his presence with our voices and hearts."[24]

Grudem's association of the voice with the heart is not without significance: "For out of the overflow of [the] heart [the] voice speaks [literally, gives utterance]" (Luke 6:45). Jesus' contrast of a good man and an evil man demonstrate that this is a universal principle. Purity in worship is not an option. But let us take great care that our own priorities and perceptions do not become the primary factors for determining what constitutes such purity. To lord it over those we consider inferior to us or incapable of attaining our lofty standard is itself impure, if for no other reason that it, too, fails to glorify God. My grandmother used to tell me that self-praise is no recommendation. Jesus put it this way:

24. Grudem, *Systematic Theology*, 1,003.

"For everyone who exalts himself will be humbled, and he who humbles himself will be exalted" (see Luke 18:9–14).

An Unwelcome Kind of Separation

Death—even the threat of death—is quite a humbling experience. Although the same may be said of the relationship between favor and merit, punishment that runs disproportionately to misdemeanor is not justice. Serious breaches of responsibility demand serious penalties, and this was serious in both respects. It was also literal in its original context. But how serious and how literal is it for us? First of all, it is not for me to propose a measure of gravity as if such incidents were subject to a scale by degrees. Suffice to say that the breach of covenantal obligations is always a serious matter. Secondly, how do we define "literal"? For Nadab and Abihu, their experience of physical death as a consequence of their sin was both literal and immediate.

What about Adam and Eve? The covenantal requirement for them seemed even more simple, though the prescribed penalty for disobedience was ostensibly the same:

> And the Lord commanded the man, "You are free to eat from any tree from the garden; but you must not eat from the tree of the knowledge of good and evil, for when you eat of it you will die."[25]

The narrative that follows is familiar to all of us, I'm sure. The upshot is that Adam did eat of the forbidden fruit, yet his physical death was not immediate. But the principle of death and decay entering the universe was instantaneous. It came in three distinct but related ways: physical, spiritual, and eternal. Adam and Eve (and everyone since) did eventually die physically. The possibility of eternal death for some also became real. But spiritual death also entered the fray, even for our first parents.

At its most basic, death equates to separation from God, the concept of a vertiginous distance between the Creator and the creation. Such distance cannot always necessarily be measured laterally except as a metaphor for detachment of intimacy. Adam and Eve never again walked with God after the fall as they had done before it. Ultimately, they did die physically, as covenant breakers. However, they also died as covenant members, who still retained something of the attendant benefits of their

25. Gen 2:16–17.

covenantal status between the issuing of the death penalty and its exercise. Just for the record, I believe that Nadab and Abihu also died as God's covenant children, as did that whole generation who failed to enter the land of promise, including Moses. They died in immaturity, many of them in rebellion, but they also died as partakers of the divine covenant. Physical death and a measure of spiritual death was their punishment, not eternal death.

"Death" Can Be Infectious

Even in the New Testament, death is not always presented as the antithesis to life but does always incorporate a measure of temporal or temporary detachment from God. In his first letter to Timothy, the apostle Paul gives specific instructions about how to deal with widows in the church. Take special note of that: they were in the church. As such, they belonged to the new covenant community of the redeemed. And yet, one group of widows, those who live for pleasure, are described as being "dead even while [they] live" (1 Tim 5:6). Precisely what is meant by this only becomes clear when we read it in the context of its contrast: "The widow who is really in need and left all alone puts her hope in God and continues night and day to pray and to ask God for help" (v. 5).

May I suggest that the premise remains valid beyond the example cited. One of the many lessons I learned at Bible college was that a need does not constitute a call. Given that this was issued in the context of outreach activity at what was essentially a missionary training establishment was quite remarkable, but the principle is more far-reaching than evangelistic endeavors only. It is true across a wide range of issues. Paul's counsel to Timothy regarding the local church's responsibility in respect of widows is summed up perfectly by Philip Towner:

> But practical need alone was insufficient grounds for receiving financial help from the church. In order to guard its testimony in society, the church could . . . subsidize only the activities of widows with exemplary lives of faith. Therefore, to qualify for support the widow had to lead a life that testified to a genuine relationship with God.[26]

To what extent Paul's appraisal of the worthy widow may or may not have been culturally conditioned, and how such an evaluation may or

26. Towner, *1–2 Timothy & Titus*, 116–17.

may not be applicable today, the fact remains that the features attached to it are of value to our study here. If the pleasure-seeking widows are described as being dead though they live, those deserving of support must be described as alive, though dealing with death. Similarly, the qualities perceived as attracting such consideration on the part of the worthy widows need only be inverted to see why undeserving widows were much less esteemed.

Without the need to be reminded, Timothy would have no doubt linked Paul's specific instruction here to the more general advice just a few verses earlier: "Give proper recognition to those widows who are really in need" (1 Tim 5:3). The NIV is almost alone in offering us "proper recognition"; others are split between "support" (e.g., HCSB, CEV) and "honor" (e.g., KJV, NASB). The original Greek is *timao*, which derives from a verb meaning to prize highly or to fix a worthy value upon.[27]

It would be easy to dismiss the worthy widow's character as a product of her circumstances. This may well be true, though it seems to me rather that her worthiness was a product of her character traits, the circumstances of her widowhood being merely incidental in bringing them to fuller expression. So, wherein lies the essential difference between these two types of widows? It cannot be relationship per se because, as we have already established, they were both in the church. Their maintaining or abandonment of fellowship could hold the key, but I think it goes further back than that.

Fearful to Be Wise

I believe the primary distinction is the widows' respective abundance and deficiency of wisdom, more specifically, their willingness or reluctance to take the first step toward its attainment. Let us look briefly at two couplets from the book of Proverbs:

> The fear of the Lord is the beginning of wisdom and knowledge of the Holy One is understanding.[28]
>
> The fear of the Lord is the beginning of knowledge, but fools despise wisdom and discipline.[29]

27. See Vine, *Expository Dictionary*, 882.
28. Prov 9:10.
29. Prov 1:7.

Derek Kidner is correct to point out that the use of the word "beginning" here is as "the first and controlling principle, rather than a stage which one leaves behind,"[30] but that does not negate it also as a relatively inchoate entry point, beyond which one may anticipate further development. Interestingly, Charles Bridges defines this "fear of the Lord" as:

> that affectionate reverence, by which the child of God bends himself humbly and carefully to the Father's law.[31]

It is not entirely coincidental, then, that my experience has been such that those in the church who might be described as being "dead even while [they] live," widows or not, have also demonstrated a singular lack of due reverence for the presence of God. Nor, perhaps, that the types of churches that seem to have more than their fair share of individuals who fit the description have been those with an overall tendency toward a party spirit, assuming an air of cataleptic nonchalance, where almost anything goes.

The remedy is in our own hands. If we want to be rid of every trace of defilement and the sanction it evokes, then we must submit ourselves to God's prescribed cleansing process. Much of the account for failure to do so must also be laid at the door of some church leaders. Water is one of those rare biblical symbols that represents both the word and the Spirit of God. It is not the responsibility of servants to perform sleight of hand pulpit tricks or indulge in theatrical histrionics, but simply to provide water. It truly is a matter of life and death, even though they live.

SUMMARY

As we step away from the brazen laver, we remove ourselves also from the vicinity of God's instruments of judgment. As priests, we now have access to the Holy Place, the furnishings of which await us in the next three chapters. We do so not as those unjudged, but as members and partakers of the new covenant and, therefore, having been judged in Christ and found acceptable to approach God's presence. In studies of this kind, I have found that the brazen laver is seldom afforded the respect it is due, often relegated to a few lines in passing, as if its symbolism extended no further than a token dip in the bowl. I trust we have seen that it was far

30. Kidner, *Proverbs*, 16.
31. Bridges, *Proverbs*, 3–4.

more meaningful than that, if for no other reason than God regarded it so. After all, the threat of capital punishment is not dispensed lightly. Now suitably cleansed, let us stride confidently and assuredly into chapter 4.

4

The Table of Presence

Welcome to the Holy Place! So glad you could make it! This is not the journey's end, but it does provide a necessary transition between where you have come from and your ultimate destination. As you look around, you will notice that there are three items of furniture here and not so much as a milligram of bronze to be found in any of them. Here is the relevant reading:

> Make a table of acacia wood—two cubits long, a cubit wide, and a cubit and a half high. Overlay it with pure gold and make a gold molding around it. Also make around it a rim a handbreadth wide and put a gold molding on the rim. Make four gold rings for the table and fasten them to the four corners, where the four legs are. The rings are to be close to the rim to hold the poles used in carrying the table. Make the poles of acacia wood, overlay them with gold and carry the table with them. And make its plates and dishes of pure gold, as well as its pitchers and bowls for the pouring out of offerings. Put the bread of the Presence on this table to be before me at all times.[1]

1. Exod 25:23–30.

THE TABLE

That was quite a lengthy reading because it gives a highly detailed description of the design of the table, but also takes into account more practical requirements, such as transportation. We will see a little something of God's culinary prowess in the following section, where the ingredients and recipe for the bread are similarly specific. The table was situated to the right (i.e., north side) as you entered the Holy Place, directly opposite the lampstand. It is the only item of furniture there not to be made entirely of gold, though it gives the appearance that it is. We shall see later that the only item in the Holiest Place, the ark of the covenant, shared this feature (or, at least, its lowest component did), as did their respective carrying poles.

Symbolism as Old as Adam

So, acacia wood overlaid with pure gold: what is the significance? From the perspective of those with a modicum of understanding regarding the New Testament, it is all too easy to superimpose our perception of Christ as the antitype back onto its type. Thus, we may see the acacia wood as representing his incorruptible manhood, yet willingly subservient to his divine nature, symbolized by the flawless gold, as the only one of whom it is said bore the "exact representation" of God's image (Heb 1:3; Col 1:15). However, this would not have been known to the generation of God's people to whom the blueprint for the tabernacle's construction first came. And yet, it is doubtful that it would have been without some symbolic meaning for them also.

At that time, any notion of a second Adam was entirely beyond the Israelites' capacity to comprehend, but what about the first Adam? At what point in history Moses received his revelation of the creation account is unclear, though Jewish tradition suggests that it was immediately prior to the giving of the Torah (Exod 24:4). Irrespective of how true this is, it is not unreasonable to imagine that verbal speculation would have abounded concerning their origin, or that the prior existence of Adam might have been known to them, including their genetic relationship to him. Also, though I can think of no clearer example where an antitype might symbolize both its type and another earlier antitype, neither am I able to bring to mind any legitimate reason why it might be considered implausible.

A Place of Trust

The table as a whole is often symbolic of communion. In the New Testament, of course, this is nowhere more obvious than at the table of Communion with an uppercase *C*. But throughout Scripture, tables are employed to reflect communion with a small *c*, particularly the existence of attendant trust. Sharing a meal around a table was even then a distinctive of Hebrew hospitality, but it was also typically pregnant with meaning. The very issuing of an invitation reflected an understanding of commonality, its acceptance confirming the fact by both parties. Conversely, the absence or rejection of an invitation signaled the lack of such a bond.

Trust is seldom an all-or-nothing quality from the outset; it is usually extended in measure and by degrees. I have a number of acquaintances and those who might be described as peripheral friends, to whom I would be happy to extend an invitation to share a meal. Not many of those would manage to sample my whisky collection as an aperitif; fewer still as a digestif. One who would definitely do so—and has on many occasions—is my best friend, Russ. With one notable exception, there is no one I trust more, and I'm sure that trust is reciprocated. But my trust is measured. It is not quite 100 percent, but it is well into the high nineties. Again, I'm pretty confident that he would say the same of me. For example, I would not trust him to drive my car unsupervised without the risk to my subsequently being faced with a hefty speeding fine. I'm not sure I would leave him too long unattended in the company of my whisky collection either.

Coming closer than anyone else alive to that elusive 100 percent is my wife, Barbara, though even she does not quite make it. To be fair to her, any degree of mistrust on my part is down to what she might consider to be for my own good; she thinks she is better placed to make that judgment than I am. I would make an incredibly skinny vegetarian, if it wasn't for the fact that I like meat and have never suffered any conviction for doing so. If I venture into the kitchen when Barbara is preparing a meal, I don't want to see anything green unless it's a pea, a Brussels sprout, or a spinach leaf. Okay, I'm also fine with zucchini and peppers but, strictly speaking, they are classified as fruit, so they don't count. Occasionally, I have suspected Barbara of masking or disguising the existence of contraband vegetables, such as broccoli or green beans, by shredding them extremely finely and hiding them in a shepherd's pie, of all places. My trust has limits; such wanton betrayal lies beyond them.

Trustworthiness Demands Trust

With tongue firmly removed from cheek, let us consider a couple of biblical examples where the phrase "table of trust" might apply. The first comes to us with musical accompaniment, probably the lyre (Heb. *kinnor*):

> Even though I walk through the valley of the shadow of death, I will fear no evil, for you are with me; your rod and your staff, they comfort me. You prepare a table before me in the presence of my enemies. You anoint my head with oil; my cup overflows. Surely goodness and love will follow me all the days of my life, and I will dwell in the house of the Lord for ever.[2]

A poetic metaphor maybe, but if ever there was a table that demonstrated the existence of trust, the establishing of communion, then it was this one. That trust was mutual, but in the direction from David toward his God it was also complete and unwavering. Why was this? Simply because the object of his trust was not a thing but a person, and that person was eminently trustworthy. His presence removes fear; his instruments of solace and correction bring comfort. But notice where the table is set: not only in the general vicinity of hostility, which might otherwise give rise to a measure of anxiety or trepidation, but more specifically "in the presence of [David's] enemies," and yet it was the safest of havens.

This psalm is rich in covenant terminology, though some of it is admittedly lost in the NIV translation. The "love," which David is assured will accompany "goodness" to the end of his days, is *hesed*, a better translation of which is "covenant loyalty" (see NASB, NET, HCSB). Because they are intrinsic to God's nature, it could be argued that goodness and faithfulness require no outward manifestation by which they must be validated: God would still be good and faithful even if there was no one toward whom he might express either quality. From our perspective, however, we can only truly know his goodness and faithfulness through good and faithful deeds (though it must also be acknowledged that our fallen nature often suppresses our perception of them).

2. Ps 23:4–6.

Entertaining Guests

The second example to which I wish to draw the reader's attention fails to mention the word "table," though many of the features we have discussed so far are certainly present, with a few more besides. Although difficult to date with any precision, it is widely acknowledged that the incidents we are about to consider took place over six hundred years earlier than the tabernacle's construction.

We are about to visit Abraham and his wife, Sarah; or rather, we are about to observe as three strangers visit them (Gen 18). Many commentators believe the three "men" to have included angelic appearances in the company of a Christophanic leader (that is, a preincarnate physical appearance of the second person of the Godhead). Their subsequent role in the imminent destruction of Sodom and Gomorrah casts little doubt on such a supposition. When they appeared, Abraham seemed to recognize some superior quality (v. 2), as he quickly sought to attend to their needs (v. 4). He invited them to stay, to which they offered no resistance (v. 5), and gave instructions to his wife for baking some bread (v. 6), while he went off to prepare a meal (v. 7). They enjoyed fellowship together and, suitably refreshed, the visitors set off on the remainder of their journey (vv. 22, 33).

A little later, the two angels who had been sent on ahead came across Abraham's nephew, Lot (Gen 19). Contrast the two experiences: Abraham had been "sitting at the entrance to his tent" (18:1b), Lot "was sitting in the gateway of the city" (19:1b); both men offered hospitality to their would-be guests (18:3; 19:2); they accepted Abraham's invitation without hesitation (18:5c), but acceded to Lot's request only reluctantly (19:2c–3a). But there is another difference that requires its own treatment: Abraham's wife, Sarah, was very much involved in the preparations for their honored guests (18:6, 9), but Lot's wife is conspicuous only by her absence until they are advised to flee the city (19:5). She may just as well have been a pillar of salt (v. 26).

Now, I have something of a mischievous streak. Coupled with a similarly impish overactive imagination, this has often placed me in a difficult situation entirely of my own making. I also have a tendency to think more quickly than I can give verbal expression to those thoughts, which has served only to compound the problem. So, I'm afraid I must ask you to indulge me for a moment. I cannot help but read this passage concerning Lot's visitors without imagining them dropping in on a marital tiff. Under intense silent pressure, Lot has taken himself off to cool down in the hope that his return will be to a more placid atmosphere. Then he bumps into the heavenly duo. Feeling he must at least give an air of spirituality, he invites them round for coffee (I know, bear with me). Sensing some unpleasantness afoot, they try to get out of it, but he prevails, perhaps anticipating that their presence will help to diffuse the domestic unpleasantness in which he finds himself. Arriving home with guests in tow, he tentatively unzips the tent flap (ditto), peers inside, and announces, "Darling, God's agents have come to stay the night!" to which his wife snarls, "See to them yourself; I'm busy!"

Supper with the Lord

Nonsense? Probably! So, what sensible lesson can we learn from what we actually know of the contrast between the two incidents? It is simply this: God is most at home where home is a more accurate reflection of heaven. Carrying that idea through to the New Testament, if we had access to some sort of comfortometer device, I wonder what spread of readings it would give of Jesus' recorded communion episodes. I'm guessing the times he spent around the table in the company of the religious leaders of his day would register quite low, while having the opposite effect with the likes of Lazarus and his sisters. Not that such comfort—or lack thereof—would necessarily be an indicator of threat to his command of the situation, so much as one of relative ease with his surroundings.

Unconvinced? Then let us take a closer look. Luke documents two occasions of Jesus being invited to eat in the home of a Pharisee. On the second occasion it is recorded that he was being carefully watched (Luke 14:1), though the unfolding of events in the first episode suggests he was under surveillance there, too (Luke 7:39). Both times he had to challenge the thinking or behavior (or both) of the religious leaders in attendance (7:44–47; 14:7–14), each time lauding the humility of the non-religious as a better example. Hardly heavenly, was it?

Although admittedly largely cultural, the biblical act of eating with someone at the same table conveyed also a statement of identification. Look at Paul's counsel to the believers at Corinth when one of their number had been exposed as guilty of sexual impropriety:

> But now I am writing to you that you must not associate with anyone who calls himself a brother but is sexually immoral or

> greedy, an idolater or a slanderer, a drunkard or a swindler. With such a man do not even eat.[3]

It is clear from the context—both immediate and more wide-ranging—that Paul's primary concern is essentially two-fold: the ultimate restoration to fellowship of the guilty party, and the protection of the covenant community from charges of guilt by association, thus endangering the effectiveness of the proclamation of the gospel.

In the same letter, Paul gives voice to similar concerns regarding impropriety around the table of the Lord's Supper (1 Cor 11:17–33). It seems they were guilty of everything except eating and drinking in remembrance of their Savior. It was a reputation of which to be ashamed; it was also one for which they would be held to account (v. 34). As the meal signified covenant relationship in its purest form—both vertically and horizontally—the Corinthians' conduct effectively invalidated their participation in it (v. 20). We do well to heed Bruce's evaluation of the situation:

> It was no more possible for the Lord's Supper to be eaten in an atmosphere of social discrimination than it was for the same people to "partake of the table of the Lord and the table of demons" (10:21). The Eucharist could be profaned by faction as certainly as by idolatry.[4]

THE SHEWBREAD

> Take fine flour and bake twelve loaves of bread, using two-tenths of an ephah for each loaf. Set them in two rows, six in each row, on the table of pure gold before the Lord. Along each row put some pure incense as a memorial portion to represent the bread and to be an offering made to the Lord by fire. This bread is to be set out before the Lord regularly, Sabbath after Sabbath, on behalf of the Israelites as a lasting ordinance. It belongs to Aaron and his sons, who are to eat it in a holy place, because it is a most holy part of their regular share of the offerings made to the Lord by fire.[5]

3. 1 Cor 5:11.
4. Bruce, *1 & 2 Corinthians*, 110.
5. Lev 24:5–9.

A Less Prescribed Approach

My wife is an excellent cook. Whatever she serves on the plate is good food. Perhaps too good for anyone with pretensions about restraining an already burgeoning waistline. When I say "good," I mean that it is always wholesome and never less than flavorsome. Maybe it would not earn many awards for presentation, though she is so adept at learning and applying new techniques that I am certain she could rise to that challenge if required. As it stands, her philosophy and mine are well married. At mealtimes, I prefer to have my taste buds tantalized than send my retinas into rapture.

Sometimes, Barbara will allow me into the kitchen and we'll experiment together. An oft-repeated query is: "I wonder what this would taste like with that." Occasionally, we get it right the first time; more often than not, it is the eventual product of trial and error, with a heaped tablespoon of tasting and evaluation thrown in. Otherwise, cooking times and the measuring of ingredients very rarely enter the equation: if it was too much last time, we just add a little less this. Much of my wife's expertise in such matters has come with years of experience. Only in a very few culinary disciplines does she appear less haphazard, baking being one of them.

Dealing with the Leftovers and the Lollers

The recipe for the shewbread did not come about by Moses trawling the storehouse of his childhood memory, his eyes swimming in a pool of unshed tears, to find sunny Sunday afternoons spent on the banks of the Nile with Pharaoh's favorite maiden great-aunt. It was according to divine order, designed in the bakehouse of heaven. God was in the detail—quite literally. The provision was made in accordance with his instructions, but what does that provision symbolize?

Before we consider that question, there are some other issues that are not only easier to resolve, but will also aid us in our greater quest. The first is both obvious and reasonably self-explanatory: the bread was replaced on a regular basis. My current cat, Dora, is almost ten years old. She is pampered more than any feline we have cared for, which is quite an achievement in itself. We adopted her as a two-year-old from a local rescue agency and pretty much continued the regime she had become used to, which included a diet of dry food only, taking care to avoid budget brands. Any snobbery attached to this is hers, not ours. She simply will not eat anything but the best, but does enjoy a variety of flavors.

The advantage of dry food over wet is that it can be left out almost indefinitely and just requires topping up at bedtime. There is an awful lot of waste with wet food. There was an awful lot of waste with Dora's predecessor, Florence, especially after her brother, Ebenezer, gave up on mopping up duties by gorging himself to the front of the queue at that great cattery in the sky. Ebb and Flo (yes, really) would not touch dry food, no matter how much a kilo had been paid for it. Theirs, too, was changed once a day, but required a complete emptying and refurbishment. With just Florence to cater for, I would guess that more found its way into the garbage than into her tummy. The shewbread was not topped up; whatever remained of the previous Sabbath's deposit, after the priests had taken their share, was disposed of and the whole batch replaced.

The second thing to note is that there were no items for repose in this part of the tabernacle either. Although the bread was for the priests' consumption and was not only permitted but commanded that they should "eat it in a holy place," this holy place was not thereby designated the staff lounge. This is not because the bread itself commanded inherent reverence, except insofar that it was the bread of God's presence (Heb. *lehem happanim*; literally, "bread of the face"). But the manner in which the priests were expected to eat of it suggested also a continual service, both toward God and on behalf of their fellow Israelites. They were, in effect, covenant intermediaries. The association of bread with covenant ratification was not new to God's people at that time, and it is considerably less so today.

Representing the Symbolic

Slightly more difficult to grasp might be the fact that, as well as serving as a symbol, the bread itself required representation. This was the role of the pure incense, placed alongside each of the two rows of bread (Lev 24:7). If the bread symbolized God's prevailing sustenance, then the incense served as a reminder to both parties that its permanence and surety was not dependent upon the chemical reaction of a few natural ingredients.

The phrase employed is not without significance, especially in the original. For "memorial portion" read *le'azkarah*, which occurs in this form only here, though this and other variants are found on seven occasions in the Old Testament, six of which are in the book of Leviticus. It derives from a root that is known from cultic contexts elsewhere, particularly where part of a greater whole was being presented as a token offering by way of invocation. Richard Averbeck concludes thus:

> If the grain was offered raw, then incense was to be added to the memorial portion to lend it an especially pleasing aroma as it burned on the altar (Lev 2:1–2, 15–16). The assumption seems to be that if it was already cooked, there would have been a naturally pleasing aroma rising from the bread itself, without adding incense.[6]

This is obviously not the case here. However, it is helpful in leading us to find agreement with Rabbi Jacob Milgrom when he asserts that the pure incense was, indeed, a token commemorative portion, reminding the offerer that "the entire cereal offering should really go up in smoke and that the portion that does is *pars pro toto*: it stands for the remainder."[7] As an aside, and though not in itself conclusive, it does introduce a different argument to the "This is my body/blood" debate of the New Testament (Luke 22:19; 1 Cor 11:24; see also Heb 10:3), especially as the same Greek word used for "remembrance" (i.e., *anamnesis*) also translates *azkarah* and its variants in the Septuagint.

Hunger Satisfaction

Now to return to the provision itself and what it symbolized. Having heard the word discussed a number of times before I actually saw it in print, part of my early Christian experience was spent imagining the perks of priesthood, whereby these thirteenth-century BC stalwarts of the faith would gather a couple of hours before lunch, each armed with their version of the Thermos flask, around the table of shortbread. Seeing "shewbread" didn't exactly despoil my vision or add much by way of further illumination. It was only when I acquired a more modern translation and was confronted with "showbread" that the penny began to drop.

The prescribed bread was perpetually on show (until it was eaten or replaced). But it also made a show by representing the Presence of God (thus, bread of the Presence). It is often assumed that there were twelve loaves to represent the twelve tribes of Israel. While this is the most likely

6. In VanGemeren, *Old Testament Theology & Exegesis*, 1:336.

7. Milgrom, *Leviticus 1–16*, 182.

explanation (see also Exod 24:4), the fact that there is no definitive expression to that end renders us able only to say that they correspond with the twelve tribes rather than dogmatically assert their representation.

Arguably the most well-known of Jesus' "I am" sayings came in the context of the crowd demanding more food after the feeding of the five thousand (John 6:1–15, 25–59). Alluding not directly to the bread of the tabernacle, but another divine provision in the wilderness (i.e., the manna), Jesus identified himself as "the bread of life" (v. 35a). He did not leave his audience to guess what he might have meant by that, but went on to explain: "He who comes to me will never go hungry, and he who believes in me will never be thirsty" (v. 35b). Just as natural bread satisfies physical hunger, so God's provision of metaphysical bread satisfies our spiritual hunger (see vv. 32–33).

Its effectiveness, however, is dependent upon more than provision and accessibility. God has taken the initiative, but we must respond to that by availing ourselves of the opportunity afforded to us. The miracle of the loaves was also a parabolic illustration, but the distribution, which was so central to the release of miraculous power within him, can also misdirect our attention. Jesus is rightly called the life giver, but he gives life not as some dispenser of a product that lies essentially outside of himself, like some heavenly errand boy dishing out market freebies. The life (Gk. *zōē*) is himself, which he also has the power to sustain. How amazing that this bread of life should be born in Bethlehem, that is, the house of bread!

But we must come to him. One of my amazing talents is for the incredible ignorance I am able to demonstrate with very little effort for all things horticultural. So much so that my wife refuses to accept any offers I may rarely make to help in the garden beyond the watering can, digging up old roots, or mowing the lawn, and only then under close supervision. But I can appreciate the end product of other people's endeavors. I could sit for inordinately lengthy spells watching birds feed, bees pollenate, butterflies flutter by, and frogs hop from one pond to another.

I am particularly attracted to arrays of garden color. My favorite plant has to be the sunflower. The sunflower is so named, not because its glorious appearance resembles a stylized image of the sun, but because it will always instinctively turn its face toward the sun to receive what it requires in order to maximize its potential. This same quality is required of us in relation to the bread of life: that we turn to him.

Getting the Best from Your Daily Bread

So, the living Word, the *logos*, is also the bread of life. The written word is also often spoken of as having the same qualities, in that it is able to feed, nourish, and sustain. The inference is reasonable enough, but is there any definitive biblical evidence to support the claim? Actually, Scripture seems more to be contrasted than identified with bread. Take these two examples: The first were Jesus' own words, quoted in the midst of arguably his greatest trial outside of the cross:

> It is written, "Man shall not live on bread alone, but on every word that comes from the mouth of God."[8]

> I have not departed from the commands of [God's] lips; I have treasured the words of his mouth more than my daily bread.[9]

Job's concluding phrase is one that will resonate with anyone who knows the Lord's prayer (Matt 6:9–13). As a metaphor, it represents the necessities rather than the luxuries in life; more specifically, our dependence upon God's power to provide. It is often also alluded to as the very thing with which Job contrasted it: the word(s) of God. I have no difficulty in accepting it as such, but with one significant caveat: it is possible to be exposed to God's written word as an expression of the bread of life and to receive no meaningful sustenance from it. Here are eight pointers on how to avoid some of the obstacles to being fed:

- Ensure your chosen environment is conducive to receiving instruction. As far as is practicable, it should be a place where you are able to focus, free from external distractions.
- Cultivate an attitude of humility. The most sagacious Bible scholars I know are also the least arrogant; this is no coincidence.
- Don't treat God's word like a daily promise box. I'm sure we've all heard stories like the one about the guy who knew no better than to receive divine guidance by randomly opening his Bible, believing the first things upon which his eyes alighted constituted God's instructions for the day. At a particularly troublesome time in his life, he opened his Bible, whereupon his eyes fell: "Judas went out and hanged himself" (Matt 27:5). Not wholly convinced, he tried

8. Matt 4:4.
9. Job 23:12.

again: "Go and do likewise" (Luke 10:37). Increasingly hesitant, he adopted a third time lucky approach: "That thou doest, do quickly!" (John 13:27). He thereafter abandoned this method.

- Avoid scanning Scripture solely for sermon pointers or to prove/disprove doctrinal issues. Trust the One whose hand feeds you to know what you need better than you do.
- Don't be afraid to ask questions of the author. Given his role in its inspiration, it might be an idea to consider addressing your queries to the Holy Spirit; and don't be too proud or doctrinally/constitutionally bound to listen to the answers.
- Resist the temptation to search as proxy advisor to others. There is a reason for private devotions to be so named. Unless there is an existing bond of trust, those who approach claiming to have a word for me often go away disappointed to find that I have a couple of words for them, too.
- Prioritize character development above increased knowledge. Understanding is for application, not gratification; we are not given insight so that we can impress the elders or attract the interest of a potential date at the next round of the inter-church Bible trivia competition.
- Expect to receive good things. I was once assigned as prayer partner to someone whose spirit seemed to have entered into a permanent residency contract somewhere between dudgeon and umbrage. Each time she began to pray, I half expected her to conclude with the invocation that the Almighty would "Give us this day our daily dread!"

GOD THE PROVIDER AND THE PROVISION

This section is more to do with the bread on the table than the table upon which the bread is set. That said, however, it must also be acknowledged that everything Israel possessed, both collectively and as individuals that comprised the community, was theirs by divine provision. This remained true even when third party conduits were involved, such as the acquiring of precious metals and clothing materials from their captives prior to leaving Egypt (see Exod 3:20–22; 12:35–36). God had foretold what would happen through Moses and events worked out precisely as he had said. But the promise first came centuries earlier:

> Then the Lord said to [Abram], "Know for certain that your descendants will be strangers in a country not their own, and they will be enslaved and ill-treated four hundred years. But I will punish the nation they serve as slaves, and afterwards they will come out with great possessions."[10]

Provision According to Need

We see just how "great" when the people responded to Moses' invitation to contribute to the tabernacle's construction (Exod 25:1–9; 35:4–29). Their offerings included both component parts used in the construction of the Table of Presence: gold and acacia wood. We have already mentioned the obvious symbolism attached to each in the previous section, but it is worth mentioning here something of the qualities of the timber of choice. The *shittah* tree grew in the deserts of Sinai and those of the Jordan River valley. The wood is hard, incredibly dense, making it indestructible by insects, and has a fine, exquisite grain. It was extraordinarily verdant in arid places, often attaining a height of twenty feet, with spectacular yellow flora. The wood's resistance to pest invasion made it an ideal candidate in which to encase mummies inside the coffin. God's provision is not without design.

The materials required for the bread are a little more tricky to explain, but not beyond reason. Let me begin by saying that I believe in the principle of divine provision by means of miraculous intervention, but there is no biblical suggestion that this was the case here. If it was, it would hardly be likely to escape having been mentioned. Given the fact that the tabernacle's construction was completed just one year after the Israelites had left Egypt, it is possible that the first batch of ingredients used were brought with them, though unlikely. Even with divine protection for the duration of the wilderness experience, sufficient wheat and oil for nigh on forty years would have needed something of the size of a modern intercontinental delivery wagon for transportation.

So, what are those reasonable explanations? Well, first of all, the whole thirty-nine years' supply was not required on day one. Their more immediate needs could have been met from their recent encounter with

10. Gen 15:13–14.

the Amalekites at Rephidim (Exod 17:8–16). Although there is no mention of plunder, it is not an altogether improbable notion. Subsequent needs could also have been met through later interaction, both hostile and friendly. The Israelites' protracted journey took them via and in the vicinity of many other territories, the nations of which may well have been open to the idea of trading some of the jewelry, livestock, and other produce of Egyptian origin in exchange for wheat and other items.

A further possibility has been raised. It is known that wild wheat grew in some of the regions Israel passed through. Although not widely available—and requiring more culinary preparation than cultivated species—there may have been sufficient to supplement what they were able to access from other sources already mentioned. The only objection I can see to this would be its apparent negation of the command to use "choice flour" in the baking of the showbread (Lev 24:5a NET), suggesting a superior quality cereal. Most other versions, however, render this "fine flour," each translating the Hebrew *solet*, which refers to the finely ground heart of the grain only, as distinct from *qemah*, "which denotes the whole kernel or bran, ground together with the heart of the grain."[11]

So, plunder, trade, or wild wheat? Probably a combination of all three with none to the exclusion of the others. But we must continually bear in mind that whether my conclusion is accurate or there were other means of accessibility that I have not considered, ultimately God was the source of Israel's provision; he was their provider.

No Help Required

It is not without a degree of some irony that both the means to accessing the ingredients to produce the symbol and what the finished product is designed to symbolize both point to the same thing: God as Provider. There are many themes that run as a constant thread throughout Scripture, and this is one of them. It goes back as far as the early chapters of Genesis, from God taking the initiative to find a suitable helpmeet for Adam to ensuring that a more adequate covering was found to hide their shame in the immediate aftermath of the fall. I remain unconvinced that Adam and Eve's nakedness was the problem per se, except insofar that it displayed their procreative organs, which thereafter would reproduce

11. In VanGemeren, *Old Testament Theology & Exegesis*, 3:269.

after their own sinful kind. God had created Adam in his own image; Adam would create in his own, too.

Arguably the most dramatic episode to demonstrate God's provision in those early chapters of Genesis concerned an incident that took place on Mount Moriah. The context is one we do well to observe. In many Christian circles of my acquaintance, the word *provision* suffers from the same exploitative misuse as does *faith*. At the root of their abuse lies a "What's in it for me?" mentality. As far as faith is concerned, I can do no better than direct the reader to that well-known heroes of the faith chapter (Heb 11) and note what was in it for them. For now, we will content ourselves with what the Bible has to say about God's provision; back to Mount Moriah.

When Abraham's wife, Sarah, gave birth to Isaac, they were both of an age where the idea of parenthood would under other circumstances have been a thing of the past. But God had made a promise to them, even in their old age. Their respective responses were as diverse as they were dramatic: Sarah thought it was a cruel joke, and Abraham thought God might need a little help to bring about his promise. They were both wrong. Sarah's laughter turned to cries of labor pains and Abraham was left with an unruly son, Ishmael, not the child of promise, but of fleshly pursuit. When Isaac was a young adolescent, God said to Abraham:

> Take your son, your only son, Isaac, whom you love, and go to the region of Moriah. Sacrifice him there as a burnt offering on one of the mountains I will tell you about.[12]

Here beginneth the first lesson: "your only son"? What about Ishmael? Strictly speaking, Isaac was not even the firstborn. But whatever others may say to the contrary, Ishmael was never recognized in the divine continuum. As far as God was concerned, the son he asked Abraham to take with him to sacrifice on Moriah was the only son he had. So, the two of them saddled up a donkey, called a couple of servants to join them on the journey, prepared the wood for the offering, and they all set off together. When Isaac asked about the sacrificial animal, his still young voice unsteady in its register, Abraham's trust remained in God's provision (Gen 22:8), though his commitment to obey never wavered. And God did provide: "So Abraham called that place The Lord Will Provide" (v. 14a), that is, *Jehovah Jireh*.

12. Gen 22:2.

When I was at Bible college, there was a lawn quadrant between the male students' residential quarters and the dining hall/meeting room. To the left as you made your way to the main block was the on-site bakehouse, directly opposite the college library. There was a wall to the side of each of these two buildings. On one, inscribed in the mortar, were the words *Ebenezer (hitherto hath the Lord helped us)*, and on the other *Jehovah Jireh*. God's provision in its original context was not one of paying the utility bill on time, arranging a sufficient supply of confectionary for the forthcoming road trip, making sure I can boast the largest yacht in the marina, or the lowest handicap at my local golf club: it was annexed to sacrifice.

Perfect Fulfilment

When it comes to God demonstrating his dual role of provision and provider there is no clearer example than the greatest sacrifice of all. It took place a little over two thousand years ago on a cross just outside Jerusalem's walls. The Latin name for the site was *Calvariae Locus*, from which our English "Calvary" is derived. The common Greek term was *Golgotha* (i.e., "place of the skull"). It was not a pleasant place, but Romans were hardly noted for their aesthetic considerations when it came to identifying places or means of execution.

So, the Bread of life had his life taken at a place about as far removed as imaginable from the tabernacle's Table of Presence. Despite the best intentions of artists and sculptors down the centuries, keen to display something of the retention of his beauty and dignity, the crucified Christ was not a pretty sight. A crown of twisted thorns forced into his brow; pierced bones mixed with blood exposed where the nails had punctured his hands and feet; his weary, forlorn and forsaken, spear-pierced naked body hanging there in sweaty desperation for his temporal needs temporarily to be attended to. No, the combined efforts of Zurbarán, Velázquez, and Dalí could never accurately capture this. But, as my good friend Alan Scotland said on a recent *TBN Presents* broadcast: "A hungry man may have many causes for complaint but, if he is offered bread, the shape of the loaf isn't one of them." And yet, in that state, the Son of Man frightened death to death.

Unlocking the Pantry Door

In Jesus, God provided what humanity needed most: a Savior. As the second Person of the trinitarian Godhead, he became also that provision. Moreover, in so doing, he fulfilled every aspect of the Old Testament provider/provision motif. For all those who acknowledge him thus, all other provisions are theirs for the asking, but not without certain conditional caveats. The first is uncompromising trust:

> Trust in the Lord with all your heart and lean not on your own understanding; in all your ways acknowledge him, and he will make your paths straight.[13]

The kind of trust of which Solomon speaks is akin to faith. The Hebrew is *betah*, the basic meaning of which is security without deviation, but with the implication of helplessness otherwise. Jesus carried this idea through when comparing the worries of life's needs with the Father's provision in nature. Perhaps some of us might be better advised to consider once again "the birds of the air" and "the lilies of the field," rather than the peddled propaganda of the name-it-and-claim-it brigade (see Matt 6:25–34).

The second proviso is a legitimate appropriation of Scripture regarding its promises. Let us look briefly at a couple of texts by way of example. The first is often cited as the premise for the sowing and reaping principle: "Remember this: Whoever sows sparingly will also reap sparingly and whoever sows generously will also reap generously" (2 Cor 9:6). The number of times I have heard this cited as an argument to promote the "sow a pushbike, reap a Ferrari" school of (un)biblical economics is quite alarming. The context is about needs being met through sacrificial service, not whims being indulged. Even the anticipated harvest is spoken of as one of righteousness (v. 10).

As if there was any doubt, Paul clarifies the situation further and in demonstrably less subtle tones in his letter to the Galatian believers:

> Do not be deceived: God cannot be mocked. A man reaps what he sows. The one who sows to please his sinful nature, from that nature will reap destruction; the one who sows to please the Spirit will reap eternal life. Let us not become weary in doing good, for at the proper time we will reap a harvest if we do not give up. Therefore, as we have opportunity, let us do good

13. Prov 3:5–6.

> to all people, especially to those who belong to the family of believers.[14]

The final example comes as a warning against the formulaic approach to seeking God's provision. Here is the text:

> I tell you the truth, anyone who has faith in me will do what I have been doing. He will do even greater things than these, because I am going to the Father. And I will do whatever you ask in my name, so that the Son may bring glory to the Father. You may ask for anything in my name, and I will do it.[15]

What do we imagine this simple phrase to mean: "in my name"? The most common misuse in my experience has been to treat "the name of Jesus" like a magical appendage to prayer, almost as if it were a spiritual "Abracadabra," transforming every desire into a certain expectation. This it is not. To pray in the name of another is to do so as a proxy representative on their behalf and with their authorization. Captains of war in medieval England would travel from town to town on horseback at the head of their troops, issuing edicts in the king's name. It was with his authority that they were delegated to make his will known throughout the land. The same principle applies here: to make requests of the Father in Jesus' name we must first discern his will regarding those things for which we pray (more concerning this in chapter 6).

GOD'S WATCHFUL EYE

We have seen that the Table of Shewbread is also known as the Table of Presence. This can be a misleading term, especially in view of God's omnipresence and what we may infer from it. To be all-present suggests that he is nowhere absent. And yet, from the perspective of subjective experience, a sense of God's presence does seem to be by degrees. We are more acutely aware of it on some occasions than on others. This appears to be the essence of what is implied when Scripture suggests that he removes himself from certain situations or from the experience of some individuals for a season: he is not absent per se, but nor does he at those times invest his presence with sensory awareness. We might even say at such times that his presence is devoid of numinosity.

14. Gal 6:7–10.

15. John 14:12–14.

He Knows, You Know

Outside of a Christian environment, I have enjoyed something of a varied employment experience, including colliery mechanical apprentice, insurance agent, paramedic, high school exams invigilator, and examiner. As you might imagine, I have also endured my fair share of ribbing and ridicule because of my Christian profession. Some of it has been lighthearted, though much of it has bordered on hostile. An example of the former took place when I was working on the ambulances. My colleague for this particular shift was a senior officer, Harry, with whom other workmates found little common ground. If Harry was trying to think of something just beyond his powers of recall—such as an address, a location, or where he last saw his first aid bag—his facial features contorted into the grimace of pained concentration. His only other claim to fame, as far as I could tell, was the sporting of a beard that defied being sheared.

I got on reasonably well with Harry, though I never allowed myself to be completely unguarded in his company. He had a dry sense of humor, which others failed to recognize, let alone appreciate. Harry knew of my Christian conviction and, though never cruel, he was not averse to the odd cutting quip. Always with a keen eye for what he perceived to be any potential slip or lowering of my defenses, however slight, whereupon he would be in with a mocking index finger raised to the skies and, in a broad Barnsley accent: "He's watchin' thi, tha knows!" Well, he was watching me, and I did know, but not because Harry had said so, though I learned to be grateful for the reminder.

Attainment through Alertness

Of course, God is not only omnipresent, but also omniscient. He knows all things and he knows them perfectly, even the as yet otherwise unknown things. But as events unfold in time, nothing escapes God's attention. We might say that he watches over his creation. But the psalmist is careful to emphasize the especial manner with which he casts a caring eye over the elect:

> For the Lord watches over the way of the righteous, but the way of the wicked will perish.[16]

16. Ps 1:6.

> He will not let your foot slip—he who watches over you will not slumber; indeed, he who watches over Israel will neither slumber nor sleep.[17]

> The Lord watches over all who love him, but all the wicked he will destroy.[18]

In general terms, the shewbread on the table was symbolic of God's provision. The fact that there were twelve loaves lends itself to the suggestion that they represented the twelve tribes of Israel. An argument could even be made that their equal size (as far as the baking process allows) speaks of God's impartial favor toward each tribe, irrespective of their numbers (e.g., Dan and Judah). More specifically, the provision of bread refers to his sustenance, which we now find in his word, both living (Christ Jesus) and written (the Bible). This is what God had to say through the prophet Jeremiah: "You have seen correctly, for I watch over my word to accomplish it" (Jer 1:12 HCSB).

Commentators are correct to identify this "word" with the specific message being brought to and subsequently through Jeremiah concerning the almond branch (Jer 1:11). However, I remain unconvinced that this negates the underlying principle in more far-reaching applications concerning the revelation of God's word in Scripture. If anything, it is enhanced by it. Irving Jensen seems to be in agreement:

> The connection of the vision and the application may be seen in the fact that the almond tree, blossoming around January, was the first tree to awaken from the long winter's night, its blossoms appear before the leaves. The symbol of awakeness befitted God's Word, for though His people had settled into a dark, cold sleep of spiritual dearth, His Word was ever awake, watched over by Him, bringing about its daily unalterable fulfillment of sovereign design.[19]

Beneficiaries of God's Vigilance

But what exactly do we understand by the phrase "God watches over his word?" Although it does not appear in any of the three texts cited above

17. Ps 121:3–4.
18. Ps 145:20.
19. Jensen, *Jeremiah and Lamentations*, 20–21.

from the Psalms, the most common Hebrew verb to be translated "to watch" is *shaqad*. The essence of *shaqad* is to be engaged in a sleepless vigil or to guard attentively. Such a state of alertness, however, is never the end itself, but has other objectives in view. Some of these are included in the texts. Let us consider some more that might be observed in relation to God's watchfulness over his written word:

Preservation

This idea is at the forefront of all three cited texts from the Psalms, but particularly so the last two. The Hebrew words employed are *somereka* and *sowmer*. Both derived from a root meaning a given or undertaken responsibility to faithfully keep, the fidelity of which is not so much in the promise itself as in the capacity to fulfil that promise. It is used elsewhere of Adam's guardianship in the garden (Gen 2:15), a shepherd's care for his flock (1 Sam 17:20), city watchmen (Ps 127:1; Isa 21:11–12), Sabbath observance (Isa 56:2, 6), and God's covenant keeping (Deut 7:9; Dan 9:4).

God's perfect power renders him the only one capable of perfect preservation, thus: "You will keep in perfect peace him whose mind is steadfast, because he trusts in you" (Isa 26:3). The guarantee is not the one whose trust is steadfast, that is the condition; the assurance is the one in whom he trusts. Thus, God is entirely trustworthy when it comes to the preservation of his written word. And yet, there are examples where his word does not seem to have been preserved with personal integrity by others or without predisposition toward pet themes. How can this be?

This touches on the inspiration of Scripture, especially in relation to its infallibility and inerrancy. Both qualities have become subject to misunderstanding and/or misappropriation. In an attempt to avoid such pitfalls, it is important to begin by defining how I understand the terms used, before issuing an overarching caveat that, I believe, covers both. Infallibility is "the quality of neither deceiving nor being deceived,"[20] (etymologically a compound of the Latin *in* and *fallo*). In relation to Scripture, its infallibility consists in the absence of intention to mislead. Where this seems not to be the case, the fault invariably lies with a lack of proper interpretive measures, such as failure to recognize type, symbolism, linguistic nuance, context, or genre.

20. Packer, *God Has Spoken*, 111.

Inerrancy is even more self-explanatory; it simply means that Scripture is without error, substantially, historically, morally, or spiritually. The caveat to Scripture's acknowledged inspiration, with reference to both its infallibility and its inerrancy, is that these are true of the manuscripts as originally given. Subsequent errors of translation, unintentional or otherwise, fall outside such a claim. Wayne Grudem defines inerrancy thus:

> The inerrancy of Scripture means that Scripture in the original manuscripts does not affirm anything that is contrary to fact.[21]

Is it, therefore, misleading to speak of the Bible as inerrant when such a term applies only to documents that are no longer extant? First of all, this is how the term has always been applied and understood. Secondly, despite the caveat—and, indeed, the valid reasons for it—God has preserved in Scripture the intention of his heart in producing its original form, wherein lies its prevailing authority.

Perseverance

To maintain the alliteration, other terms I might have chosen include persistent or the prevailing nature of God's word. What do I mean by that? Precisely this: unless conditionally annexed, God's word cannot be hindered in its progress, and he watches over it to ensure that outcome. This may come as a surprise to some. We can all think of texts where we, as Christian believers, are encouraged to persevere (e.g., Rom 5:3; Heb 12:1), or examples of godly men and women in the Bible who maintained their witness with tremendous fortitude (see 1 Sam 1:1–20; Job 2:10). However, we are speaking here not of what God's word reveals of others, but of itself. This is what Isaiah said: "The grass withers and the flowers fall, but the word of our God stands for ever" (Isa 40:8).

This was a message of comfort to God's still covenant people, a reminder of his steadfast love toward them in their particular situation. So, is it thereby restricted in its application? Well, the apostle Peter certainly wasn't of that opinion. He cited Isaiah's words more than seven hundred years later in the context of reminding his readers of how they had been reconciled to God:

21. Grudem, *Systematic Theology*, 90.

> For you have been born again, not of perishable seed, but of imperishable, through the living and enduring word of God . . . and this is the word that was preached to you.[22]

There is possibly an element of progressive revelation in Peter's counsel. We must bear in mind, however, that he was essentially the apostle to the Gentiles, among whom will have been some former pagans. His concluding reference to "the word" seems to be specifically identified with the gospel message, by which his original readership came to faith, but there is no reason to believe that this was consistent throughout his argument. It is the same kind of thing as when a parent is giving instruction to a child about the source of yesterday's meal: "This is a lamb; you remember the lamb you had last night with the mint sauce, potatoes, carrots, peas, and gravy?" There is no suggestion that the child had been expected to eat a whole lamb to themselves. It is but an identifiable sample.

Alec Motyer says this of Isaiah's text:

> Just as the flower fades under adverse conditions, so the moral and spiritual constitution comes under testing. Furthermore, what Isaiah says about "all flesh" [v. 6] he notes to be equally true of those from whom more would be expected: the Lord's people show the same moral instability . . . . [B]y marvellous contrast, there is a changeless factor in the world: "the word of our God."[23]

Productivity

> As the rain and snow come down from heaven, and do not return to it without watering the earth and making it bud and flourish, so that it yields seed for the sower and bread for the eater, so is my word that goes out from my mouth: It will not return to me empty, but will accomplish what I desire and achieve the purpose for which I sent it.[24]

The first thing to notice here is what proportion of the initial objective is attained: all of it. Until you realize what—or, rather, who—you are dealing with, that is quite a remarkable statistic. For a short time, my stint as an ambulance paramedic involved me being seconded to a lower

22. 1 Pet 1:23, 25b.
23. Motyer, *Isaiah*, 277.
24. Isa 55:10–11.

managerial position. Any instructions to staff that were met with more than a 75 percent favorable response were deemed to have been successful. There seems little wonder, then, that these words through Isaiah were preceded by "For my thoughts are not your thoughts, neither are your ways my ways" (Isa 55:8).

This may well be cited as a hallmark of Scripture's authority; I prefer to think that it speaks more of God's sovereignty, from which Scripture's authority is derived. Even the analogy chosen to illustrate the word's productivity is not incidental. Precipitation enables growth and life (see also John 6:63); it is never without effect. Similarly, God's words are never wasted; small talk is not on the agenda. At the same time, however, our response to what he says must be a cautious one. That may seem a strange thing for me to say in the context of believing God without reservation. Allow me to explain.

Believing what God has said and believing what we think he has said can be poles apart. Human imagination can be a wonderfully creative tool, but it can also lead us down paths of its own design. God's sovereign power is subject only to God's sovereign will; that will is governed by no external constraints, including any frailty of interpretive skills on our part. This is both a challenge and a comfort. The challenge is that we get on board with his revealed will at the earliest opportunity; the comfort is that, having done so and adjusted our prayer life accordingly, we come to realize how unassailable God's will is.

God's will is "good, pleasing and perfect" (Rom 12:2). It is, therefore, beyond improvement by modification. We can come to know it "by the renewing of [our] mind[s]." And one major contributory factor in the process of renewing our minds is to feed upon the revealed word of God in Scripture. It will realize its objective; he watches over it to that end.

CONSEQUENCES OF INATTENTION

Ignorance Not so Blissful

History is only superficially concerned with the past; its main object is to understand humanity through time. In around 950 BC, Solomon's Temple was built, effectively rendering the temporary tabernacle obsolete. Just over three hundred years after this, a remarkable though terrible discovery was made. By now, the kingdom had been divided into north (Israel) and south (Judah). Judah's kingship was a mixture of good and bad, while the northern territory knew no good kings. In 622 BC, Josiah succeeded his father in the south after Amon's officials had conspired to kill him (2 Kgs 21:23–24). Josiah was only eight years of age when he took the throne. By the time the events of his reign were being recorded, he earned this appraisal: "[Josiah] did what was right in the eyes of the Lord and walked in all the ways of his father David, not turning to the right or to the left" (22:2). In fact, he was the last godly king before Judah's exile and is entirely deserving of the space allocated to him by the historian.

One of the central paths Josiah took involved the discovery, in the eighteenth year of his reign (2 Kgs 22:3), of the Book of the Law of Moses. The book was actually found in the temple by the high priest, Hilkiah, and reported to Shaphan, the king's secretary (v. 8a). Shaphan read the document twice, first in private (v. 8b) and then to Josiah (v. 10). The precise nature of the contents of the Book of the Law continues to fuel debate, as does conjecture over whether its earlier discovery might have made a difference to Judah's subsequent history. Speculation here both is unnecessary and would prove utterly futile. We learn all we need to know from Josiah's response:

> When the king heard the words of the Book of the Law, he tore his robes. He gave these orders to Hilkiah the priest, Ahikam son of Shaphan, Acbor son of Micaiah, Shaphan the secretary and Asaiah the king's attendant: "Go and enquire of the Lord for me and for the people and for all Judah about what is written in this book that has been found. Great is the Lord's anger that burns against us because our fathers have not obeyed the words of this book; they have not acted in accordance with all that is written there concerning us."[25]

Just how great the Lord's anger was is revealed a few verses further on through the prophetess, Huldah:

> Because they have forsaken me and burned incense to other gods and provoked me to anger by all the idols their hands have made, my anger will burn against this place and will not be quenched.[26]

There then follows notice of a reprieve for Josiah because of the contritious manner with which he had responded to news of the Book's discovery. We learn much, however, of God's perspective concerning his

25. 2 Kgs 22:11–13.

26. 2 Kgs 22:17.

people's negligence. First of all, the personal inference cannot be overlooked: he equates their neglect of his law with them having forsaken him. Secondly, a natural consequence of them abandoning their covenantal duty to the one true God is that the void must be filled elsewhere, and so they aligned their allegiance in the direction of false gods of their own choosing and making.

The principle underscoring this practice has been repeated throughout history. At no time has it been more evident than in the current age, where denial of the divine has progressed (*sic*!) to narcissistic self-indulgence. The gods of the age are those commercially designed to address the pleasure-seeking needs of the populace, while at the same time lining the pockets of the even more extravagant demands of their corporate production teams. That individual Christians, and in some cases whole church organizations, have so willingly jumped on the zeitgeist bandwagon is no cause for glee. This is especially so in the light of God's declaration here. Is it applicable to our generation? You be the judge: "These things happened to them as examples and were written down as warnings for us, on whom the fulfilment of the ages has come" (1 Cor 10:11).

Looking Back before We Can Look Ahead

Having already considered the advantages of due diligence, it seems to require little exercise of our lateral thinking to realize that the consequences of inattention include a commensurate reduction of value in those benefits. Let us return to the tabernacle. We saw in earlier chapters the correlation in the outer court between the altar and the laver, insofar that satisfying the demands of the one provided accessibility to the other (albeit only for the priests). Here in the Holy Place, the three items of furniture also correlate. Without preempting too much of the following chapter, the illumination provided by the lampstand is vital to a correct understanding of what takes place both here at the Table of Presence and in relation to the altar of incense.

We shall also see in the final chapter that God's chosen location in which to reside was the Holy of Holies, above the mercy seat, between the cherubim (see Exod 25:21–22). Here we see especially God's sole provision for us to have direct communication with him; there is no other way, no less arduous route, no alternative private back door. You either come by his designated mode and method or not at all. In relation to the symbolism currently under consideration, these two features are linked thus: our capacity to commune with the God of the word is inextricably annexed to our absorption of the word of God. Or, to put it negatively, where the word of God does not govern our path, our capability to fellowship with the Father is commensurately diminished.

In terms of our understanding of God's purpose in creating humanity, this is somber business. His purpose for us cannot be divorced from his reason for creating us. According to the Shorter Westminster Catechism of 1647, in response to the question "What is the chief end of man?" comes the two-fold reply: "The chief end of man is to glorify God and enjoy him forever." The first part is objective, the second subjective. But notice also the order: the subjective is derived from the objective, not vice versa. Although not taken directly from the Bible, the convened assembly responsible for the Catechism's compilation was careful to derive its premises from Scripture's contents (see Ps 86:9; 144:15; 1 Cor 10:31; Phil 4:4). It is my conviction that such glorification and enjoyment are only possible on the basis of humanity's restored communion with God through Christ.

Communion Precedes Enjoyment

David's experience was a checkered one by any standard. Scripture records his triumphs with relish, but is equally not silent concerning his failings of character and failures in conduct. But he was a humble man and an honest man; so much so, that he might also be described as his own worst critic. The sense of God's presence was very dear to him. Here is what he had to say of it:

> You have made known to me the path of life; you fill me with joy in your presence, with eternal pleasures at your right hand.[27]

Twenty-five words in which are posited three benefits to communion with God: behavioral revelation, temporal joy, and a deposit of pleasure that stretches into eternity. All these would have been absent without David's resolve to give attention to his primary responsibility: communion with God. Let us take a closer look at each one in turn and some of the implications attendant upon them:

27. Ps 16:11.

How to live

God's mode of making anything known to us is identical to that experienced by David—revelation. And yet, there are differences. Identical, yet different? Yes, and the differences come in two key areas. First of all, for us the potential distractions are far greater. Global shrinking is a metaphor for how much easier it is becoming to communicate and conduct business affairs with the rest of the world. Economies are so interdependent that a crisis on one side of the world right now affects most of the rest of it within the hour. And no one is immune or exempt from its effects, not even Christians. Any doubts on that score will have been quickly put to bed during the recent coronavirus pandemic.

Secondly—and more positively—the boundaries of revelation have been expanded considerably since David's time. Bruce Milne defines revelation as "the unveiling of something hidden, so that it may be seen and known for what it is."[28] The purpose of divine revelation is to make God known to us; it is necessary because without it we could not possibly know him. He does so in a number of ways: through the physical universe (Rom 1:18–32), in human morality (2:14–15), in the unfolding of world events (Acts 17:26–27), and in the commonality of religious desire (Eccl 3:11). Together, these constitute general revelation: the notion of God's existence.

Special revelation, however, is not concerned so much with knowing about God as it is coming to know him, his ways, and his requirements of us. As such, he communicates with us directly in two ways: in the person of his Son, the living Word (see John 1:1–2, 18; 17:3; Matt 11:27); and through Scripture, the written word (1 Cor 10:11; 2 Tim 3:16). In both of these ways, we have the potential advantage over David; if we fail to avail ourselves of them, we are poorer than he. For example, how can Scripture teach, rebuke, correct, and train without our applying ourselves to its study?

Joy in God's presence

The kind of joy there is to be had in God's presence is beyond description; our best efforts fail to do it justice, for it transcends comparison. For that reason, it is perhaps easier to explain what it is not. It is not the fullest

28. Milne, *Know the Truth*, 19.

expression of joy imaginable, for the extent of it cannot be imagined, yet it is the only experience that can truly be described as joyful. Although the memory of having been in God's presence is a wonderful thing in its own right, surpassing all other joyful recollections, it comes nowhere near to matching the actual experience of it.

Nor is this kind of joy to be equated with frivolity or superficial merriment induced or conditioned by temporal pleasures. Although it is an emotion triggered by an experience, the joyfulness is focused on the experience itself rather than what is produced by it. Neither is it governed by or dependent upon circumstance. In this regard, it might be regarded as somewhat akin to contentment. Consider Paul's words to the believers at Philippi, and notice how emphatic he is in his command: "Rejoice in the Lord always. I will say it again: Rejoice!" (Phil 4:4). He is just as insistent to the Thessalonians:

> Be joyful always; pray continually; give thanks in all circumstances, for this is God's will for you in Christ Jesus.[29]

Paul was not being just a cheery leader with an aptitude for encouragement. Nor was he guilty of proclaiming platitudes devoid of experiential substance. Hard graft, facing death on a regular basis, frequent flogging and beating, shipwreck, endangered by the elements and his enemies alike, enduring many sleepless nights, and knowing many times what it was like to have his physical needs denied him (see 2 Cor 11:16–29). Did I miss anything out? Ah, yes: multiple imprisonments. On one occasion, his feet-cuffed cellmate was Silas. Their response to this gross miscarriage of justice? "At about midnight [they] were praying and singing hymns to God" (Acts 16:25a). The joy of God's presence is unconfined and pervades natural constraints.

Eternity now?

Although the concept of an afterlife was incipient in David's time, it would not be true to say that it was entirely absent. Tremper Longman appears to share that opinion:

29. 1 Thess 5:16–18.

> Even in its Old Testament context, the idea of not seeing decay and enjoying eternal pleasures in God's presence seems to point to something beyond the grave.[30]

Maybe I am missing something that is staring me in the face, but I honestly don't see how this portion of Ps 16:11 (or any of it, for that matter) can in any legitimate way be linked to having all our needs met with abundance, as is sometimes claimed. This is not to say that I necessarily refute the suggestion per se, nor do I dismiss the idea of Christians enjoying a foretaste of heaven in the present, just not on the basis of David's words here cited. To my mind, a much stronger case could be made for a transfer in the opposite direction, thereby linking David's prayer and the counsel of Jesus in his sermon on the mount:

> Do not store up for yourselves treasures on earth, where moth and rust destroy, and where thieves break in and steal. But store up for yourselves treasures in heaven, where moth and rust do not destroy, and where thieves do not break in and steal. For where your treasure is, there your heart will be also.[31]

Jesus first addresses the earthly before directing our attention to the heavenly; he does so by issuing a negative command, followed by a positive one. But there is no middle ground, no opportunity to hedge one's bets. By failing to be obedient in concerning ourselves primarily with heavenly matters, which would be secure in God's keeping, we thereby take the opposite path, our heart's treasure being vulnerable to "all those agencies and processes that cause earthly treasures to diminish in value and finally to cease completely to serve their purpose."[32]

SUMMARY

"The Table and the Shewbread" sounds like a sixteenth-century play by the Bard of Avon. Even the Table of Shewbread disguises what each constituent part symbolizes. Thus, I prefer the Table of Presence. I trust that I have shown in each of the sections of this chapter that the intimate sense of God's presence in reality was never intended to be merely abstract; the design has always been for communion between the Creator and his

30. Longman, *Psalms*, 106.
31. Matt 6:19–21.
32. Hendriksen, *Matthew*, 344.

creation. In every Old Testament type, we see God take the initiative to make his presence known through revelation that communion might be its product. Not only does he provide the means by which that might be facilitated, but the symbol of it also points to him as the actual provision. Nowhere is this more clearly evident than in the New Testament fulfilment of the antitype in Christ Jesus, "who for the joy [of restored communion] set before him endured the cross" (Heb 12:2).

5

The Golden Lampstand

There were no windows in the Holy Place. It was a place of shadows, both metaphorically and literally. Its only light came from the *Minora*, variously translated as candlestick or lampstand. My only objection to the former is that our current understanding of the term is far removed from when the text was first translated into English. As an ignitable wick embedded in animal fat, candles as we know them first made an appearance around 500 BC. As similar devices of other components, the name of which might be derived from the Latin verb *candere* (i.e., to shine or glow), the existence of "candles" may well have predated this. For the sake of clarity, I will persist with the use of "lampstand." The golden lampstand was positioned alongside the south wall of the Holy Place, directly opposite the Table of Presence.

THE LAMP AND THE WORD

Another incredibly detailed description with which the reader might want to compare your translation of choice:

> Make a lampstand of pure gold and hammer it out, base and shaft; its flower-like cups, buds and blossoms shall be of one piece with it. Six branches are to extend from the sides of the lampstand—three on one side and three on the other. Three cups shaped like almond flowers with buds and blossoms are

> to be on one branch, three on the next branch, and the same for all six branches extending from the lampstand. And on the lampstand there are to be four cups shaped like almond flowers with buds and blossoms. One bud shall be under the first pair of branches extending from the lampstand, a second bud under the second pair, and a third bud under the third pair—six branches in all. The buds and branches shall all be of one piece with the lampstand, hammered out of pure gold. Then make its seven lamps and set them upon it so that they light the space in front of it. Its wick trimmers and trays are to be of pure gold. A talent of pure gold is to be used for the lampstand and all these accessories.[1]

A Costly Correlation

This is the first major piece of furniture we come to in the tabernacle that is made entirely of gold. It was not just any grade or quality of gold the Israelites could lay their hands on, nor was it alloyed with other metals. What they had in their possession fit the bill perfectly: it was pure gold (Heb. *tahor zahab*). Pure in this context should not be identified with gold in its raw state, but that which has been subject to the most rigorous of refining processes. Of the fifty-eight occasions where *tahor* is used as an adjective in the Old Testament, almost half of them (i.e., twenty-six) are to be found in these later chapters of Exodus in connection with the tabernacle, qualifying the nouns *gold* and *incense*.

The weight of gold used in the construction of the lampstand and its accessories totaled around seventy-five pounds, which is marginally over thirty-four kilograms. This is about equivalent to the average weight for a boy approaching his eleventh birthday. In terms of monetary value, the amount of gold of that quality required to make a lampstand of the same dimensions today would cost in the region of 1.8 million pounds (i.e., a smidgen over 2.25 million dollars).

We have already established that there were three specific items in the Holy Place: the Table of Presence, the golden lampstand, and the altar of incense. Each had a unique function, but the lampstand shared one particular distinction with no other: it was the only item of furniture that was designed to improve our capacity to appreciate the others within its domain. We shall see the relationship between this fact and the role of the

1. Exod 25:31–39.

Holy Spirit in due course. For now, we must content ourselves with the significance of the interrelationship between the lampstand and the table of shewbread or, more specifically, what is symbolized by each.

Enlightenment the Product of Illumination

Illumination and enlightenment are often used interchangeably. Although I can appreciate occasions where this might be valid, especially when employed as nouns, I believe their verb forms often give rise to a subtle difference. One such occasion is highly significant in our study of the mutual interdependence that exists between the lampstand and the shewbread, and their respective antitypes. To illuminate merely provides the light by which we might see; to be enlightened, on the other hand, is the state of having been informed (usually, though not necessarily, by an external agency) regarding something of that which is or has been viewed.

This distinction is consistent with Hebrew idiom, seen in a number of places, especially the poetic writings. For example, what at first appears to be a repeating couplet actually highlights the difference:

> Your word is a lamp to my feet and a light to my path.[2]

> For these commands are a lamp, this teaching is a light.[3]

For obvious reasons, the lamp had to be lit in order to provide light, but that is assumed in both citations above. However, different (though admittedly related) words are used for "lamp" and "light." The former is *nerah*, from a primitive root verb meaning "to break up" (as in darkness or the way a furrow breaks up the soil in preparation for sowing). The latter translates *or*, which is literally a bright shining natural light, but is often used metaphorically of light given to the eyes, that is, a teaching that finds fulfilment in having been fully expressed or acted upon.

Just as the lampstand supplied a light source by which the sustenance provided by the shewbread might more readily be identified (we shall see how later), so God illuminates Scripture whereby it might enlighten us. The responsibility is then ours to act appropriately and in accordance

2. Ps 119:105.

3. Prov 6:23.

with that enlightenment. James taught this, by way of parabolic illustration, in the first chapter of his epistle:

> Do not merely listen to the word and so deceive yourselves. Do what it says. Anyone who listens to the word but does not do what it says is like a man who looks into a mirror and, after looking at himself, goes away and immediately forgets what he looks like. But the man who looks intently into the perfect law that gives freedom, and continues to do this, not forgetting what he has heard, but doing it—he will be blessed in what he does.[4]

Okay, confession time: had I been given to gambling, I would have considered it relatively risk-free to have staked a sizeable amount on Jesus having uttered those words. It is certainly reminiscent of some of his teachings. This is particularly true of the closing promise, a truth not lost on George Stulac when relating it to the teaching of the Beatitudes:

> Jesus based blessedness specifically on the coming of his kingdom, and the blessedness was often identified in paradoxical contrast to the world's usual standards for happiness. Jesus made it a point to declare "blessed" those who were poor, mourning and persecuted, and his promise of blessing carries this Christian content. True blessedness—the joy of Christ's kingdom—comes not by escaping trials, but by doing the word of the Lord.[5]

Light Earns the Divine Approval

Theologians often speak of the law of first mention, many placing great store by it as a principle of interpretation. The underlying premise is that the first time a motif or type of event is referred to in Scripture contains in the narrative of its circumstances a seed of information that equips us to understand all like subsequent episodes. The first reference to a relationship between illumination and the word of God could hardly occur any earlier. It comes to us in the first chapter of Genesis. In fact, it was also the first day of creation:

> And God said, "Let there be light." And there was light. God saw that the light was good. And he separated the light from the darkness. God called the light "day," and the darkness he called

4. Jas 1:22–25.

5. Stulac, *James*, 79.

"night." And there was evening and there was morning—the first day.[6]

"Well, I can see the light, but where is the word?" In the command to come into existence, by which the previously non-existent light was immediately brought into effect by God's Spirit. Now, what is the first thing you notice? Rather helpfully, Derek Kidner points out that the creation of the light "appropriately marks the first step from chaos to order."[7] For me, however, it is the fact that there also appears to be an apparent role reversal. In the tabernacle, the lampstand is the dominant object, with everything else in its domain, including the table of shewbread, subject to it. Here, the word of God is the more forceful of the two. But is it truly a case of roles reversed or are we, too, in need of enlightenment? Notice that in both cases, whether objectively or subjectively, the light is the servant of the word, not vice versa.

We are then told that when God saw the product of his command, he declared it to be good. This might be slightly misleading. It almost gives the impression that it could have been anything other than good, or that God was a little taken aback by light's goodness, like some cheap afternoon game show contestant who has the runner-up prize revealed to him for the first time. What lies at the heart of the declaration is that when God saw the actual realization of the command, it was just as good as he had imagined it prior to calling it into existence. (Of course, I apply sequential thought process to the divine Being only anthropomorphically.)

This was also ultimately for the benefit of humanity, even though Adam's creation was almost a week away (or twenty-two verses). Of course, the rest of the created order would also be aided by the creation of light, and that before Adam arrived on the scene. But, as the pinnacle of all that was to be, humanity would be the primary beneficiary of light's existence. It was created first in order to contribute toward the perfect environment into which Adam and Eve might be introduced. It certainly was not to help God to see what he was doing, as I recently heard being taught to a Sunday school class.

6. Gen 1:3–5.

7. Kidner, *Genesis*, 51.

Acting within the Parameters of Our Vision

One of the major obstacles I have found to moving from illumination to enlightenment is not disobedience per se, except insofar that it is a product of cognitive dissonance. In this context, cognitive dissonance is where apparently contradictory views are held in tension awaiting resolution. This is not always a negative condition if such views are located in the same place and exist because no satisfactory conclusion may be drawn on the basis of the evidence currently available. The problem arises when such views are held in different parts of the same person, such as when your heart believes one thing and the head believes another.

Is there an answer? For many years, I heard it preached that faith must conquer—or, at the very least, subdue—reason. That was the real battleground: to get the mind on board with the heart by any means possible, even if that involves the latter riding roughshod over the former. Well the mind is the battleground, and it is won over by arduous, though arguably less callous, means.

On one occasion, Jesus was confronted by a man whose son was in desperate need of deliverance (see Mark 9:14–27). Presumably, having heard reports of this miracle-working prophet, the man had asked his disciples to help, but to no overtly positive avail. So, he approached Jesus directly, his faith having already taken something of a nosedive: "if you can do anything, take pity on us and help us" (v. 22b). Jesus then opened up a dialogue in his own inimitable way without so much as asking a question, but it evoked a response: "Everything is possible for him who believes" (v. 23b).

The man's reply has troubled me for decades until recently: "I do believe; help me overcome my unbelief" (v. 24b). What could this possibly mean? I am now firmly of the conviction that the man's heart believed, but his mind required convincing. Jesus acted upon the mustard seed of faith that existed anyway, but what did the man really need for his mind to catch up with his heart? I'm guessing the realization of the miracle would have done it, but elsewhere the apostle Paul doesn't talk about the mind being switched off, ignored, or relegated to the back row of the decision-making process. Rather, he counsels his Roman readership to be transformed in their thinking by its renewal (Rom 12:2). I believe that cognitive dissonance is one of the major obstacles to a positive outcome in prayer; if we cannot find agreement in ourselves between what the heart believes and what the head acknowledges to be true, how can we expect God to say "Amen!" to it?

A cautionary note: God has his own program of recovery for us, which may not correspond with our opinion (or those of others) of what it should be. He is not primarily in the business of goosebumps; he seems to be more concerned with what we might become than in giving us a buzz. Thus, we will find more often than not that the illumination of certain parts of his word are designed to enlighten us with regards to transforming our characters, rather than titillating our command of his greatness. "Ah!" but you say, "I thought the chief end of man was to glorify God and enjoy him forever?" Yes, it is, but I don't think I'm being too presumptuous or disrespectful by suggesting that God's foremost objective for hitherto fallen, but now new, creations is to match them with characteristics befitting their newfound status.

We all have ways of responding to new discoveries in Scripture, whether that is a nugget of information about God's nature, the bridging of a historical gap in our understanding, an ever-expanding amazement at the wonder of Jesus, or the revelation of endurance or humility on the part of an Old Testament prophet. They usually range from "Wow!" to "Hallelujah!" I am as appreciative of those occasions as anyone else. When it comes to being challenged, however, either on a troublesome character issue or a cherished doctrinal position, our response is often one of stunned silence. Let us not remain dumb for too long before we thank God for bringing it to our attention, embracing it for what it is, and moving forward in the enlightenment it has brought. And remember, it was not God's responsibility in the tabernacle to replenish the oil, clean the glass, or trim the wicks: it was that of the priests.

THE LIGHT OF THE WORLD

Jesus is the antitype of which the golden lampstand in the tabernacle was a type; he fulfilled its illuminatory function:

> When Jesus spoke again to the people, he said, "I am the light of the world. Whoever follows me will never walk in darkness, but will have the light of life."[8]

Or did he?

8. John 8:12.

> Now when [Jesus] saw the crowds, he went up on a mountainside and sat down. His disciples came to him, and he began to teach them, saying . . . "You are the light of the world. A city on a hill cannot be hidden. Neither do people light a lamp and put it under a bowl. Instead they put it on a stand, and it gives light to everyone in the house. In the same way, let your light shine before men, that they may see your good deeds and praise your Father in heaven."[9]

A Kingdom Initiative from the Beginning

So, which is it to be? Jesus or the people of God? The answer is a resounding "Yes!" In new covenant terms, it is the people of God because it is Jesus, but more of that in due course. For now, we must consider the fact that this was always the design of election for God's people, even under the old covenant. Scripture reveals to us three domains of God's purpose in creation, the last two a progressive development of its predecessor: the garden, the land, and the world. The primary purpose of each is a subject I rarely touch upon in my writing: evangelism. The reason is quite simple: it is an area upon which I am remarkably underqualified to pass practical comment. But it is also a topic that I believe is grossly misunderstood, even by some who have no qualms about being recognized as evangelists (often with a capital *E*).

I have nothing but respect for the likes of George Whitefield, Dwight L. Moody, and Billy Graham, but to hear some speak of them would seem to suggest that God suddenly woke up in the mid-eighteenth century to the possibility that mission might be a good idea. Nor was it only a product of the gospel age, or at least, not what we might understand by that term as an exclusively New Testament concept. It went back even further than Israel's abortive effort in Canaan to Adam's mandate in the garden.

The garden of Eden may well have constituted the known world as it was to its inhabitants initially, but that did not make it the whole world per se. It was just the cultivated piece of land given to Adam as a base from which eventually to extend God's purpose further. That purpose consisted in the establishing of his government throughout the earth. But note how when Adam failed, there was no plan B, just a modified plan A.

9. Matt 5:1–2, 14–16.

Making God Known through His Mighty Deeds

Fast forward to Israel's second water crossing. The previous generation having passed through the Red Sea on their way out of Egypt under Moses, those now under the command of Joshua experienced a similar miracle in their journey out of the wilderness, through the Jordan, and into Canaan. Once safely across, they were required to set up a memorial altar at Gilgal, so that when successive generations, both of Israel and other peoples, enquired as to their meaning, they would be told of God's miraculous intervention:

> [Joshua] said to the Israelites, "In the future when your descendants ask their fathers, 'What do these stones mean?' tell them, 'Israel crossed the Jordan on dry ground.' For the Lord your God dried up the Jordan before you until you had crossed over. The Lord your God did to the Jordan just what he had done to the Red Sea when he dried it up before us until we had crossed over. He did this so that all the peoples of the earth might know that the hand of the Lord is powerful and so that you might always fear the Lord your God."[10]

This was effectively Israel's great commission: to make God's might known. That they largely failed to do so has caused some to speak of it as nothing more than an intermediate divine purpose. The implications of such terminology include the premise that God's design for natural Israel under the old covenant was always to provide us with examples of how not to respond to him and the consequences of failure. This became the case, as Paul makes clear (1 Cor 10:11), but there is no suggestion that that was the decreed intention.

Israel was required to take Canaan by conquest where necessary. One episode that captivates this concept perfectly is often lost in our presentation of it to children. When faced with the Philistines at Socoh in Judah, the Israelite forces may well have hoped for an amicable settlement. The best the Philistine champion, Goliath, could offer was a two-man battle, one from either side; to the winner the spoils. Israel's confidence plummeted at the sight of this nine-foot-tall colossus. David just happened to be in the vicinity when Goliath was shouting out his threats. He was only there to bring supplies to his brothers; he was neither battle-hardened nor trained in tactical warfare. All he had was his unshakable faith in God's covenant promises.

10. Josh 4:21–24.

Of course, we all know how the narrative unfolds, and probably have done from a tender age: David took the Philistine's life with a carefully aimed slingshot, striking Goliath in the forehead, from which he fell dead. What was David's primary motivation? To avenge Israel? To vindicate God? Let me put it another way: how well do we really know the story? Prior to taking aim, this is what David said to the Philistine champion:

> You come against me with sword and spear and javelin, but I come against you in the name of the Lord Almighty, the God of the armies of Israel, whom you have defied. This day the Lord will hand you over to me, and I'll strike you down and cut off your head. Today I will give the carcasses of the Philistine army to the birds of the air and the beasts of the earth, and the whole world will know that there is a God in Israel. All those gathered here will know that it is not by sword or spear that the Lord saves; for the battle is the Lord's, and he will give all of you into our hands.[11]

There it is again: "and the whole world will know." The NIV is poor here; the relationship between the consequence and the condition is not so obvious as suggested by the original. Other translations have it better, replacing "and" with "(so) that" (e.g., ESV, KJV, NASB), or "then" (CEV, HCSB, GNT). Nor was it a mere triumphalistic embellishment designed to inspire hope among the forlorn; it was a revelation of evangelistic mission.

A More Peaceable Era

David's reign is often regarded as the golden age of Israel's history. I disagree. I think his conquests paved the way for that, but the fruits of it were enjoyed during the reign of his son, Solomon. They are both types of Christ, but in different ways. It might even be argued that David and Solomon are two sides of the same type, the father representing the conquering Christ, the son the Christ reigning in the peace having been attained in conquest. David had had it in his heart to build a more permanent residence for God's presence than the tabernacle. The idea was not dismissed completely, but he was not to be the one to build it, for he had blood on his hands, some of it innocent.

11. 1 Sam 17:45–47.

And so, Solomon was appointed to the task of completing the temple, under God's supervision. Having done so, Solomon presented a lengthy prayer of dedication, which included a suggestion of his understanding of God's kingdom purpose:

> As for the foreigner who does not belong to your people but has come from a distant land because of your name—for men will hear of your name and your mighty hand and your outstretched arm—when he comes and prays towards this temple, then hear from heaven, your dwelling-place, and do whatever the foreigner asks of you, so that all the peoples of the earth may know your name and fear you, as do your own people Israel, and may know that this house I have built bears your Name . . . . And may these words of mine, which I have prayed before the Lord, be near to the Lord our God day and night, that he may uphold the cause of his people Israel according to each day's need, so that all the peoples of the earth may know that the Lord is God and there is no other.[12]

Twice here we have the same phrase: "so that all the peoples of the earth may know." One prominent foreigner who came from a distant land because of the Lord's renown was the Queen of Sheba (1 Kgs 10:1–10). She was not the only one to seek advantage from the repository of wisdom God had invested in Solomon . . . :

> King Solomon was greater in riches and wisdom than all the other kings of the earth. The whole world sought audience with Solomon to hear the wisdom God had put in his heart.[13]

. . . but she does hold especial significance. Jesus cites her thus in the context of his own superiority to Solomon:

> The queen of the south shall rise up with this generation, and shall condemn it; for she came from the uttermost parts of the earth to hear the wisdom of Solomon; and behold, a greater than Solomon is here.[14]

12. 1 Kgs 8:41–43, 59–60.
13. 1 Kgs 10:23–24.
14. Matt 12:42 KJV.

The Cross Was Necessary, but the Resurrection Is Vital

Matthew and Luke are the only two Gospel writers to refer to the Queen of Sheba; she appears nowhere else in the whole of the New Testament. That phrase, "uttermost parts of the earth" ("ends of the earth" in other translations) does appear outside of the Gospel accounts, twice in the book of Acts (1:8; 13:47), and once in Paul's letter to the Romans (10:18). Arguably the most well known to many Christians is to be found on the lips of Jesus himself, on the occasion of him promising empowerment for the task before the early disciples, immediately prior to his ascension:

> But ye shall receive power, after that the Holy Ghost is come upon you; and ye shall be witnesses unto me both in Jerusalem, and in all Judaea, and in Samaria, and unto the uttermost part of the earth.[15]

This is a slightly different version given by Luke of the same event recorded in his Gospel account (Luke 24:45–49), but the material facts are all there. Matthew also gives an account of it, though one key feature is made more overt: what we now speak of as the great commission of the church (Matt 28:16–20) is a product of Christ's authority on earth matching that which he enjoys in heaven (v. 18). This is reminiscent of the prayer Jesus taught his disciples, where God's kingdom rule is described in similar terms: his "will be[ing] done on earth as it is [done] in heaven" (6:9–13). It is, in effect, an affirmation of the believer's calling in accordance with the divine purpose, which is to fulfil the original mandate for humanity.

This, too, is not plan B, C, or Z, nor even so much plan A modified, but rather perfected. It will be achieved through evangelism, though we might have to realign our understanding of that term on more biblical grounds than is often the case. The cross of Christ is essential to our standing before God, without which we would still be in Adam and, therefore, in sin. But a gospel message that ends there is a deficient one and, in my opinion, has a tendency to produce a diminished Christian experience, largely devoid of life.

At the risk of coming across as overly dogmatic, I would challenge any reader to find me a New Testament example of the gospel being preached where there was not at least an allusion to the resurrection. In most cases, it is emphasized. And yet, this has not been my experience,

15. Acts 1:8 KJV.

nor would I guess that of many readers. Instead, Sunday evenings and the climax of week-long rallies culminate with a pathos-laden invitation to revisit Calvary: "Jesus raised two hands for you; cannot you lift one for him? How about a little finger?" "He carried his crucifix all the way to Golgotha for your benefit; all he asks now is that you bring your burden of sin to the front of the auditorium that you might be rid of it."

Please don't misunderstand me. I'm grateful for all that was achieved at the cross. But if the mission of Christ had ended there, much of the rest of the New Testament would have been written very differently. All those Pauline passages about being a new creation would have disappeared, because the basis for them is being in Christ (e.g., 2 Cor 5:17), which is only possible because of the resurrection (Rom 6:4). A gospel that ends with the crucifixion might still have been considered good news, but not nearly as good as it presently is. We would not have been a new creation in Christ, but a cleaned-up version of the old one in pre-fallen Adam, with all the same potential to repeat his folly. If we are truly to be ambassadors of God's message to a world in darkness, then let us illuminate it in its entirety. Jesus does not covet our sympathy; he commands life.

FUELED BY GOD'S SPIRIT

> Command the Israelites to bring you clear oil of pressed olives for the light so that the lamps may be kept burning. In the Tent of Meeting, outside the curtain that is in front of the Testimony, Aaron and his sons are to keep the lamps burning before the Lord from evening until morning. This is to be a lasting ordinance among the Israelites for the generations to come.[16]

Oil as a Symbol

People and priest alike had one responsibility each: the people were to bring the oil and the priests were to ensure that the lamps were kept burning throughout the night. However, their respective capacities to fulfil their tasks were dependent upon other factors: the priests could only keep the lamps burning if the people brought the oil, and the people could only bring the oil if they had also made the necessary preparation.

16. Exod 27:20–21.

This involved crushing unripe olives in a mortar and squeezing the pulpy mass in a porous cloth bag, through which the oil would thereby drain into a suitable receptacle.

The practical usefulness of oil to the ancient Israelite should not be underestimated. It was used as a skin emollient, to provide nutritional value to foodstuffs, and for cooking. Olive oil was often reserved for religious applications, most notably being added to offerings (e.g., Lev 2:1–2) and, as here, providing fuel for lighting lamps. It must be noted that oil was strictly forbidden alongside sin offerings (Lev 5:11). Also, as a general rule, any reference to oil in Scripture must be understood to be olive oil, unless otherwise stated (e.g., Esth 2:12).

What we are considering here is the use of oil in Scripture as a symbol or metaphor for the Holy Spirit. I have become aware in recent times of objections to this premise, based on a number of not entirely unreasonable factors. The first of these is that the Bible makes no explicit declaration that oil is to be equated with the Spirit. This is, of course, true, but no more so than any other widely acknowledged and accepted symbol or type. The bases of further complaints are closely linked: there are other symbols for the Holy Spirit, and oil can be seen to be symbolic of other things, the evidence for both being more strongly supported by Scripture's testimony. Again, this is true, but hardly grounds for rejection of the premise that oil is often used as a symbol for the Holy Spirit. There is no claim for exclusive application regarding biblical symbolism; to the best of my knowledge, there never has been among serious students of the word.

Perhaps the most convincing argument in favor of the symbolism is to be seen in the act of anointing with oil. The act itself was often a symbol of dedication, separation, purification and/or consecration for God's service. Kings and priests alike were subject to such anointings, the latter having the blood of the ordination ram sprinkled over them and their garments (Lev 8:30). There is a subtle difference between the protocol for anointing the priests for ordination (which included Aaron) and that for consecrating the high priest (Aaron alone): the priests had oil and blood sprinkled over them, the high priest only oil (see v. 12). It must be remembered, however, that the high priest had already engaged with the twin application as part of his consecration for priesthood.

It is in this act of anointing—or, more specifically, what is represented by it—that gives us our clearest marker of the oil being used as a symbol of the Holy Spirit. Oil was usually applied for anointing where blood had previously cleansed (see Lev 14:14–18). This act was also rich in symbolism: the right ear lobe (speaking of giving heed to godly instruction), the right thumb (indicative of righteous activity), and the big toe of the right foot (a reference to our earthly pilgrimage).

From Temptation to Triumph

It is not without significance, nor is it merely coincidental, that having returned from being baptized by John in the Jordan, Jesus was led by the Holy Spirit (of whom it is recorded he was full—Luke 4:1), to be tempted by the devil in the wilderness. Count them off: three temptations, to which Jesus responded in accordance with the above parallels:

- "Man shall not live by bread alone, but on every word that comes from the mouth of God" (Matt 4:4)—godly instruction;
- "Worship the Lord your God and serve him only" (Luke 4:8)—compromised righteousness is tantamount to unrighteousness; and
- "Do not put the Lord your God to the test" (Luke 4:12)—Jesus had been challenged to indulge his position by taking a path contrary to divine leading.

Satan's strategy for temptation seldom alters: the promise of the rewards for maturity without the need to engage with the maturation process demanded by God. Having thus proved his cleansing, "Jesus returned to Galilee in the power of the Spirit" (Luke 4:14). He then made his way to Nazareth and, on the first Sabbath after his arrival, identified himself with this reading from the prophet Isaiah:

> The Spirit of the Lord is on me, because he has anointed me to preach good news to the poor. He has sent me to proclaim freedom for the prisoners and recovery of sight for the blind, to release the oppressed, to proclaim the year of the Lord's favor.[17]

The word structure leans more toward the Holy Spirit's anointing being one of commissioning rather than empowering, though an English translation of the Ethiopic version has "by whom he hath anointed me." It seems likely that both are intended, the source of each being the same. What concerns us most for now is that we grasp that the anointing to come Jesus' way, however that was constituted, was no more by virtue of

17. Luke 4:18–19; Isa 61:1–2.

oil than his preparatory cleansing had come through sacrificial blood. It was the Spirit of God. Thus we can establish a legitimate connection between (olive) oil as a recognizable symbol for the Holy Spirit, at least in the area of anointing.

No Better Luminary

Can the same be said of illumination? Perhaps I might be permitted to put it another way: in view of the above, is there any reason why we may not also consider (olive) oil, as used to fuel the golden lampstand in the tabernacle, to be a recognizable symbol of the Holy Spirit's illuminative properties? Moreover, when it comes to type and antitype, who or what else could it be?

The most important questions we now face, in relation to this study, are concerned with recognizing the Spirit's illumination and taking such appropriate action in response to it as to ensure a positive advantage. Jesus helps us with the first part:

> But the Counsellor, the Holy Spirit, whom the Father will send in my name, will teach you all things and remind you of everything I have said to you . . . . When he comes, he will convict the world of guilt in regard to sin and righteousness and judgment: in regard to sin, because men do not believe in me; in regard to righteousness, because I am going to the Father, where you can see me no longer; and in regard to judgment, because the prince of this world now stands condemned . . . when he, the Spirit of truth comes, he will guide you into all truth.[18]

Herein lies the illuminatory function of the Holy Spirit toward humankind, both believers and unbelievers: instruction, conviction, and direction. Let us look at each in turn:

The Holy Spirit teaches and reminds

Let us consider these verses in reverse order. When Jesus spoke these words, it was to a small group of disciples, whose company he had enjoyed for around three and a half years. They had shared the joy of the crowds and endured as much as he the hostility of the religious leaders. They had learned first-hand who he was, what he had come to do, and

18. John 14:26; 16:8–11, 13a.

how it must be done in accordance with divine protocols. It would be these things of which they would subsequently be reminded.

The things of which we can be reminded are very different, though the principle behind their recollection remains the same. The early disciples had a bank of memories from which to draw because they had made a conscious decision to spend time with Jesus, whereby their investment grew. It did so by means of communion and communication. We, too, can add to our resources through prayer and the word of God. The Spirit's capacity to illuminate is not restricted by our negligence in this regard, but he can hardly be expected to re-mind us of things that we have not been mindful of in the first instance.

The scope of the Holy Spirit's teaching is about as comprehensive as it could be: "all things." I must confess to a little mocking ridicule as a young Christian. When older believers spoke of always discovering something fresh in God's word, I was disinclined to accept their testimony. One such mature sage took me to one side and gave me some sound advice: "The wisest of men are not those who claim to know it all, but those who admit how little they know in relative terms." Between us, the Holy Spirit and I continue to prove his veracity. So much so, in fact, that I never cease to be challenged by Jesus' parabolic illustration, when:

> He said to [his disciples], "Therefore, every teacher of the law who has been instructed about the kingdom of heaven is like the owner of a house who brings out of his storeroom new treasures as well as old."[19]

The Holy Spirit convicts

The world stands convicted of guilt, it is the Holy Spirit who brings about that conviction, and he does so in regard to three specific areas: sin, righteousness, and judgment. But we are also told why this is the case. Not difficult to understand, is it? And yet, I struggled for years to get my head around the intricacies of the three "becauses." Even when I thought I had, having a mental grasp of a concept and finding a way to articulate that are not the same thing at all. Here goes . . .

The first one is relatively easy. The world stands convicted of guilt in regard to sin, because they continue to abide in Adam's fallen state. For whatever reason—and none qualify also as an excuse—they have failed

19. Matt 13:52.

to avail themselves of God's provision that it might be otherwise. They do not believe in Jesus. More specifically, they do not believe in the atoning efficacy of his sacrificial death and subsequent resurrection; it is highly likely that they do not even believe in the necessity of either.

The world also stands convicted of sin in regard to righteousness. Nothing tricky so far. But why is this especially so in the light of Jesus' return to the Father? We need to read this in the context that would have been understood by its original audience. Jesus was about to be crucified as a wrongdoer in the eyes of those who sought his death. As far as they were concerned, Jesus "ought to die!" (John 19:7). To them, he was unrighteous. The resurrection vindicated him, but God's stamp of approval was affirmed by means of the ascension. He truly is "the Holy and Righteous One" (see Acts 3:14).

The guilt of which the world stands convicted is not only progressive, but also each phase is predicated on the previous step: a warped standard of righteousness flows naturally from sin, the products of both being flawed judgment. The root of the Greek word translated "judgment" is *krisis*, which means to deduce something by means of critical appraisal. If the process is not governed by divine revelation (even unwittingly), then it can only be defective, however favorable, aesthetically pleasant, or conducive to worldly paradigms of secular morality the outcome might appear to be. The world is convicted as guilty in regard to such judgment because the one who instigated them stands condemned.

The Holy Spirit guides

We must establish some features concerning the direction of the Holy Spirit's guidance. The first may seem too obvious to mention, but it does need spelling out. Jesus said: "He will guide you into all truth." The clue was in the name he ascribed: "the Spirit of truth." He does not guide us into error. This is not to say that whatever we find ourselves associated with, having claimed to have been following his lead, thereby becomes truth, however otherwise erroneous. That would be a nonsense. But it is a nonsense with which I have been sadly familiar. "I believe God has called me to . . . " and what follows is diametrically opposed to the revelation of God's word in the area of godly conduct for believers, even to the extent that some seem incapable of distinguishing between the pure and the prurient. If this is or has been you, or someone you know, however close you might be to them, then let me assure you with as much Christian love as I can muster, the Spirit of truth was not the guide.

The second feature is that the word "guide" translates the Greek *hodegos*, a noun derived from a verb, meaning "to lead the way." Imagine a blind person being guided across a busy road. The guide does not forcefully push from behind, but gently leads the way by going on ahead, yet still close enough to maintain contact. It is precisely in this manner that the Holy Spirit guides into all truth (that is, "the whole body of redemptive revelation"[20]).

With these in mind, I'll close this section with ten ways to discern and/or respond to the Spirit's leading:

- Be open to the possibility of him doing so through unconventional means.
- Although he may lead us out of our comfort zones, it is seldom in the absence of a peaceful resolve.
- If in any doubt, ask for secondary confirmation, but beware of interpreting "signs" that do not exist.
- Be patient—the now or never "deal" is usually best left alone (the Holy Spirit is neither a bully nor a used-car salesman).
- Try to avoid the Gideon's fleece routine, unless specifically invited to employ it.
- Steer clear of "directions" that deflect from God's glory to others; it simply is not his way.
- Don't add to or subtract from what you honestly believe to have received from him; presumptuous supposition, however innocent, is never a good idea.
- Engage with the Spirit's revealed purpose where required, but otherwise allow it to unfold in his good time.
- If the way ahead seems unclear, a step of faith in the revealed direction may unlock further steps; if not, prayer is never a bad thing.
- Spiritual matters are spiritually discerned for the benefit of ourselves or others (usually the latter); they are not tools with which to indulge the sinful nature.

20. Hendriksen, *John*, 328.

THE SEVEN-FOLD SPIRIT

> Make a lampstand of pure gold and hammer it out, base and shaft; its flower-like cups, buds and blossoms shall be of one piece with it . . . . Then make its seven lamps and set them upon it so that they light the space in front of it.[21]

> A shoot will come up from the stump of Jesse; from his roots a Branch will bear fruit. The Spirit of the Lord will rest on him—the Spirit of wisdom and of understanding; the Spirit of counsel and of power; the Spirit of knowledge and of the fear of the Lord—and he will delight in the fear of the Lord.[22]

> John, to the seven churches in the province of Asia: Grace and peace to you from him who is, and who was, and who is to come, and from the seven-fold Spirit before his throne . . .[23]

All the translations I have seen give "seven spirits" (or similar) for the citation from Revelation. Although this is accurate, I have opted for the reading in most margins as potentially less misleading and more representative of what we know from elsewhere. I also propose to take my seven characteristics from the Isaiah rendering. While the three pairs seem to be drawn together under the opening umbrella term (i.e., "the Spirit of the Lord"), this is not out of keeping with the structure of the lampstand in the tabernacle, which had one central stem, from which came three pairs of branches.

The Spirit of the Lord

The key feature regarding the Spirit of God is his triune status within the Being of the divine Godhead. He is co-equal and co-eternal with the Father and the Son, and all the "omnis" are similarly applicable. In terms of triune co-equality, I think Louis Berkhof puts it best when he says: "The whole undivided essence of God belongs equally to each of the three persons."[24] Thus, all the perfections, without exception, that may be

21. Exod 25:31, 37.
22. Isa 11:1–3.
23. Rev 1:4 (alternative reading in margin).
24. Berkhof, *Systematic Theology*, 88.

identified as being attributable to God belong to Father, Son, and Holy Spirit alike.

We shall be looking specifically in this section at six other characteristics of the Holy Spirit, in accordance with Isaiah's representation of him, and because that number equates to the image of the lampstand in the tabernacle. But we should not imagine these to exhaust the Spirit's nature, role within the Godhead, or functions in relation to humanity. For example, if God the Father is a God of grace, then so too is the Holy Spirit a Spirit of grace; if Jesus is appropriately described as the Son of righteousness, then we do the Holy Spirit a great disservice by failing to recognize him also to be a Spirit of righteousness.

In the Old Testament, when individuals were given a task by divine appointment that required skills or resources beyond their natural means, "the Spirit of the Lord came upon" them (Heb. *wattehi alaw*, literally "became above," e.g., Othniel—Judg 3:10; see also Luke 1:35), often accentuating the link between God's declared intention and its fulfilment. This usually involved a temporary enabling, which terminated when the need was no longer pressing. The word structure of Isaiah's prophecy concerning the coming Messiah, however, was that "the Spirit of the Lord will rest on him" (*wenahah alaw*, literally "find a place of abode upon which to remain").

The Spirit of Wisdom

The first thing I must establish here is that the Holy Spirit's impartation of gift, fruit, or virtue is not like some ethereal and otherwise distant Santa Claus figure being called upon to fulfil the role of the Father's mail carrier. What he gives he does so from within himself. And so, when we receive wisdom from the Spirit of wisdom it is because wisdom contributes toward the essence of his personal nature.

In the introduction, I distinguished between knowledge, understanding, and wisdom. All three may be regarded as intellectual virtues, but they are not all purely theoretical. After twenty-five years of marriage, I pretty much know what makes my wife tick. I also have a shrewd understanding of the whys and wherefores. For example, I know that she does not take kindly to public humiliation, however slight the acrimony or small the audience, and irrespective of how defiantly the source may claim "I was only jesting!" I suspect the reasons for such a release of emotional rage include Barbara's convent school education, being subject to certain mental cruelties inflicted by the tongues of some teachers. I understand! If I am wise, I will respond to my knowledge and understanding by ensuring that, as far as it is within my gift, she is shielded from the likelihood of such circumstances.

The book of Proverbs is rightly lauded as one of the five pieces of wisdom literature in the Hebrew Scriptures. Its value is not so much in the revealing of information about nature or human behavior, but how we might respond to their unveiling to our advantage. We are shown how to give practical application to the material placed at our disposal. The principal compiler of the book of Proverbs was the second most wise man that ever lived; the most sagacious was Jesus. It is no coincidence that they each derived their erudition from the same source: the Spirit of wisdom.

The Spirit of Understanding

If ever wisdom and understanding were to appear symbolized as branches of a lampstand, they would surely be coupled together. Despite my earlier distinction, they are mutually interdependent. If understanding requires wisdom to make its theory of some practical use, then wisdom needs understanding as the sure theoretical premise upon which to act. At the root of the Hebrew noun *binah* is the capacity to perceive, a quality through which comes discernment. This is not always regarded with positive consequences, as corrupted human nature through sin has rendered our rationale susceptible to faulty discernment based on defective skills of perception. Perhaps it is for this reason that Solomon advises against a high level of reliance upon natural thought processes (Prov 3:5). He certainly valued the kind of understanding that comes by divine revelation (4:7).

One of the many concerns with which I have been confronted in this regard has been an apparent assumption by some Christians that their experience of the Holy Spirit includes a baptism of the brain. The record suggests otherwise. But that has not prevented some from presuming that anything they may now imagine or express brings with it an automatic "Thus saith the Lord" appendage. Such notions deserve to be discarded. God's thoughts are not our thoughts (Isa 55:8–9) any more under the new covenant than they were under the old. They still become known only by revelation. If baptism in the Holy Spirit negated this requirement or made spiritual understanding an instinctive endowment, then Paul's letters to the Corinthian believers would have been much shorter. Charismatic Corinthians? Well, this is what Paul had to say of their understanding of such matters: "Now concerning spiritual gifts, brethren, I do not want you to be ignorant" (1 Cor 12:1 NKJV), before going on to correct their *mis*understanding.

The Spirit of Counsel

At first glance, the role of the Holy Spirit as Counselor appears very familiar to us. Most readers will surely be reminded of Jesus' promise to the disciples that he would ask the Father to send them another Counselor, whom he identifies as the Holy Spirit (John 14:16, 26; 16:5–7 NIV, HCSB). But we must be careful not to jump to hasty conclusions. The only link between this and the aforementioned passage in Isaiah is the person of the Holy Spirit.

The Johannine citations are better translated "Comforter" or "Helper" (e.g., KJV, NASB, ESV), each a more accurate translation of the Greek *paraklesis*. It simply means "one who is called alongside,"[25] the context suggesting with what end in view (e.g., reconciliation, exhortation, encouragement). In the Septuagint, *paraklesis* most often translates the Hebrew *naham* (to offer comfort, having been moved to pity). Thus, *paraklesis* is more akin to one who consoles than one who counsels.

The Isaianic passage does not employ *naham*, however, but *esah*. Here, "Spirit of counsel" is not only acceptable but preferred. The primary meaning of *esah* as a verb is to consult with or advise, usually in accordance with a predetermined plan or design. It finds prominence in the writings of the later prophets, but is not entirely absent before that time. This is an example of how Solomon used it:

> Many are the plans in a man's heart, but it is the Lord's purpose that prevails.[26]

Unlike *naham*, *esah* is most frequently translated by *boule* in the Septuagint, which retains the sense of the Hebrew perfectly, though again dependent upon the context. At its most basic, *boule* must be translated

25. See Vine, *Expository Dictionary*, 199.

26. Prov 19:21.

"will" or "volition," but came to mean by extension "the result of a deliberation in the sense of a decision of the will, a resolution, a counsel or an edict."[27]

The Spirit of Power

As in the previous couplet, this pairing makes perfect logical sense. Having a plan that is devised in accordance with a predetermined will is one thing (and I am not a stranger to it), but having the resources with which to execute that plan is an entirely different matter (as I have often learned). Here, there is no ambiguity of translation. Both the Hebrew *gevurah* and the Greek *dunamis* convey essentially the same meaning: an inner capacity of resourcefulness that surpasses the anticipated norm. Expressions that demonstrate this are often described as miraculous or wonders contrary to nature, by which we mean that they are over and beyond what we might otherwise expect in the natural order of things. Other derivations of use, especially of *gevurah*, include those occupying preeminent positions, someone who is exceptionally strong or valiant, and in relation to militaristic activity (i.e., strength for war).

Inextricably linked to power are two key features: authority and responsibility. Neither come as arduous tasks to the Holy Spirit, for they are each inherent to him within the commune of the triune Godhead: he is both authoritative and responsible in the exercise of his power, ensuring that such deeds conform to the purpose of God. Perhaps the clearest example of this is to be found in the act of creation, where the Spirit exercised his power in response to the expressed will of God: "Let there be . . ."

But what of us? Do we yearn, even with prayer and fasting, to see God's power being demonstrated among us so that he shall be glorified on account of it, or that we might thereby become vindicated in our commitment to him? The latter finds no commendation in Scripture.

The Spirit of Knowledge

When I first announced that I was contemplating going to Bible college as a raw twenty-year-old, with only a little over three years Christian experience behind me, it was to a mixed reception. Apart from suddenly

27. In Brown, *Dictionary of New Testament Theology*, 3:1,015.

becoming attractive to members of the opposite sex, for no other apparent reason, I was also met with a wholly unexpected measure of hostility from others. I had anticipated harsh conversations with my grandparents, but this was Christians within the church into which I had been birthed. "Knowledge is a dangerous thing!" they argued, as if the misquotation would stop me in God's tracks. Only later did I come to realize that it is "a little learning" (i.e., imperfect or incomplete understanding) that is likely to herald such a risk. Later still did I discover that the pithy saying owed nothing to Solomon's wit, but that of eighteenth-century English satirist Alexander Pope.

There are two Greek words translated "knowledge" in our Bibles. They are not unrelated, and yet they stand poles apart; they are *gnosis* and *epignosis*. This is how Trench distinguishes between them:

> In comparing *epignosis* with *gnosis*, the *epi* must be regarded as an intensive use of a preposition that gives the compound word a greater strength than the simple word alone possesses . . . Paul exchanged *ginosko*, which expresses present and fragmentary knowledge, for *epignosomai* when he wished to refer to future knowledge that is intuitive and perfect (1 Cor 13:12).[28]

The kind of knowledge owned by the Holy Spirit is more than mere awareness of information; it is of the latter kind discussed by Trench. And it is this that he makes available to us through revelation. Nathanael Culverwell clarifies the matter even further:

> *Epignosis* is the complete comprehension after the first knowledge [*gnosin*] of a matter. It is bringing me better acquainted with a thing I knew before; a more exact viewing of an object that I saw before afar off. That little portion of knowledge which we had here shall be much improved, our eye shall be raised to see the same things more strongly and clearly.[29]

The Spirit of the Fear of the Lord

As a concept, the fear of the Lord is much misconstrued, and yet its reality is essential to the pilgrim's progress. For the Christian, fear of God's wrath because of sin has been removed (Eph 2:3; 1 Thess 1:10); for us,

28. Trench, *Synonyms*, 300.
29. Culverwell, *Spiritual Optics*, 180.

the fear of the Lord now consists of nothing more frightening (or less so) than reverential respect for the presence and personal Being of God. It is to regard him as awesome with all of that word's etymological implication, before it became diluted of meaning by being used to describe such things as a favorite or unusual ice cream flavor. Our experience of the presence of God should be truly awe-full.

I realize it is almost a generational rite of passage to speak fondly of "the good old days," and to bemoan a perceived current lack of some of their most cherished features. If I was to be allowed just one, then it would be this: a restoration of godly fear. What is perhaps most frustrating is that my experience of its relative absence is to be found in those church settings that are also the most vociferous about the need for spiritual revival. Any concerted reading of the history of Christian revivals will be rewarded with the realization that such occasions were consistently accompanied—some might even argue, precipitated—by a heightened sense of veneration for the things of God.

But Paul employs the phrase in a slightly different—though not entirely unrelated—context, most notably to the believers at Corinth:

> Having therefore these promises, dearly beloved, let us cleanse ourselves from all filthiness of the flesh and spirit, perfecting holiness in the fear of God.[30]

The Greek word here is *phobos*, from which we derive our English "phobia." Vine describes Paul's use as:

> . . . not a mere fear of His power and righteous retribution, but a wholesome dread of displeasing Him, a fear which banishes the terror that shrinks from His presence . . . and which influences the disposition and attitude of one whose circumstances are guided by trust in God, through the indwelling Spirit of God.[31]

EACH CHURCH A LAMPSTAND

The premise of this section is based upon John's revelatory disclosure:

> I, John . . . turned round to see the voice that was speaking to me. And when I turned I saw seven golden lampstands, and among the lampstands was someone "like a son of man," dressed

30. 2 Cor 7:1.

31. Vine, *Expository Dictionary*, 414.

> in a robe reaching down to his feet and with a golden sash round his chest . . . . In his right hand he held seven stars, and out of his mouth came a sharp double-edged sword . . . . When I saw him I fell at his feet as though dead. Then he placed his right arm on me and said: "Do not be afraid. I am the First and the Last. I am the Living One, and behold I am alive for ever and ever . . . . The mystery of the seven stars that you saw in my right hand and of the seven golden lampstands is this: The seven stars are the angels of the seven churches, and the seven lampstands are the seven churches."[32]

There then follows an appraisal of each of the local churches in question at Ephesus (Rev 2:1–7), Smyrna (vv. 8–11), Pergamum (vv. 12–17), Thyatira (vv. 18–29), Sardis (3:1–6), Philadelphia (vv. 7–13), and Laodicea (vv. 14–22).

Although each local church has its own distinctives, in general terms it is a microcosmic facsimile of the larger body of Christ to which it belongs—or should be. It is a strange quirk of nature that the very first thing one sees when a lamp is switched on is the lamp itself. This is not its design, of course, but what we see initially may help to determine what and how much that envisions us beyond itself; or does it obscure our sight rather than helping us to observe?

What Does God See in the Church?

Let me narrow that down a little: what do you imagine God sees when he looks at you as an individual believer and, therefore, a representative member of the church? Perhaps your natural disposition tends toward overconfidence and you imagine yourself as an answer to God's prayers. It is almost as if he has been awaiting your arrival so that he could finally get the job done. In fact, if only you had been around sooner, then we could all be resting on our own little cloud, smoking cigars, and sipping champagne, like some indefatigable victim of the cartoonist's pen and penchant. (Well, if we're going to be ridiculous, we may as well go the whole way.)

Maybe you are not anywhere near being so narcissistic; quite the opposite, in fact. You have become so used to having your faults identified and laid before the public gaze, that you are beginning to wonder if you might be God's solitary mistake. For you, blameworthiness is not an

32. Rev 1:9–20.

occasional experience, but a lifelong condition. If the snack vendor at work becomes inoperative, the first question on everyone's lips is: "When did you use it last?" At school, your reputation was so widespread that, even after you had been left for some time, if a problem arose your involvement was cited as its probable cause. At home, your parents always readjusted their plans to allow for what they mockingly called "the Joey/Mary factor." And now your whole life is seasoned that way, your personality interminably cicatriced by a perception of abandoned geniality. Your Christian experience is such that it is seldom fun and never funny.

Very few of us represent these extremes, though most would tend toward one or the other, even if we lie closer to the middle. We also have a proclivity to gravitate toward those of like temperament, both socially and in our choice of local church expression. The difficulty is then compounded when we project that image onto what we believe God sees in us, individually and corporately. But God's ways are not our ways, his thoughts are not our thoughts (Isa 55:8–9), and what he sees is vastly different from what we see.

When I was about to make the step up from ambulance technician to paramedic, I had to go on several skills improvement programs. One of these was an advanced driving course, where we were taught to drive safely at speed, negotiate hazardous weather conditions, and be more acutely conscious of our highway environment. The one phrase that was hammered home more than any other was "peripheral vision." What this amounted to in practice was making a mental note of all that was in front of us, to the side of us, and—by extensive use of rearview mirrors—what was immediately behind us. Being aware meant being prepared for every eventuality, such as an unaccompanied child suddenly stepping into the road to chase a wayward balloon.

God's vision is perfect. Let me put it another way: God's vision is without imperfection, imaginable or beyond our comprehension. What does that mean? Well, we cannot know what it means concerning those features that lie outside our capacity to understand, so we must content ourselves with what has been revealed. First of all, God's vision is not restricted or incomplete. He sees things that have happened or are happening of which we are blissfully unaware; our view of anything in either dimension (i.e., past or present) is largely conditioned by spatial presence or hearsay, even if the latter comes via a reliable source.

God's view of things is also not limited to past or presently unfolding events, but includes the future, both actual and possible. This may account for why he is so immeasurably more optimistic about what he sees when he looks at the church. He hasn't had to read the book of Revelation: he inspired its writing. God also unveiled something of how he sees the church to the apostle Paul:

> And God placed all things under [Christ's] feet and appointed him to be head over everything for the church, which is his body, the fulness of him who fills everything in every way.[33]

If the church is Christ's body, under whose feet are his enemies to be trampled? As far as I am aware, this appraisal has been neither abrogated nor rescinded: "God is not a man that he should lie, nor a son of man, that he should change his mind" (Num 23:19a).

What Does the Mirror Reveal?

God's vision of the church is annexed to his purpose for it. Can the same be said of us? Is what we see governed by a recognition of divine purpose or an admission of failure to live up to the high standards dictated by that same purpose? Again, allow me to rephrase: are we living by faith or by sight? The strange thing about this question is that faith does not negate sight, but embraces a different kind of viewing ability. Faith allows us to tap into how God sees things, within the confines of divine revelation, of course.

Where supernatural tools are either unavailable to or remain unaccessed by us, then all we have left at our disposal are natural instincts, which are not always reliable. Our view of the church is thereby determined by our exposure to local expressions of it, often only the one to which we demonstrate some measure of allegiance. If that is the case, what do you consider to be its purpose? The answer to that question will largely be governed by how the church is defined in your thinking: is it the redeemed community of God's people, as suggested by Scripture, or do you imagine it simply to be the building on the high street with a steeple, stained glass, and a stuffy seating arrangement? Here are just some of the ideas I have heard from those who would fit strongly into the latter category concerning the purpose of the church:

- "Somewhere to catch up with friends and acquaintances";
- "A place to have a good old sing-song";

33. Eph 1:22–23.

- "Free cake and coffee afterward";
- "It's where I've always gone, so there's an air of nostalgia about my visits";
- "I was christened there, so it's effectively *my* church";
- "Where else am I going to meet members of the opposite sex in a religious context?";
- "I've pre-paid a plot of land for my funeral, and I like to keep an eye on it."

I suppose each one has a purpose of sorts, but they're hardly likely to revolutionize society. What concerns me greatly is that some of those who correctly identify the church as the people of God speak in similar terms regarding its purpose. This is how they, too, see it, especially in terms of it being gathered together in one location on a more than once-weekly basis:

- "Somewhere to catch up with friends and acquaintances";
- "A place to have a good time";
- "I particularly enjoy the monthly student lunches";
- "It would take some special vibe to convince me to go to a different church";
- "I was baptized here, so there's a long-standing relationship";
- "I play guitar in the worship band, so it's an ideal place to impress the chicks";
- "The pastor is a cool dude; he believes exactly the same as me on most doctrines of any importance."

Perhaps it is time for Christians to rediscover what Scripture says about the church, instead of having our understanding of it molded by other influences. When we perceive the church as nothing more strategic than a Sunday morning (and/or evening) social venue, to which we transfer our Friday night allegiance, then I think it is safe to say that our alignment with God's design is somewhat askew. A little earlier in the same chapter as mentioned above, Paul writes to the Ephesian believers of the revelation of a mystery in the following terms:

> And [God] made known to us the mystery of his will according to his good pleasure, which he purposed in Christ, to be put

> into effect when the times will have reached their fulfilment—to bring all things in heaven and earth together under one head, even Christ.[34]

This is our mandate. When the church to which you belong takes a long, hard look at itself in the mirror, does it see a parochial reflection or one with a kingdom objective?

How Do We Look to Outsiders?

I have never felt particularly comfortable engaging with street evangelism. I'm not very good at communicating with strangers about anything; small talk does not come easily to me. However, as a first-year Bible college student, Saturday afternoons were given over to grinning and bearing it near the bus station in downtown Swansea. I would say that I looked forward to Saturday evenings when it was all over, except that those were used to follow up any afternoon contacts at the coffee bar of the local Baptist church. Sundays were welcomed with relish, and not just the sort on offer at the California Express burger bar.

On one slightly less nightmarish occasion, I seemed to be making good progress with a bit of a hippy type, not much older than myself. I had learned the hard way that some of those we were likely to meet had a fondness for stringing us along with false declarations, but this one felt different somehow. We were also encouraged not to prattle on indefinitely, but invite questions of our targets (I mean, candidates). Jason's was one for which I was totally unprepared: "I live out of town, in the such-and-such district. If I get saved, will I have to go to so-and-so church?" As far as Jason was concerned, Jesus was groovy, but "so-and-so church" was a "No, No!"

I never did discover exactly what Jason found so off-putting about "so-and-so church." Maybe it was nothing more sinister than he knew someone who went there he would rather avoid. Perhaps the fellowship in question had a reputation for so-called heavy shepherding, or possibly there had been a well-publicized issue of marital infidelity. I didn't know (so it can't have been that well publicized) and, ultimately, I didn't care about the details. But Jason's reservation over forty years ago has troubled me ever since. How many others were there? How many more since? And

34. Eph 1:9–10.

what happens to that number when the horizons are extended beyond the South Wales coastal area?

The following Friday morning, we had our scheduled weekly lecture on evangelism. I lingered behind at the end (sacrificially forfeiting my usual place near the front of the lunch queue), hoping to air my concerns with the inimitable David Shepherd. Expressing zeal and frustration in near equal amounts, he responded with a typical: "You should have told him not to look at the church, but to look to Jesus." Despite my tender years, it was not the first time I had heard that phrase used in similar circumstances, nor was it to be the last. In fact, it was repeated only last week. But does it come with biblical conviction? I think not!

Many years ago, I belonged to a house-style fellowship that had a not entirely unwarranted reputation with other believers in the area. At the very top of their hit parade of insults against us were that we were a "Bless me!" group. Although unintentional, I later discovered that to be regarded thus was not necessarily a negative feature:

> May God be gracious to us and bless us and make his face shine upon us, that your ways may be known on earth, your salvation among nations.[35]

A little earlier, we considered the approach of the Queen of Sheba to Solomon's throne. Scripture records of her visit that "she was overwhelmed" (1 Kgs 10:5). This follows a whole catalogue of features that may be said to have aroused such an emotion, the very first being Solomon's wisdom (v. 4). I wonder if the world stands aghast at the repository of wisdom the church has to offer. Too often we fail to be sufficiently sagacious even to realize the evangelistic significance of unity. And yet, Jesus' prayer is hardly cloaked in ambiguity:

> My prayer is not for [the disciples] alone. I pray also for those who will believe in me through their message, that all of them may be one, Father, just as you are in me and I am in you. May they also be in us so that the world may believe that you have sent me . . . . May they be brought to complete unity to let the world know that you sent me and have loved them even as you have loved me.[36]

35. Ps 67:1–2.

36. John 17:20–21, 23b.

Scripture does not invite us to proffer mental assent only to the doctrine of unity. We can intellectually agree with the idea of it, but be riven with division where it really matters—in practice.

SUMMARY

The purpose of illumination is self-evident: it is to facilitate improved vision. That vision includes the object providing the light, but is not restricted to it. In fact, its primary function is to direct attention away from itself. I was once forced to suppress a sardonic smile when passing a church building that was thitherto known to me and had noticed that its name had been changed. No longer Community Bible Church, it had now become Lighthouse Christian Fellowship. If any light source was designed with no other purpose in mind than to divert interest from it, then it has to be a lighthouse: "Keep away! Danger beckons!" it announces.

Just as the lampstand lit up the Holy Place to aid the priests in their daily tasks in relation to the shewbread and the altar of incense, so the Holy Spirit enables believers to see spiritual matters with increased clarity. In so doing, he gives direction, identifies issues in need of remedial attention, instructs and informs us, and reveals Christ's character in increasing measure that it might cause an intensification of our desire both to worship him and—as much as it is within our capacity—to emulate him.

6

The Altar of Incense

THE ALTAR OF INCENSE was the final piece in the Holy Place, its position directly in front of the veil (i.e., west side), signifying access to the presence of God. Theodore Epp has this to say of the altar's placement:

> Since the Holy of Holies was God's dwelling place, the nearest one could be to the Holy of Holies without being in it was the altar of incense.[1]

The horns at each corner were a symbol of strength by means of invested authority. Together, the three pieces of furniture in the Holy Place symbolized a triumvirate of fellowship based on mutual interrelationship:

- The Table of Presence—instruction by the word of God;
- The golden lampstand—illumination by the Holy Spirit; and
- The altar of incense—the offering of worship in accordance with divine design.

Please read Exod 30:1–10 in preparation for all that follows . . .

A FRAGRANT INCENSE

. . . now moving on to verse 34:

1. Epp, *Portraits of Christ*, 126.

> Then the Lord said to Moses, "Take fragrant spices—gum resin, onycha and galbanum—and pure frankincense, all in equal amounts, and make a fragrant blend of incense, the work of a perfumer. It is to be salted and pure and sacred. Grind some of it to powder and place it in front of the Testimony in the Tent of Meeting, where I will meet with you. It shall be most holy to you. Do not make any incense with this formula for yourselves; consider it holy to the Lord. Whoever makes any like it to enjoy its fragrance must be cut off from his people."[2]

Holy, Holy Prayers

It is no accident, nor is it without significance that the anointing oil is described as "holy" or "sacred" (Exod 30:31), but the incense is identified as "most holy" (v. 36). Our English translations reflect the original Hebrew, where *qodes* is coupled with *qadasim* to effectively compound the effect in the latter (thus, the incense was regarded as holy, holy).

The beginning of verse 35 may provide a clue to our understanding of the end of the previous verse. As only a sample of the whole mixture was taken at a time to be ground (i.e., "some of it"), it must be presumed that the addition of salt was to preserve the rest for future use. The sodium chloride content may also have facilitated the burning of the incense, as suggested by Alan Cole.[3] Aside from these practical considerations, the covenantal symbolism cannot easily be overlooked (see also Lev 2:13).

There is no attempt in the Hebrew Scriptures to provide a definitive explanation for the cultic symbolism in the use of incense. Even in the New Testament, it is not until the very last book that our thirst for knowledge is quenched. It is one of those occasions when, once you know, you realize that there were clues all along. Here is how John breaks the news to us:

> And when he had taken [the scroll], the four living creatures and the twenty-four elders fell down before the Lamb. Each one had a harp and they were holding golden bowls full of incense, which are the prayers of the saints.[4]

One of those earlier hints came from the imploring lips of David:

2. Exod 30:34–38.
3. Cole, *Exodus*, 216.
4. Rev 5:8.

> O Lord, I call to you; come quickly to me. Hear my voice when I call to you. May my prayer be set before you like incense; may the lifting up of my hands be like the evening sacrifice.[5]

More Than a Vehicle for Requests

The question might reasonably be asked how far the parameters of prayer extend. Our interest is primarily evoked by a tendency to think of prayer almost exclusively in terms of invocation to satisfy a desire, whether needful or otherwise. We must first ask what the respective original readerships of the psalmist and the revelator might have understood by the words translated "prayer." Indeed, what did the authors themselves intend by them?

The words used by each are *tepillati* (Hebrew) and *proseuchai* (Greek). The former is found seventy-seven times in the Old Testament, each occasion related to petition or plea, often associated with intercession. *Proseuchai* finds its way into our New Testament less than half as many times and conveys a more general application: simply of communication with God. Other terms are used for more specific types of prayer, such as *erotao* (to make a request), *deesis* (supplication), *enteuxis* (intercession), and *deomai* (beseech in order to fulfil a desire).[6]

Perhaps unsurprisingly, Wayne Grudem's definition of prayer fits perfectly with the above translation of *proseuchai*: "Prayer is personal communication with God."[7] Notice the preposition in both cases: it is "with," not "to." This being the case, maybe "communion" would be a more suitable subject noun than "communication," reflecting the fact that conversation is not merely one way. Grudem goes on to make this point well:

> What we call "prayer" includes prayers of request for ourselves or for others . . . confession of sin, praises and thanksgiving, and also God communicating to us indications of his response.

It is difficult for me to gauge the overriding emphasis of my prayer life over the years. I guess it will have been governed largely by the circumstances in which I found myself at any given time. In terms of God's

5. Ps 141:1–2.

6. See Vine, *Expository Dictionary*, 871–72.

7. Grudem, *Systematic Theology*, 376.

responses, however, the task seems much simpler. It concerns the receipt of clearer insight into misunderstood passages from the Bible, for which I am most grateful.

Developing a Conducive Environment

We cannot be responsible for God communicating with us, except insofar that we make room for opportunities whereby he might do so. Or can we? Our conduct can impinge on the effectiveness of prayer, both positively and negatively. This is not to suggest a kind of brownie points system, whereby divine favor is extended toward those who have proved their worthiness as recipients. But Scripture does suggest that some issues can become barriers to effective prayer:

- an unforgiving disposition toward others (Matt 6:12–15; Mark 11:25–26);
- requests that are designed to promote self-indulgence (Phil 2:3–4; Jas 4:2–3);
- dishonoring marital partners (1 Pet 3:7);
- unrepentant sin (Ps 66:7–9; Isa 59:2);
- unbelief (Heb 11:6; Jas 1:5–7); and
- disobedience (Prov 28:9; 1 John 5:14–15).

Some of the texts cited above suggest a positive inversion to the principle being posited. It does not seem unreasonable to assume that this is equally true of all of them: forgiveness toward others releases God's forgiveness toward us, intercessory requests are likely to be met with success, honoring of the marital covenant removes barriers to God's ear, repentance paves the way for prayers to be heard, faith and obedience likewise, and seeking God's will is to be recommended as a prerequisite to an effective prayer life.

There are lessons to be learned, too, without straying too far from the environment of the tabernacle. It might be helpful for us to re-read a couple of verses from that opening citation:

> Aaron must burn fragrant incense on the altar every morning when he tends the lamps. He must burn incense again when he

> lights the lamps at twilight so that incense will burn regularly before the Lord for the generations to come.[8]

First of all, I remain unconvinced that the connection between commanding the high priest to add incense to the burning altar and his duties concerning the tending of the lamps is either accidental or merely one of practical convenience. If prayers are anything then they are essentially spiritual. Unbelieving politicians and atheistic journalists seeking to reassure listeners that their prayers are with those bereaved in tragic circumstances might give some immediate comfort, if only to those with a keen eye on the viewing figures, but they are otherwise meaningless.

Secondly, the NIV use of the word "regularly" is an unfortunate translation, as it suggests "at regular intervals" (see also ESV). Certainly, the ground incense mixture was added to the fire twice a day, but the occasion of the burning itself is better expressed by other versions, which more accurately translate the Hebrew *tamid* as "constant" or "continual" (e.g., KJV, NASB, YLT). The relationship between this perpetuality and that of prayer is not difficult to find:

> Be joyful always; pray continually; give thanks in all circumstances, for this is God's will for you in Christ Jesus.[9]

This idea of ceaseless prayer was not just something Paul consigned to an apostolic benediction when he was trying to run his letter toward an amicable conclusion (see Rom 1:9–10; Eph 6:18). Nor was his counsel abstract advice with little or no practical experience (2 Tim 1:3). To pray without ceasing requires a continual measure of fellowship. Modern technology aside, the only way I can always be in a position whereby I can communicate with my wife is if I am never absent from her.

Follow the Leader

If we want to discover what this means in real terms, Jesus provided the best possible model. By way of instruction, he taught his disciples how to pray in what we often describe as the Lord's Prayer (Matt 6:9–13), but Jesus' whole life was a practical demonstration of prayer without equal. Let us take a look at some of its features by way of example:

8. Exod 30:7–8.
9. 1 Thess 5:16–18; see also 1:2–3; 2:13.

Jesus prioritized prayer over his social life

Jesus was not anti-sociable. He enjoyed the company of others, whether at the synagogue, at weddings, or in the home of friends. Indeed, social interaction is a God-given need shared by humanity. But neither did Jesus complain of having insufficient time at his disposal to pray or regard prayer as interfering with his social life. He often sought to be alone with his Father, frequently in the immediate aftermath of occasions that might otherwise give rise to social engagement, such as after the feeding of the five thousand:

> Immediately, Jesus made the disciples get into the boat and go ahead of him to the other side, while he dismissed the crowd. After he had dismissed them, he went up on a mountainside by himself to pray.[10]

Jesus prioritized prayer over the need for physical rest

Let us remain with the above-cited incident a little longer. The rest of that concluding verse tells us that by the time Jesus found himself alone, it was evening (Matt 14:23b). It had already been a long day. Even the feeding of the five thousand was an interruption to his mourning at the news of his cousin's recent beheading (vv. 1–14). He then "went up on a mountainside to pray" (v. 23a). There is absolutely no mention or suggestion that Jesus slept at any point in the narrative. Now, I am fully aware that absence of evidence is no evidence of absence, but I posit it only for consideration.

The next established time frame we have is when Jesus went out to his disciples on the water, "during the fourth watch of the night" (i.e., between three and six in the morning). Could it be that he had spent all night in prayer? He was certainly no stranger to the "very early" morning prayer appointment (Mark 1:35).

Jesus prioritized prayer over satisfying his physical appetite

Jesus was also familiar with the accompaniment of fasting with his prayers. On one occasion, he had just been talking with a Samaritan woman,

10. Matt 14:22–23a.

when his disciples rejoined him in a state of some alarm. Whether to conceal their embarrassment, provide an excuse to absent themselves from her company, or a genuine concern for Jesus' welfare, they said to him: "Rabbi, eat something" (John 4:31b). Their sense of urgency is compounded by the use of both *eroton* and *legontes*, suggesting a legitimate worry. But notice Jesus' response:

> "I have food to eat that you know nothing about . . . . My food," said Jesus, "is to do the will of him who sent me and to finish his work."[11]

Jesus prayed in the midst of suffering

Ah, suffering: the charismatic gift that seems to have eluded the attention of many twenty-first-century mega-church leaders, content rather to intone a litany to an untroubled Christian existence! That notwithstanding, I suppose this is one area with which most of the rest of us might readily identify. Even the ardent atheist seems to find little difficulty in seeking God's face when confronted with no other alternative. But prayer was always Jesus' first and only option. When we think of his suffering in relation to prayer, probably our minds are turned first to the anguish of Gethsemane (Matt 26:36–44) or the agonies of the cross (Luke 23:34, 46). But look at how the writer to the Hebrews records Jesus' life of prayer:

> During the days of Jesus' life on earth, he offered up prayers and petitions with loud cries and tears to the one who could save him from death, and he was heard because of his reverent submission.[12]

Whether it was the antipathy of the Pharisees or the apathy of the multitudes, Jesus' sufferings began long before Holy Week. For us, the suffering may come as the result of the loss of a loved one, the end of a personal relationship, the onset of a debilitating medical condition, or unreasonable aversion to our Christian testimony. It seems there is always something to pray for; therefore, always pray!

11. John 4:32b, 34.
12. Heb 5:7.

Jesus prayed in the throes of joy

This is the other side of the same coin as just discussed, and perhaps the one we find least identifiable. After all, who prays when things are going well, right? Well, our exemplar-in-chief did! Having heard the report of the seventy-two he had earlier sent out with his authority, Luke says this of Jesus' response:

> At that time Jesus, full of joy through the Holy Spirit, said, "I praise you, Father, Lord of heaven and earth, because you have hidden these things from the wise and learned, and revealed them to little children. Yes, Father, for this was your good pleasure."[13]

Success—even within an ostensibly Christian milieu—can be a most seductive force. Where suffering can effect morbidity, the joy of accomplishment can drive us to extravagance. Recognizing its true source and giving immediate thanks is a potent antidote to the potential for desolation wrought by ingratitude (Matt 23:37–39). Prayer is only optional if we are prepared to pay the price for its neglect.

Jesus prayed when he was popular

In some ways, this might be seen as an extension to the above. Let us return to the scene immediately after the five thousand plus had been fed. Now imagine that same scene being repeated at a modern-day Christian convention by a preacher of some note. What a marketing opportunity! All the years of hardship, disappointments, turmoil, study, and prayer have been leading to this. You had seen others come and go, but this was your time. Put the books out on display, post flyers around the town, because look who just announced his arrival.

Take away the obvious twenty-first-century allusions, and it is not so much of a stretch to see some of Jesus' company thinking that way. When Matthew records that Jesus "made the disciples get into the boat" and "dismissed the crowd" (Matt 14:22–23), though two different Greek words are used (*enankasen* and *apolyse*), there is a similar sense of urgency attached to each. The first conveys compulsion, as in "he drove them away," while the latter is also used elsewhere for divorce. If ever he needed to be alone with his Father, it was now.

13. Luke 10:21.

Jesus prayed when he was unpopular

This is familiar territory for many of us. Faced with the choice of *vox populi* or *vox Dei*, then the *vox populi* can be as "unpopuli" as it likes. This was certainly true of Jesus, and in marked distinction. Apart from one or two individuals here and there, the religious authorities always seemed threatened by Jesus' existence, and not without good cause. It is the testimony of history that those given to religious observance fear the truly spiritual. It should come as no surprise to us, and I'm sure it was no shock to Jesus. Having healed a man of a shriveled hand on the Sabbath, the Pharisees "were furious and began to discuss with one another what they might do to Jesus" (Luke 6:6–11).

But there is a clearly identifiable diminishing of popularity among the people from the beginning to the end of his short-lived ministry. This was true even among those who came only for the outward display of miracles. There was a 20 percent reduction between the first public feeding and its sequel. In the early days, Jesus' healing of the sick and deliverance of the demon possessed had attracted an intense desire among the people for him to remain with them (Luke 4:38–42). By the end, they were crying for a stay of execution for a common criminal that Jesus might die (23:18). How did he respond? "Father forgive them, for they know not what they are doing" (v. 34).

Jesus prayed when facing major decisions

Solomon was not the wisest man that ever lived; that accolade belongs to Jesus. And yet, when confronted with the need to make major decisions—and despite the fact that he was true God of true God—he did not rely upon natural sagacity. It is more implied than explicit, even in the original tongue, but Jesus' choice of the twelve disciples from among his followers does not appear to have been the result of anything but a prayerful decision:

> One of those days Jesus went out to a mountainside to pray, and spent the night praying to God. When morning came, he called his disciples to him and chose twelve of them, whom he also designated apostles.[14]

14. Luke 6:12–13.

We may infer from the fact that it took all night to conclude with twelve names that prayer for Jesus was a communicative process, included among which was the opportunity for the Father to respond. Maybe they discussed the possibilities together; perhaps Jesus required some convincing with one or two of them. There are a couple about whom I might have expressed doubts. We don't know. We do know that Jesus prayed.

BEFORE THE LORD

> Put the altar [of incense] in front of the curtain that is before the ark of the Testimony—before the atonement cover that is over the Testimony—where I will meet with you. Aaron must burn fragrant incense on the altar every morning when he tends the lamps. He must burn incense again when he lights the lamps at twilight so that incense will burn regularly before the Lord for generations to come.[15]

I would not want to preempt anything I might prefer to include elsewhere, but the position of the incense altar is important. First, a brief mention about the use of the word "Testimony." This related to the stone tablets contained within the ark, on which were inscribed the Ten Commandments of the Sinaitic covenant. These did not constitute some pre-tech listicle, over which its recipients were obliged merely to cast a cursory glance. The original Hebrew is thought to have derived from a Babylonian forensic term, meaning "covenant stipulations." Thus, "ark of the covenant" and "ark of the Testimony" are to be treated as synonymous terms.

Close to God's Presence

What concerns us most here, however, is that phrase "before the ark." We shall see that the ark was the place in which God invested his especial presence among his people, Israel. More specifically, it was above the mercy seat—here described as "the atonement cover"—and between the guardian cherubim. In effect, save for the curtain that stood separating them, the stipulated position of the incense altar was before (i.e., in front

15. Exod 30:6–8.

of) the Lord's presence. Therefore, "before the ark" (v. 6) and "before the Lord" (v. 8) also amount to the same thing.

The Hebrew word translated "before" in this type of context (i.e., to be in the immediate presence of) is *lipne*. It appears in the Old Testament almost six hundred times in this form alone, with variants accounting for another fifteen hundred occasions. There is no deviation of meaning, whether the one before whom one stands is Yahweh, kings, prophets, priests, royal ambassadors, one's own wife or husband, parents or children. It is the object to which the word *before* is attached that gives it significance, not the word itself.

In relation to prayerfulness or religious obligation, any object other than the Lord is cited only by way of prohibition. Old Testament priests had a duty to conduct their covenantal responsibilities first for themselves and then as representative intermediaries on behalf of the community, but it was before the Lord that they stood in the carrying out of those duties and no one else. Moreover, there is no conclusive biblical evidence to support the idea that this has changed in principle under the new covenant, except where it is explicitly stated. Each individual is now their own priest, with direct access to God through the provision of but one Mediator, the man Christ Jesus. We still stand before the Lord, not high-ranking ministerial officials, long-deceased Christian martyrs, any of the first-century disciples, or close family members. We stand before Christ and Christ alone.

The question I now want to pose is this: Is it possible to be in the vicinity of the Lord, even with a sense of devotion or measure of commitment, and yet be not truly before him? Try to avoid the temptation to read any further before you have had time to reflect upon the question and arrived at some sort of resolution to it.

I think it is possible. I have experienced it in the company of others several times, and probably been the guilty party myself on a number of occasions. Let us take a look at three examples, one from the Old Testament and two from the New.

This Woman Is Not Drunk, as You Suppose

Samuel's story as a great Old Testament prophet will be well known to many readers. The role he played as a leading statesman in Israel will no doubt be at the forefront of our thinking whenever his name is mentioned.

His anointing to confirm the appointments of Saul and David as Israel's first kings will probably dominate our thoughts. But I want to take you back to before he was conceived, to his mother's desire for a son.

Please read 1 Sam 1:1–17.

Hannah's desperation was possibly fueled in some measure by the fact that her rival for her husband's affection was able to give him children, whereas she was barren. While this is not irrelevant, it was merely the crisis that precipitated a genuine cry to God to come to her aid. Hannah was limited in where she was allowed to roam inside the tabernacle. But as much as any priest of that generation, she truly did come before the Lord.

Hannah was spotted by Eli as he rested from his priestly duties. Just how committed he was to them when he was not resting will become clear to us in due course, but the narrative as it unfolds here provides a clue. When it came to intuitive discernment, Eli was ill equipped to distinguish between an agitated woman pouring out the agonies of her soul and a drunken beggar. Thank God he chooses to bypass those entrusted to act on his behalf from time to time. Joyce Baldwin makes the following observation:

> There is an instructive contrast between the Hannah who, distraught and averse to food, went to pray, and the Hannah who returned to join the family. Though outwardly her circumstances had not changed, she was now joyous and resolute, full of assurance that her prayer would be answered.[16]

God honored Hannah's integrity, the answer to her prayer proving in many ways also to be that of the entire nation: Samuel was born at the appointed time, and God had shown that he had not been finished with Hannah (Samuel means "God has heard" or "heard by God"). For very different reasons, neither was God finished with Eli. In the very next chapter, we are told that "a man of God came to Eli" and prophesied to him (1 Sam 2:27). We are told nothing more than that of the prophet's identity, and it must suffice. He spoke of divine retribution upon Eli's house for the neglect of their priestly duties, the sign of which would be the death of his two sons on the same day (v. 34).

Eli's sons, Hophni and Phinehas, did die together, at the battle with the Philistines in which the ark of the covenant was captured and Israel was defeated (1 Sam 4:10–11). But the judgment upon Eli's house did

16. Baldwin, *1 and 2 Samuel*, 17.

not end there. When the old man (now ninety-eight) heard the news, he fell off his chair, broke his neck, and died (vv. 17–18). Phinehas' wife was about to give birth at the time and she, too, died at the point of delivery, but not before she named her soon to be orphaned son "Ichabod, saying 'The glory has departed from Israel'" (vv. 19–22).

A Beautiful Thing

Each of the gospel writers gives an account of the occasion where a woman poured perfume on Jesus from an alabaster jar. The differences in some of the details suggest more than a varied perspective of the same event. For that reason, I would like to draw your attention to Matthew's account.

Please read Matt 26:6–16.

Here, the woman is unnamed, as in Mark (14:3–9) and Luke (7:37–38). Her identity was obviously not considered sufficiently important to the efficacy of the narrative; it may even have been omitted because it was regarded as a potential distraction. John's naming of Mary hardly clarifies matters (John 12:1–8). It would be prudent, therefore, to stay within the boundaries of what we have revealed to us.

If all the gospel accounts relate to the same event, we learn that the perfume content of the alabaster jar was "very precious" (Gk. *barytimou*—Matt 26:7 KJV), "very costly" (*polytelous*—Mark 14:3 KJV), and "of pure nard" (*nardou pistikes*—John 12:3). And there was "about a pint" of the stuff! If they were not the same incident, then more than one woman held Jesus in such high esteem (or the same woman was even more incredibly lavish).

But notice the company. Could it be that the disciples had become so used to being around Jesus that the novelty of his presence was beginning to wear off? Did they imagine that whatever they did was neither consonant with nor an affront to his dignity? Might their embarrassment at having their indifference highlighted have contributed toward their flagrant display of animosity? Perhaps! If so, then Jesus' appraisal of the situation will have done nothing to alleviate their shame:

> Why are you bothering this woman? She has done a beautiful thing to me.[17]

17. Matt 26:10b.

It was Judas Iscariot, the group treasurer, who voiced the fiercest complaint, and his motives for doing so were not as honorable as he sought to convey. But he was not isolated in his criticism. In fact, the only one who was alone was the one before whom the woman stood in recognition of her Lord: Jesus. It delighted her heart simply to be in his presence. To hear his commendation of her lavish act of love would possibly have unleashed a joy almost beyond the capacity of any human to bear.

Of all the adjectives at Jesus' disposal, why did he choose this one? The Greek *kalos* "describes that which is beautiful as being well proportioned in all its parts, or intrinsically excellent."[18] Not for the first time, I think William Hendriksen captures the mood best:

> The opportunity to show love and honor to Jesus in the state of humiliation had almost vanished. Gethsemane, Gabbatha, and Golgotha were just around the corner. What [the woman] had done was therefore right, beautiful even, for it was prompted by thankfulness of heart. It was also unique in the thoughtfulness it revealed. Moreover, it was regal in its lavishness. Last but not least, it was marvelous in its timeliness.[19]

That such an act of beauty should trigger one so heinous belongs forever consigned to the realm of mystery. But that is precisely what happened. Judas could stand it no longer. He had spent a long time in the vicinity without truly recognizing that he stood before the Lord:

> Then one of the Twelve—the one called Judas Iscariot—went to the chief priests and asked, "What are you willing to give me if I hand [Jesus] over to you?"[20]

Busyness the Enemy of Intimacy

Not long after I became a Christian, I bought an album by Chuck Girard, entitled *The Stand*. The third track on side one was something I regarded at the time as a poignant ditty, called "Busy Day." My girlfriend at the time hated it. In retrospect, I think it may have been more pointed than poignant.

Please read Luke 10:38–42.

18. Vine, *Expository Dictionary*, 97.
19. Hendriksen, *Matthew*, 900.
20. Matt 26:14–15a.

Before we go any further, I have something of a confession to make, which at one time I would only have ventured to do in the company of trusted friends. For many years, I read this thinking that Jesus was maybe being a tad harsh. I had more than a little sympathy for Martha. That in itself may seem strange to those who know me, because my natural compassion would be extended toward Mary, but I almost envied the Marthas of this world for getting on with things.

I want to draw your attention first to two conjunctions, one of which does not appear in the NIV. This is how it appears in some other translations:

> And [Martha] had a sister called Mary, who also sat at Jesus' feet and heard his word. But Martha was distracted with much serving . . .[21]

The two words are "also" and "but," apparently incongruous, but with much significance. Although it is more implied than stated, the "also" of Mary's siting at Jesus' feet suggests this was in addition to another activity. The most obvious candidate for this would be that she, too, along with her sister Martha, welcomed Jesus into their home. The "but" is less ambiguous. Not only are we given the detail of what it constituted, but it is seen in sharp contrast to what Mary chose to do instead or, perhaps just as significantly, where she opted to be. What choice would you have made: standing by the Aga, or sitting agog in the presence of Jesus?

Before you answer that, allow me to describe the scene more fully. Martha was not an unbeliever. Outside of his closest group of disciples, Jesus' entire social circle probably extended not much further than this family from Bethany. On the occasion of discovering that her brother was sick, John tells us that "Jesus loved Martha and her sister and Lazarus" (John 11:5). And yet, Martha had an officious streak about her. Given the opportunities of more recent times, I have no doubt that she would have made a very good career professional, dotting every i and crossing every t. Not waiting to be told what to do, she would have instinctively known before anyone else. She even presumed to know what Jesus wanted better than he.

But it was Mary who attracted Jesus' commendation. For all her apparent vulnerability, Mary had learned the secret of sitting at the Lord's feet, not to be puffed up by knowledge alone, but built up in love. She hung on every word, recognizing that this man's word had a habit of

21. Luke 10:39–40a NKJV; see also NASB, YLT.

providing the basis for everything that would follow. She listened to him, not to be critical of syntax or analytically rearranging the parts into a more digestible snack for later, but devotionally.

DESIGNATED OFFERINGS ONLY

Let us remind ourselves of the formula:

> Then the Lord said to Moses, "Take fragrant spices—gum resin, onycha and galbanum—and pure frankincense, all in equal amounts, and make a fragrant blend of incense, the work of a perfumer. It is to be salted and pure and sacred. Grind some of it to powder and place it in front of the Testimony in the Tent of Meeting, where I will meet with you. It shall be most holy to you. Do not make any incense with this formula for yourselves; consider it holy to the Lord. Whoever makes any like it to enjoy its fragrance must be cut off from his people."[22]

The specific ingredients to be used are not easily identifiable, though the lesson suggested by them is. It is one not lost to Alec Motyer's erudition:

> Only when the incense is compounded with the prescribed ingredients and in their exact proportions is it acceptable to the Lord; only as such is it a sweetness for the Lord's delight.[23]

All Rights Reserved

The recipe for the incense may not be quite as detailed as that for the anointing oil (Exod 30:22–24), but its sanctity was to be preserved by the same measure of prohibition (compare vv. 31–33, 36b–38). An overarching summary covering both injunctions may be put thus: "Whoever makes either perfume or incense for use beyond that prescribed must be cut off from his people."

Precisely what such "cutting off" would entail is not made clear in the narrative. It was not the first time Israel had been introduced to the phrase. The first occasion they encountered it as a people group was also in connection with a penalty for refusing to accept divine prohibition, this time in relation to the eating of anything containing yeast during

22. Exod 30:34–38.

23. Motyer, *Message of Exodus*, 287.

the celebration of Passover (Exod 12:15). Its very first mention, however, came to Abraham, when God instituted the covenant of circumcision:

> Any uncircumcised male, who has not been circumcised in the flesh, will be cut off from his people; he has broken my covenant.[24]

This is an example of typically Hebraic idiom, where the root for the penalty is similar to that which is breached; in this case, cut a covenant (Heb. *karat berit*), and abide by its stipulations, or be cut off (*wenikrat*). The range of possibilities was not unlimited, though it was more wide-ranging than we might imagine. Here are a sample few, some of which may be compounded:

- temporary expulsion from the community (i.e., excommunication with a view to future restoration);
- to be permanently treated like an outsider, though still living within the camp boundaries;
- to face banishment through exile (could be as an individual, as part of a clan, or tribally);
- to have one's family line terminated via an incapacity to reproduce;
- to be put to death.

Of passing interest is the fact that Talmudic tradition expands upon the Old Testament proscription. It observes that a person authorized to make incense as part of what we might today call an apprenticeship would, thereby, be exempt from condemnation; only those who made it for pleasure or profit were to be cut off. Moreover, the act of smelling something holy was not itself regarded as sacrilegious, but burning the leftover incense for secular purposes after the sacrifice had been performed was forbidden. Burning the incense before the sacrifice was offered was also permitted, presumably to allow the mixture to be tested for authenticity.

The question that concerns us most here, however, is how this information relating to the shadow is relevant to those of us in the age of the substance, if at all. For that, I want us to look at three slightly different uses of a familiar phrase, all found within the Pauline epistolary:

24. Gen 17:14.

Stench or Sweet-smelling Savor?

> But thanks be to God, who always leads us in triumphal procession in Christ and through us spreads everywhere the fragrance of the knowledge of him. For we are to God the aroma of Christ among those who are being saved and those who are perishing. To the one we are the smell of death; to the other, the fragrance of life. And who is equal to such a task? Unlike so many, we do not peddle the word of God for profit. On the contrary, in Christ we speak before God with sincerity, like men sent from God.[25]

How we are perceived by others, in the context of Paul's address here, is not dependent so much on our adherence to prescribed methods of making Jesus known, as it is on whether those to whom we make him known are receptive to our message or otherwise. The same individual with the same message to two people might well be a foul smell to one and a sweet-smelling savor to the other. What really matters in this regard is that God considers us to be "the aroma of Christ."

When Paul asks, "Who is equal to such a task?" it is not a rhetorical question. He does, in fact, provide the answer himself a few verses later: "Not that we are competent in ourselves to claim anything for ourselves, but our competence comes from God" (2 Cor 3:5). God favors those who recognize their dependence upon him. But there is another clue provided immediately after the question has been posited. It comes as a disqualifying feature, suggesting a mark of those who are not "equal to such a task": those who "peddle the word of God for profit" (2:17a). Might it be said that those who fall into this category are guilty of using the correct formula, but for personal advantage?

The phrase "peddle . . . for profit" is a translation plus interpretation of the Greek *kapeleuontes*, though the final part (i.e., "for profit") is strongly implied. Other translations give "corrupt" (as a verb—KJV), "adulterating" (adjective—YLT), and "hucksters" (plural noun—NLT). The verb *kapeleuontes* is derived from *pleonexia*, itself a compound of *pleon* (more) and *echo* (have). When put together, *pleonexia* indicates the desire to have more rather than its perceived attainment. Thus, suggested synonyms might include greed, avarice, and covetousness. The means to that end must be seen in sharp contrast to Paul's claim for himself and his companions, for it is far removed from sincere. The verb form of

25. 2 Cor 2:14–17.

pleonexia is *pleonekteo*, which Friedel Selter expresses as to "take advantage of, outwit, defraud, cheat."[26]

The targets of Paul's criticism were not those who received remuneration per se, but whose motivation to do so reduced the word of God to nothing more than a piece of merchandise, a marketable commodity to be exploited for personal gain. Sound familiar? Churches in the twenty-first century are led by human agents, some of whom seem to be on a connecting flight to beyond nonsense, whose thoughts are elevated no higher than the level of their pockets (or wherever else their fiscal accessories find safe haven). For them, the norm is what George Ritzer coined *The McDonaldization of Society*.[27] But it is not their church and, ultimately, it is not in their hands. God's prerogative will prevail, but at what cost and for whom? And, if I am correct to make the connection, what will being "cut off" mean for them?

Living between a "Therefore" and a "But"

> Be imitators of God, therefore, as dearly loved children and live a life of love, just as Christ loved us and gave himself for us as a fragrant offering and sacrifice to God. But . . .[28]

This is yet another example of the importance of context. As mentioned earlier, whenever you come across the word *therefore*, look around to see what it is there for. *Therefore* is an adverb, meaning "for that reason" or "consequently." Thus, we need to look before its entry, so that we know what follows it is a consequence of. In this case, what specific characteristics are we to mimic in God, as exemplified in the life of Christ, whereby we, too, might be regarded as "a fragrant offering"?

The list of character traits in question actually fall between two "therefores." What immediately precedes the first is the reminder of a previous instruction to "put off [the] old self . . . and to put on the new self, created to be like God in true righteousness and holiness" (Eph 4:22–24). What then follows the first "therefore" is a range of activities relating to the "old self," which must be "put off" by means of adopting more positive traits of "true righteousness."

26. In Brown, *Dictionary of New Testament Theology*, 1:137.

27. Ritzer, *McDonaldization of Society*.

28. Eph 5:1–2.

The prescribed remedial formula is important here: "put[ting] off falsehood" does not consist simply in keeping our mouth firmly closed, lest it resort to what was until now a default setting; rather we do so by making a deliberate choice to "speak truthfully" (v. 25). *Suppressio veri, suggestio falsi.* Likewise, the road away from taking what belongs to others is in the direction of resourcefulness, so that they might now become beneficiaries rather than victims (v. 28).

This, too, has a ring of familiarity about it. It echoes Jesus' encounters with two men: Zacchaeus (Luke 19:1–10) and the rich young man who had approached him with interest (Matt 19:16–22). Both were wealthy, and they each took the initiative to seek Jesus out privately. Zacchaeus knew what he was and how he had become that; he also recognized the need for restitution as the way forward. The rich young man, however, did not come with a proposal, but a question: "What must I do?" Perhaps he, too, had experienced divine conviction but hoped there might be an easier way. If so, he certainly was not prepared to tread the path of Jesus' confirmation. Salvation came to only one of the houses represented: that of the chief tax collector (Luke 19:9).

Just as the believers at Ephesus might have imagined Paul to be winding down his lesson on how to live a life in accordance with Christ's example, he gets a second wind:

> But among you there must not be even a hint of sexual immorality, or of any kind of impurity, or of greed . . . nor should there be obscenity, foolish talk or coarse joking, which are out of place, but rather thanksgiving.[29]

The disqualifying condition (i.e., "not . . . even a hint"—*mede onomazestho*) applies to all the following prohibitions, not only sexual immorality. In the original, it appears toward the end of the list, as if to emphasize its all-encompassing range, and has the effect: "let none of these things be even named among you."

A Giving Disposition

> For even when I was in Thessalonica, you sent me aid again and again when I was in need. Not that I am looking for a gift, but I am looking for what may be credited to your account. I have

29. Eph 5:3–4.

> received full payment and even more; I am amply supplied, now that I have received from Epaphroditus the gifts you sent. They are a fragrant offering, an acceptable sacrifice, pleasing to God. And my God will meet all your needs according to his glorious riches in Christ Jesus.[30]

Mutual hospitality between Christian believers that emanates from a genuinely gracious disposition rather than a grudging duty is wonderful to behold. But, apart from the coincidental phrase "fragrant offering," what links this to the altar of incense in the tabernacle? After all, that was an offering to God; these are beneficent acts between God's people. Precisely! Having previously considered "Living between a 'Therefore' and a 'But,'" we now turn our attention to note the difference between a "Baa!" and a butt.

In what proved to be the last of Jesus' kingdom parables, he related temporal behavior to eschatological reward and punishment (Matt 25:31–46). As might be expected, the good deeds of the "sheep" and the less than noble acts of the "goats" are juxtaposed sharply. But it is the object of each that attracts our attention: what each did or did not do for him. Who was it that fed him when he was hungry, or supplied refreshment for his thirst, provided warmth and security when required, clothed his nakedness, tended to him when sick, or visited him in prison? And who did none of these things?

Neither the sheep nor the goats were aware of having encountered Jesus in such dire straits. That much, at least, they had in common. Then comes the key to the conundrum:

> I tell you the truth, whatever you did/did not do for one of the least of these [brothers of mine], you did/did not do for me.[31]

How different from the way we might sometimes define acts that we imagine hold some value in the divine estimation! They are conspicuous only by their absence. The sheep are commended (and the goats reproved) not for the literary construct of their public prayers, or for declaring the mind of God with prophetic authority, or for their global reputation of being able to incite a spine-tingling sensation of God's presence among his people, or any perceived notion any of us might have that we are able to expound Scripture's meaning with scholarly erudition.

30. Phil 4:16–19.

31. Matt 25:40, 45.

But no! Their endorsement comes as a result of what William Hendriksen describes as "the faithful discharge of humble duties pertaining to day by day living."[32] In other words, workaday routine tasks. Even these proved to beyond the goats' sense of interrelational responsibility. They held no interest. But it is such things that God finds pleasing, a fragrant offering, an acceptable sacrifice, whereby the promise of needs being met in accordance with his riches in Christ Jesus is made.

ITS ORIGINAL POSITION

> Put the altar [of incense] in front of the curtain that is before the ark of the Testimony—before the atonement cover that is over the Testimony—where I will meet with you.[33]

This was on the west side of the tabernacle, in the Holy Place, with the golden lampstand on the south side, and the table of shewbread on the north side. Positioned in front of the curtain that separated the Holy Place from the Holy of Holies, the altar of incense was effectively as close as the regular priest could come to the presence of God without actually being in that presence.

Successive, more permanent constructions recognized the command of God in relation to the desert tabernacle, but also allowed for more elaborate décor and the designers' fancy. I do not wish to delve too deeply at this stage into the design of either temple (i.e., that of Solomon or the one built after Judah's return from Babylonian captivity), lest I preempt much of what I hope to cover in the following section of this chapter.

Curtain Down

An observation must be made, however, about the interior of the temple standing when Christ was crucified. This was essentially the Second Temple, the foundations of which were laid on what was understood to have been the site of the First Temple, in around 535 BC. During the sub-reign of Herod the Great, many ambitious construction projects were undertaken, including restoration and expansion plans for this Second Temple.

32. Hendriksen, *Matthew*, 888.

33. Exod 30:6.

It is, thus, sometimes referred to as Herod's Temple. Of particular interest in this regard is a comment made by Alfred Edersheim:

> Though the Rabbis never weary praising its splendour, not with one word do any of those who were contemporary indicate that its restoration was carried out by Herod the Great. So memorable an event in their history is passed over with the most absolute silence . . . . The first mention occurs in the Babylonian Talmud, and then neither gratefully nor graciously.[34]

There were many consequences of Jesus' death, more still of his resurrection, and yet more incumbent upon his ascension to his rightful place at the right hand of the Father. Both Matthew and Mark (unsurprisingly) identify a common immediate product of Jesus completing his final breath: "At that moment the curtain of the temple was torn in two from top to bottom" (Matt 27:51a; Mark 15:38; see also Luke 23:45b).

Most commentators understandably speak of this in terms of Christ providing access for all to come into the holy presence of God in the innermost sanctuary. We are often encouraged to imagine ourselves in the place of others on resurrection morning. How would you feel as one of the disciples? Or Jesus' mother? Or, as the news about the empty tomb begins to emerge, one of the guards entrusted with the task to ensure its security? Imagine instead that you are the first priest to arrive at the temple for duty after the verses cited above. What are your immediate thoughts?

Foremost among them may well have been this: there are no longer two rooms, but one. In other words, the removal of the curtain between the Holy Place and the Holy of Holies meant that everything that formerly belonged to them in isolation from each other now furnished the one vast space. The altar of incense and the ark of God were now in the same room. Neither of them had moved; they had each retained their original position. Of course, this is equally true of other items of furniture already considered, but that is not our primary concern here. In terms of type and antitype, shadow and substance, symbol and that symbolized, the prayers of the saints have a guaranteed hearing in the immediate presence of God. The barrier of impossibility no longer existed . . .

There is a caveat to that concluding sentence of the previous paragraph: . . . unless or until someone chooses to replace the curtain, either literally or metaphorically. It was torn from top to bottom, but an effective

34. Edersheim, *Temple*, 34 (the final sentence appears as a footnote).

substitute can be installed from the bottom upward, and it would require no expert drapery fitter to do so. An effective "curtain," in my opinion, is the notion that we must only pray in accordance with the divine will, so that must be determined before we may engage with the Almighty. I think this is a fallacy, but perhaps not for the reasons you might imagine.

Back to Bethany

Let us return briefly to the narrative of Jesus' visit to the house of Mary and Martha at Bethany (Luke 10:38–42). We are by now familiar with how the incident panned out and why Mary earned Jesus' commendation. But let us exercise our imaginations a little; envision with me a slightly different scenario. Jesus is welcomed into the sisters' home and, after being greeted and offered the most comfortable seat in the house, both Mary and Martha sit at his feet. They adoringly take in everything he has to say to them, lovingly catching up with his latest news, accepting instruction where it can be gleaned, and hoping he doesn't have to rush off any time soon.

Jesus then brings his little talk to a perfectly balanced cadence and, feeling a little peckish, asks if they might have a morsel of bread, and perhaps some wine. Both Martha and Mary would have then repaired to the kitchen area and prepared something in accordance with their friend's request. I'm confident most readers would agree that this would have been the preferable outcome, though it may also have seen it excluded from the canon of Scripture. But what would have rendered it more desirable? In simple terms, because the works of God must emanate from the words of God.

It is not within our gift to decide how to effect God's purpose, however obvious the route may seem. There has perhaps been no area of Christian ministry more bedeviled in this regard than that of evangelism. Jesus was careful to give specific instruction about such matters. How excited we get when we read about or hear preached texts on "the harvest [being] truly plenteous, but the laborers are few" (Matt 9:37 KJV), all leading to an altar call of "Go, therefore!" But Jesus' next words were not: "so everyone grab a sickle and get busy," or "form yourselves into gospel choirs," much less "compete against others who have the same idea"; it was: "Pray ye therefore the Lord of the harvest, that he will send forth laborers into his harvest" (v. 38). The first word is not "Go!" but "Pray!"

What is prayer? The ideal example of how to pray is to be found in what we often refer to as the Lord's prayer (Matt 6:9–13). The same text provides valuable insight into the nature and purpose of prayer, especially within a kingdom milieu. The kingdom rule of God becomes increasingly established on the earth as his will being executed here reflects its sovereignty in heaven. Thus, far from being merely an opportunity to plead for our earthly whims to be granted an audience in heaven, prayer is the vehicle by which we discern the heavenly will for earthly expression. In other words, it is not so much that we are prohibited from praying for things that lie outside of God's will, as the focus of our prayer is to have that will revealed to us.

The Johannine account of Jesus' declaration regarding the harvest is immediately preceded by his disciples' Martha-like concern for his need for nourishment: "Rabbi, eat something" (John 4:31). This is how he responded to their presumption:

> "I have food to eat that you know nothing about . . . . My food," said Jesus, "is to do the will of him who sent me and to finish his work."[35]

Curtains Replenished

The works of Jesus and the will of the Father were so finely attuned that they may almost be regarded as synonymous terms. His prayer life, as we have seen, was exemplary. By just one measure (though ultimately immeasurable), consider the extent of his consultation process. It involved no one that could not be accessed vertically. It is not my place or business to seek to induce unhealthy guilt trips; if it was, then I would be as culpable as anyone of prayer neglect. But as far as my albeit limited experience has allowed, I have discovered that most Christians—whether individually or corporately—make decisions based on a higher proportion of horizontal consultation than we do on the basis of having prayerfully sought God's counsel. Does this not effectively constitute a reintroduction of the veil that was rent in two? If so, what other "curtains" might impede our access to the Father's presence:

35. John 4:32–34.

The imposition of unauthorized intermediaries

Pastoral responsibility involves giving wise counsel to the flock under one's care, and with an increased sense of urgency if the wider testimony is likely to be called into disrepute; it does not include a requirement for a perceived supra-priestly blessing for every decision to be undertaken by those over whom such responsibility is extended, even less so in the guise of God's delegated representative (John 14:6; 1 Tim 2:5).

Forsakenness of first love

A curtain can be found in the most unlikely of places. Note the catalogue of commendations stored up for the church at Ephesus before we arrive at "Yet I hold this against you: You have forsaken your first love" (Rev 2:4). Hard work, perseverance, intolerance of wickedness and falsehood, endurance, and displays of incredible stamina (vv. 2–3) are no guarantee of immunity from the potential for idolatry, nor do they absolve the guilty party of the need for repentance thereafter (v. 5).

Unconfessed sins

The psalmist admits that the cherishing in his heart of secret sins—had they existed—would have caused his prayers to remain unheard (Ps 66:18). Isaiah had something similar to say (Isa 59:2), of which the blind man healed by Jesus reminded the Pharisees (John 9:30–33; see also v. 16). It is not without irony that a common denominator in the committing of most types of sin is our speech (Lev 19:11; Ps 39:1; Matt 5:37), when therein also lies the vehicle of penitent expression (Rom 10:9–10).

Unresolved marital conflict

Paul takes great pains to advise on appropriate domestic behavior as a means to enjoying divine favor (e.g., Eph 5:28–33; 6:1–4), but it is left to Peter to make the specific connection between godly husbandry and an unimpeded prayer life (1 Pet 3:7). A point not clear in English translations is that the husband's treatment of his wife affects the prayers of them both, not his alone; "your prayers" (literally "the prayers of you") must be seen in the context of their state of union before God as "one flesh" (Gen 2:24).

Personal neglect for any reason

Here, I must first delve—though not too deeply—into the pool of rationale: if you do not pray, you cannot expect to be heard. James was even more forthright: "You do not have, because you do not ask God" (Jas 4:2d). This curtain comes down just as easily as it went up, its remedy being similarly reasonable. It comes to us through the lips of James' brother, Jesus: "Ask and it will be given to you; seek and you will find; knock and the door will be opened to you" (Matt 7:7).

An irreverent approach

The opening lines of the Lord's prayer demonstrate the perfect antidote to disrespectful attendance in the presence of God, a recognition of who it is you are seeking to address; we may call him Father, for so he is, but his name is no less hallowed (Matt 6:9). At the root of irreverence, even if it is expressed in what Hendriksen describes as "chumminess or easy familiarity,"[36] is personal pride. We do well to heed the counsel of Solomon: "[The Lord] mocks proud mockers, but gives grace to the humble" (Prov 3:34).

An unrenewed mind

Whatever channel God may choose to use, his will in respect of anything, whether general or more specific, can only come by revelation. He opts to make those things known to us, or he elects to retain some of them in the realm of mystery. In relation to the former, he also reserves the right to implement certain conditional criteria, by which such revelation might more sympathetically be received. If one potential pathway is transformation "by the renewing of [our] mind[s]" (Rom 12:2), then it seems not unreasonable to assume the benefits of taking that route to be beyond us if we decide not to take it.

36. Hendriksen, *Matthew*, 326.

An unyielding will

"To obey is better than sacrifice," Samuel admonished Saul, after the king had made offerings that lay outside his kingly office (1 Sam 15:22). Very often, however, the two are not mutually exclusive. If Jesus in his humanity was unaware of it before, he certainly discovered in the garden of Gethsemane that obedience and sacrifice were sometimes inextricably linked (Matt 26:36–42). No such sacrifice shall ever be required again, but the principle of obedience remains valid: A will that will not yield to the will of the Father shall continue to be a barrier to that will being further revealed.

Inattention to developing fellowship based on relationship

Please note the choice of words. Fellowship and relationship are not worlds apart, but neither are they synonymous terms. My wife is my wife irrespective of any matrimonial difficulties that may take place from time to time. That is the relationship that continues to exist between us: husband and wife. I have no children and my parents are no longer with us, but please feel free to substitute mother/father/son/daughter as appropriate. Whoever it is, you have an ongoing relationship with them, but sometimes fellowship can become strained, even nonexistent. The same is true of our relationship/fellowship with God, but with one caveat: he is never the one responsible for paucity or breakdown of fellowship.

Failure to comply with known revelation

This may seem a little harsh to some, but I am of the opinion that God is not in the business of churning out sermons week after week as a kind of divinely appointed pick-'n-mix ensemble, whereby we get to choose the most soft-centered option. Revelation has a tendency to be progressive. Perhaps if we are struggling to discern God's direction for the next step in his purpose, we could do worse than re-evaluate whether we have fully complied with the requirements of the one most recently made known to us.

THE ERROR OF THE WRITER TO THE HEBREWS?

> Now the first covenant had regulations for worship and also an earthly sanctuary. A tabernacle was set up. In its first room were the lampstand, the table and the consecrated bread; this was called the Holy Place. Behind the second curtain was a room called the Most Holy Place, which had the golden altar of incense and the gold-covered ark of the covenant.[37]

Karl Barth once said that truth walks the razor edge of heresy.[38] A phrase commonly attributed to one of my favorite writers of the last century is "true truth." Francis Schaeffer used it widely and in a variety of contexts, but all with the same essential meaning. It had a similar effect to that found typically in the Hebrew language where a virtue (or variant of it) is repeated for emphasis. Schaeffer's use of "true truth" was with the intention of conveying absolute truth in distinction from variable degrees of it, whether conditional or circumstantial.

This is my understanding of the revelation of Scripture, especially with regard to its inerrancy. Where this does not appear to be the case, then it is my conviction that it is incumbent upon us to discover the "true truth" of the matter; or, at least, to make the effort to do so. The first step toward arriving at a satisfactory conclusion is to acknowledge an apparent inconsistency. The task may well prove beyond us in the short term, but we must endeavor to approach it with vigor and with integrity. We do ourselves, those we are seeking to convince, and ultimately God's honor a great disservice by closing our eyes to the problem and/or pretending no such conundrum exists. In the spirit of honesty, let us at least admit that the writer to the Hebrews herein presents us with something of a challenge. The next step is to pick up the gauntlet and face that challenge head on, without prejudice or partisanship.

Frustration Guaranteed

So, did the writer to the Hebrews get it wrong about the placement of the altar of incense? I don't believe so! But I must warn readers at the outset of this section that, though we will look at possible explanations, if I am unable to draw a definitive conclusion, I will say so. This may be alien

37. Heb 9:1–4.

38. Quoted in Sweet and Viola, *Jesus Manifesto*, 79.

territory for some, but I have no qualms about admitting that I simply do not know, if that proves to be the case, and I make no apology for it. As far as I am aware, I have no reputation to defend.

My immediate thoughts upon having this brought to my attention were along the lines of the writer imagining the scene after the veil had been torn in two as a result of the events at Calvary, but then I read it more thoroughly and found this not to be the case. The otherwise reliable Ray Stedman mentions the discrepancy, but simply corrects the author before disappointingly moving on with only a passing comment: "because it was closely associated in worship with the ark of the covenant and its mercy seat."[39] This may well be a reasonable starting point, but by itself seems unsatisfactorily superficial.

The most obvious resolution to many will have been the charge of a copyist's error. While we should never dismiss the obvious in our myopic quest for the oblivious, neither should we automatically assume that the most palpable is always necessarily the most probable. Perhaps bizarrely, if our quandary was to be resolved by discovering a scribal mistake, it would not thereby impinge upon the perception of Scripture's inerrancy, as this is acknowledged only in reference to the original documents, from which the scribe will presumably have copied in error.

But there are other concerns to which this theory gives rise. If such an error was committed early on, then why was no serious effort made to correct it, at a time when the originals would have been more readily accessible? This was attempted much later, around the fourth century, but the results convince only of a struggle to resolve texts beyond the understanding of those responsible for the "correction." Moreover, in the design of revelation, it seems incongruous to imagine such an apparent lack of divine preservation.

Perhaps a closer inspection of the various temple projects might shed further light. There were subtle differences of design between Solomon's Temple and the original tabernacle in the wilderness, as indeed there were in the Second Temple and Herod's redevelopment, though none were as significant as this text suggests.

39. Stedman, *Hebrews*, 94.

A Glimmer of Light

Our next port of call involves linguistic analysis of the text in question. Most English translations of the epistle to the Hebrews are in agreement with the NIV: that the Most Holy Place housed both the ark of the covenant and the altar of incense (e.g., NLT, NASB, ESV). Of those translations available to me, only five give a slightly different rendering: "having a golden censer" (i.e., KJV, NKJV, RV, Weymouth, and YLT).

The original Greek is *thymiaterion* and appears nowhere else in the whole of the New Testament (though a variant of it does appear in Luke 1:9–11). Although similar, the word for altar is *thysiasterion* (literally, a sacrificial table of any cultus), a derivative of the verb *thysiazo* (to sacrifice, especially by means of burning). The word used by the writer to the Hebrews (i.e., *thymiaterion*) does, indeed, mean censer, that is, either a vessel for burning incense (literally, any fragrant substance, usually but not confined to ground powder in form) or one for conveying already burning incense from one location to another. Each word retains these separate identities from the Septuagint translation of the Old Testament (e.g., 2 Chr 26:19; Ezek 8:11; Judg 2:2; 2 Kgs 16:10), though often in close proximity to each other for obvious reasons. *Thysiasterion* occurs over four hundred times, while *thymiaterion* most commonly translates *qetoret* and *qitter*, both related to "sweet smoke." Their common prefix, *thyo*, eventually "assumed the meaning to slaughter for cultic ends."[40]

Does that make a difference? Well, it makes some difference, but perhaps not as much as we might have hoped for. And it still requires a little more conjecture than that with which I would normally be content. However, it is not only feasible but also has Talmudic tradition on its side. Twice every day (morning and evening), the high priest would burn incense at the altar of incense in the Holy Place (i.e., before the veil—Exod 30:7–8). Once a year (that is, on one day in every year, not necessarily on one occasion only during that day), on the Day of Atonement, he entered the Holy of Holies, carrying some of the burning coals in a vessel designed for that purpose (a censer). Once inside, two handfuls of ground incense were added to the fire, its fragrant rising smoke atoning for him as he approached God's presence above the mercy seat, between the cherubim (Lev 16:12–13).

The argument here is that more than one censer was in use at any given time. On the Day of Atonement, the high priest took a censer from

40. In VanGemeren, *Old Testament Theology & Exegesis*, 3:417.

the altar of incense and filled it afresh to accompany him beyond the veil. This was then left there, and the previous year's censer removed from its place in the Holy of Holies, cleaned and made available for use again in the Holy Place. This would certainly remove the offense with which the author of Hebrews is normally charged, though it would thereby replace it with another: omitting to mention the altar of incense. A solution that creates more mysteries than it resolves is immeasurably less than satisfactory. Further objections that it would be inconsistent with those versions that translate *thymiaterion* as "altar" are groundless if they are actually mistranslations, which seems to be the case.

Not Short on Theories

Another possibility is that the veil may have been temporarily held back from its normal position on the Day of Atonement, affecting the resulting placement of the altar of incense, so that it appeared to be in the same locus as the ark of the covenant. This, too, would resolve the immediate difficulty as found in the writer to the Hebrews' recollection, without necessarily placing him/her in the same danger as above. But there is no known instance of this being the case by way of textual evidence; it exists only in the realm of plausibility. Moreover, much of the argument relies too heavily on treating typology as analogous, which is not the case elsewhere. We are simply not at liberty to assume typological inferences where they are not suggested more clearly than is evident here.

Falling into the same category, but arguably lower down the scale, is that the actual altar was physically moved from its normal position on the Day of Atonement. This would be a satisfactory explanation for many reasons. It would remove the allegation of error, avoid conjecture beyond its own premise, forestall any charges of unfamiliarity with Hebraic history that might otherwise be leveled against the epistle's author, and dispel some of the objections to extrabiblical evidence to the contrary, such as that found in the Jewish pseudepigraphal Apocalypse of Baruch (6:7).

However, having gone to such great lengths to support the idea that the Greek word employed by the writer to the Hebrews better fits "censer" than "altar," this suggestion falls foul of such a translation. Other arguments that claim to be in favor of this premise demonstrate a paucity of understanding regarding the original languages, which tend to speak against rather than for it.

The idea that the altar's position was referred to as being on the other side of the veil by some elaborate metaphor for its doctrinal association rather than its actual spatial location is at best fanciful. There was some degree of doctrinal association between all the items of furniture, and yet all except the altar of incense managed to retain their usual positions in the thinking of the writer to the Hebrews. This, too, falls foul of the *thymiaterion/thysiasterion* dichotomy.

I Did Warn You!

Well, now comes the moment for which I tried to prepare you a little earlier. It should hardly come as a disappointment, therefore, when I say that I really do not know the answer to the question. This is surely unsurprising; the clues, such as exist, are inconclusive. But I have shown that there are conceivable explanations, which is the whole point of the argument. Some are admittedly more likely than others. I have omitted to mention one or two that have been posited, largely because I believe they stretch the bounds of credulity too far, such as the possibility that all the Old Testament references are incorrect and the writer to the Hebrews was the only one to get it right. Indeed, I have come across one translation that changes the text of the Old Testament to accommodate this theory. You can probably see why I chose not to afford that more consideration.

There may well be other possibilities known to the reader of which I am presently unaware. Others that have yet to be considered may emerge in the fullness of time. Until and unless that happens, I am fully persuaded that what the writer to the Hebrews had in mind was not the altar of incense but the censer, as suggested by the original language. The traditional view that more than one censer was in operation at any one time when the tabernacle was operational (i.e., not in transit) is both credible and reasonable. This still subjects the Hebrews' pensmith to an "error" of sorts, but of the two with which we are faced in an either/or situation, it is the one with which I can most comfortably live. To my mind, it is not one that brings the inerrancy of Scripture into question, or at least, not by anything close to the same degree.

I realize, of course, that this will not satisfy every enquiring mind. Some may even be offended by what they consider to be the apparent ease with which I have abandoned the quest. I am reminded of a piece of advice I was given over forty years ago as a first-year Bible college student, by a lecturer upon whose shoulders I yet aspire to stand. He said something like this:

> There will come times when you will be faced with truths that carry equal weight, though they appear contrary, even contradictory. Though no resolution can immediately be found, the first temptation you must resist is to pretend that it is otherwise. Imagine that you stand by a standard-gauge railway track. The distance between each rail is fixed to accommodate the wheels of the train. You are told to walk alongside the track until the two rails come together. After a couple of miles, you realize you have been set an impossible task. In sheer desperation, and not a little futility, you look ahead into the distance. At the furthest point, before your vision completely fades, the tracks begin to rise with the terrain, before disappearing on the other side of a hill beyond the horizon. There, the tracks come together as one.[41]

SUMMARY

Teaching on the tabernacle furnishings in general is minimal in many church settings. Within that framework of absence, perhaps the altar of incense suffers more than most. Its symbolic correlation to prayer makes this quite poignant. Theodore Epp rightly speaks of the Holy Place as "the place of fellowship."[42] All the furnishings therein reflect this in their own way, their interrelationship demanding our attention to them all.

I am not an enthusiastic user of the telephone, whether landline or cell phone. Apart from calls necessitated by utility firms overcharging my account, I am an infrequent contributor to the Alexander Graham Bell benevolent foundation. Of my regular Christian callers, only one ends the conversation with anything but a cheery "Goodbye," "Speak to you again soon," or "Have a good week!" My ex-college lecturer always (i.e., without fail) invites me to join him by the altar of incense for prayer. It remains the most cherished of conversations; I almost cannot wait for its conclusion.

41. Ieuan Jones, Bible College of Wales lecture, March 10, 1981; author's personal notes.

42. Epp, *Portraits of Christ*, 125.

7

The Ark of the Covenant

I HAVE A MINOR medical condition that requires regular treatment: two different tablets per day, one to be taken immediately after breakfast and the other before bed. My wife refers to it as my bed and breakfast routine. The only hardships involved are remembering to take them and collecting a fresh supply from my local pharmacy each month. They cannot be purchased over the counter, so I am obliged to order them a few days in advance online. The prescription is then ratified by my doctor. I can come into possession of them no other way (not that I've tried).

God chose to invest his presence within the confines of the Holy of Holies at the western-most end of the tabernacle. That presence he made accessible once a year to the high priest in office, but only if he came in accordance with the divinely appointed manner: it was by prescription only. The Holy of Holies contained only one item of furniture, though it was in two parts: the ark of the covenant.

Please read Exod 25:10–22.

THE PURPOSE OF THE ARK

The specific purpose of the ark of the covenant must be viewed within the milieu of a purpose greater than itself. To arrive at a better understanding of that and the part the ark of the covenant plays annexed to it, let us take a couple of steps back to see if anything may be gleaned from the meaning of the word *ark*. Five times in the citation marked above, the Hebrew word *haaron* appears, which is translated "chest"/"ark." Its approximation to the name of Moses' brother and Israel's first high priest, Aaron, is surely no accident.

In the ancient Near East, words similar to that used here appear in relation to a box for conveying items, often used of a coffin or portable sarcophagus. It is believed by some to relate to a shared root for the type of wood used in construction (possibly cedar or pine). Another Hebrew noun is also translated "ark." This other word, *teba*, is used of a nautical vessel. Although the precise usages of *teba* and *haaron* are quite distinct, an overarching purpose may be identified: they are both places of refuge, security, and perpetuation.

Let us take a closer look at a couple of well-known examples where *teba* is used, before returning to *haaron*:

Noah's Ark

Political and nationalistic proclivities aside, has there ever been a more universally familiar seafaring vessel than this? Although different Hebrew words are translated "ark," the ark built by Noah and that constructed for the tabernacle share some remarkably similar features. The first and perhaps most obvious comes in two parts: both were made according to divine design, and there was no previous template upon which to model either. The reason for the latter requires little fathoming for each case: there had been no previous need.

Another common feature is that both arks were types of which Christ became the antitype. In respect of Noah's ark, its soteriological symbolism should not be underestimated or dismissed too readily because it is so obvious. Jesus himself drew the parallel:

> As it was in the days of Noah, so it will be at the coming of the Son of Man. For in the days before the flood, people were eating and drinking, marrying and giving in marriage, up to the day Noah entered the ark; and they knew nothing about what would happen until the flood came and took them away. That is how it will be at the coming of the Son of Man.[1]

William Hendriksen rightly alludes to the common suddenness of both incidents and "the necessity to guard against unpreparedness and

1. Matt 24:37–39.

carelessness."[2] Though one event still remains future, it is hardly as if either will have been subject to insufficient warning. Although some English translations of Jesus' words might seem to imply that Noah's generation were afforded no opportunity to repent (e.g., see NIV above), the original Greek suggests otherwise. The use of *ouk egnosan* is the third person plural (i.e., "they") aorist indicative tense of *ginosko* in the negative. Although it can mean "they did not know," it can just as easily be rendered "they did not perceive, understand the implications of, or acknowledge fully what they did know." Thus, as Hendriksen concludes: "They failed to realize their perilous situation until it was too late."[3]

In the divine perspective, the ark's objective was to protect the continuity of life on earth in the midst of judgment. Anthropocentrically, however, it might reasonably be argued that the purpose of Noah's ark was to save those who availed themselves of the divine provision whereby their salvation might be effected. It also marked a clear distinction between those who did so and those who did not, the same opportunity being made conditionally accessible to all. Some were prepared to meet its condition; others were not.

What was that condition? God himself affirms it: "Go into the ark, you and your whole family, because I have found you righteous in this generation" (Gen 7:1). The writer gives precisely the same appraisal just a few verses earlier: "This is the account of Noah. Noah was a righteous man, blameless among the people of his time, and he walked with God" (6:9). Blamelessness here is not perfection, as some older versions would have it (e.g., Vulgate), but translates the Hebrew *tamim*, which occurs over two hundred times in its various forms in the Old Testament, always in connection with moral probity directed toward fellow human beings.

That Noah was found to be righteous not only compounds his blamelessness but lifts it to another level entirely. Where it is possible to be blameless through ignorance, that in itself might not dissuade a charge of guilt. Strictly speaking, only God has the authority and insight to declare anyone righteous. Thus: "I have found you righteous" (7:1). In this context, the condition of being righteous (Heb. *tsadiyq*) cannot be divorced from committing deeds in accordance with an implied or imposed standard for such conduct. In the simplest of terms, righteousness means to do the right thing in the eyes of God. Noah alone was found

2. Hendriksen, *Matthew*, 869.

3. Hendriksen, *Matthew*, 870.

with this qualification in his entire generation ("you" of v. 1 is singular, not plural); it was this quality that was required for the new beginning and that which the ark was designed to preserve.

Jochebed's Basket

I must confess to taking something of a liberty here. Allow me to explain. The first biblical record of Moses' birth does not name his parents (Exod 2:1–10). We discover his genealogical background five chapters later when, as a grown man, God promises the Israelites' deliverance from Egypt through him (6:1, 12–20). The textual evidence seems clear enough, but it is not without certain difficulties. Identities behind the names and corresponding time lines can often be explained by the possibility of more than one person sharing the same name across the generations. However, if "Jochebed" means anything like "the glory of the Lord" (compare Ichabod—1 Sam 4:21), then this means that the name Yahweh was known prior to Moses' birth (see Exod 6:3).

Scholarly opinion is divided and minds far greater than mine cannot find agreement. The divine declaration that God did not make himself known to the early patriarchs by the name Yahweh could have one of a number of meanings beyond the obvious:

- that he did not make himself fully known to them, but only in part;
- that the name alone was known, but without the implication of what was suggested by it; or
- that the new phase of redemptive history about to unfold required further revelation than had previously been given.

Any of these are possible and none to the necessary exclusion of the others, though I recognize that some readers will remain dissatisfied. If that is the case, please imagine the heading of this subsection to read: "The Basket Provided by Moses' Mother."

Both Hebrew words translated into English as "papyrus basket" are of Egyptian origin. The word for basket finds itself mentioned only here and in connection with Noah's ark (see above). In his later prophecy against Cush, Isaiah mentions them dispatching "envoys by sea in papyrus boats" (Isa 18:2), of which Jochebed's basket may have been a forerunning facsimile. It is more likely, however, to have been similar in design to the kind of baskets common among market traders for storing lightweight commercial merchandise, such as fruit.

Whatever its etymology, it is clear that the purpose in Moses' mother's mind was very different, yet her purpose was subject to that in the mind of God. Preservation and protection dominated them both. Jochebed's was the instinctive yearning of a threatened mother; Yahweh's the resolute reshaping of historical events to bring about the plans of a sovereign Father. Indeed, we might also see Jochebed's act in these terms, though there is no indication that she would have been aware of it at the time: safeguarding the perpetuity of God's purpose through Moses.

It would make a fascinating study to consider Scripture's demonstrations of God's sovereignty in the immediate context whereof any notion of him also being a dour sobersides is summarily dismissed. This is one such example. I find it highly amusing that in the arranging of Moses' survival, his own mother is not only permitted to nurse the child on behalf of Pharaoh's daughter, but is paid for the privilege of doing so (Exod 2:7–9.). The fact that such an arrangement provided the ideal environment within which Moses might be schooled in the God of his fathers in those early years does nothing to lessen the sense of humor. Between the smiles, Alan Cole composes himself well enough to make the following observation:

> Psychologists rightly stress the importance of impressions received during the earliest years. Without this ancestral background, God's later revelation to Moses would have been rootless, and the Sinaitic Covenant could not have been seen as a sequel to, and consequence of, the Abrahamic Covenant.[4]

From Jochebed's perspective, the reward had proven worthy of the risk. Were her actions motivated by faith? There seems to have been no indication of her following a direct word of God to that effect, though it was certainly one whereby she trusted him for the outcome. Indeed, the actions immediately preceding this draw the following appraisal from our good friend, the writer to the Hebrews:

> By faith Moses' parents hid him for three months after he was born, because they saw he was no ordinary child, and they were not afraid of the king's edict.[5]

4. Cole, *Exodus*, 65.
5. Heb 11:23.

The Ark of Testimony

So far, in relation to the two arks whereby the Hebrew *teba* is translated, we have discovered three principal common features: preservation, protection, and perpetuation. It would be difficult to argue for the absence of any of these concerning the ark of the covenant. But could an argument of similar strength be made for any of them being its primary purpose?

There is certainly some evidence for their contributory involvement, without which the likelihood of attaining its primary objective would be reduced drastically. In this respect, the ark of the covenant shares its purpose with that of all the tabernacle furnishings: to foreshadow in type what would be made substance in antitype. The fulfilment of those types is constant and consistent: they all point to Jesus. Even among Jews who fail to identify Jesus as the promised Messiah, they do hold that the coming of the Anointed One (from their perspective) will give substance to all that previously typified him in the Hebrew Scriptures.

One idea that seems to have taken several steps to the right or left of Barth's razor's edge is the Mariolatrous notion that Jesus' mother is the ark of the new covenant. First of all, there is no conclusive biblical evidence for such a claim. Secondly, texts used to support such a claim are either spurious or ill-founded. Finally, given the subject matter and depth of reference, were such a claim valid, the complete absence of support in the writer to the Hebrews' treatise on shadow and substance between the two covenants is more than a little surprising.

So, what evidence is proposed to substantiate the theory? Much is made of Mary's visit to her cousin Elizabeth, especially the alleged similarities between that and David's responses to the return of the ark to Israel:

> David was afraid of the Lord that day and said, "How can the ark of the Lord ever come to me?"[6]
>
> But why am I so favored that the mother of my Lord should come to me?[7]
>
> [David] and the entire house of Israel brought up the ark of the Lord with shouts and the sound of trumpets.[8]

6. 2 Sam 6:9.
7. Luke 1:43.
8. 2 Sam 6:15.

> In a loud voice [Elizabeth] exclaimed: "Blessed are you among women, and blessed is the child you will bear!"[9]
>
> David, wearing a linen ephod, danced before the Lord with all his might . . .[10]
>
> As soon as the sound of your greeting reached my ears, the baby in my womb leaped for joy.[11]
>
> [David] was not willing to take the ark of the Lord to be with him in the City of David. Instead, he took it aside to the house of Obed-Edom the Gittite. The ark of the Lord remained in the house of Obed-Edom the Gittite for three months, and the Lord blessed him and his entire household.[12]
>
> At that time Mary got ready and hurried to a town in the hill country of Judea . . . . Mary stayed with Elizabeth for about three months and then returned home.[13]

My apologies if this causes offense to any readers, but this "evidence" smacks to me of ill-fitting jigsaw pieces being brutally engaged into an unfamiliar position. To be fair, I have heard similar levels of pseudo-correlation from some pulpits of churches with which I am more familiar, regarding other pet themes that are equally lacking in serious biblical support.

Other arguments tend to revolve around Mary's presumed role as bearer of God's glory (i.e., *Theotokos*). The essence of this is affirmed by tradition rather than finding any basis in scriptural canon, though some support in relation to the ark is claimed from the Septuagint version of the Old Testament. When the angel said to Mary that "the power of the Most High will overshadow you" (Luke 1:35), the word translated "overshadow" is *episkiasei*. It is also used of Jesus' transfiguration (9:34). The Septuagint uses this verb in connection with the glory of God on Mount Sinai (Exod 24:15), filling the tabernacle (40:34–38), and enveloping Solomon's Temple (1 Kgs 8:10–11). So, by that reckoning, not only is Mary claimed to be the ark of the new covenant, but there is just as much

9. Luke 1:42.
10. 2 Sam 6:14.
11. Luke 1:44.
12. 2 Sam 6:10–11.
13. Luke 1:39, 56.

"evidence" that she is a new Holy of Holies and temple also. Yet there is no non-conjectural biblical evidence for any of it.

Just as he is the head and initiator of the new covenant, so too is Jesus the ark of the new covenant, the purpose of the original ark being to point as a shadow to that substance. If it were otherwise, I am inclined to think the writers of the New Testament in general, and that of the letter to the Hebrews in particular, might have been let in on the secret.

MATERIALS USED IN THE ARK'S CONSTRUCTION

> Bezalel made the ark of acacia wood—two and a half cubits long, a cubit and a half wide, and a cubit and a half high. He overlaid it with pure gold, both inside and out, and made a gold molding around it. He cast four gold rings for it and fastened them to its four feet, with two rings on one side and two rings on the other. Then he made poles of acacia wood and overlaid them with gold. And he inserted the poles into the rings on the side of the ark to carry it. He made the atonement cover of pure gold—two and a half cubits long and a cubit and a half wide. Then he made two cherubim out of hammered gold at the ends of the cover. He made one cherub on one end and the second cherub on the other; at the two ends he made them of one piece with the cover. The cherubim had their wings spread upwards, overshadowing the cover with them. The cherubim faced each other, looking towards the cover.[14]

Quite a Spectacle

There is nothing particularly out of place regarding the materials used in the ark's construction. The only feature that truly stands out is the fact that its two component parts were of slightly different composition. The actual materials used were invested with a dual symbolism of sorts: they were symbolic in their own right and each was perfectly suited to the symbolism conveyed by the object of which they were made. Acacia, being an incorruptible wood that is not subject to the decaying process at the same rate as other timbers, speaks to the humanity of Christ.[15]

14. Exod 37:1–9.
15. See Conner, *Symbols and Types*, 71.

Among its symbolic uses, gold is said to represent both the divine nature and heavenly glory.[16]

Gold had been used in Egypt for ornamentation and decorative purposes for centuries by the time of the exodus. Although not without difficulty to locate, once found, its pure state, combined with a relatively uncomplicated processing system, made it a worthwhile venture. The Egyptians excelled in their capacity to work the mined ore; they also knew how to exploit an inexpensive work force in its excavation. The Israelites had first-hand experience of the latter, and presumably had been observant students of the former.

When we looked at the golden lampstand earlier, I attempted to calculate its monetary value in current terms. This was a simple matter based on a reasonable estimate of the weight of the lampstand multiplied by the current price of gold on a bullion trader website. No such estimate is possible for the atonement cover, as the dimensions at our disposal are incomplete. We have only the length and width corresponding to the dimensions of the ark it was to cover, but no depth is given. Even at the lowest possible estimate we may ascribe to the cover's depth, allowing for it to support its own weight without risk of collapse, we may say with confidence that it was the single most valuable furnishing in the whole of the tabernacle. Moreover, the task of conveying the ark from site to site, with cover and carrying poles *in situ*, would not have been one for feeble hands or the faint-hearted.

The splendor of the Holy of Holies would have been something to behold. The ark and its cover gave the appearance of gold, but it would be a mistake to imagine no other precious metal to have been used there. The bases used for the supporting framework and pillars were made of silver (see Exod 26:19, 21, 25, 32). A subtle reminder, perhaps, of the redemption cost having been met whereby access into God's presence was possible.

Identity Governs Function

As with other furnishings of similar construction, it is not difficult to see why the lower part of the ark is seen to reflect the two natures of the person of Christ, and the mercy seat is representative of the divine glory, especially in its mediatorial capacity. Indeed, given that God chose to

16. Conner, *Symbols and Types*, 69.

invest his especial presence in the locus just above the mercy seat and between the cherubim, it would not be too much of a stretch to identify the mercy seat with the throne of God (symbolically, of course).

Theodore Epp makes a valid point when he says:

> The ark of the covenant distinctly spoke of the Person of Christ—not what He has done, but who He is. When we see who and what Jesus Christ is, we will better understand and be able to evaluate His work.[17]

The truth underscoring Epp's observation may be more difficult to grasp in an age where the opposite is often deemed to be more valuable. When introduced to strangers for the first time, the opening question is often along the lines of "What do you do for a living?" If they must include my activities as part of their evaluation process of me, then arguably better questions might be: "What do you do in your spare time?" "How do you choose to relax?" or "What kind of music do you listen to when you want to destress quickly?" What we do to earn our paycheck rarely has more than a modicum of relevance to the type of person we are. Employment and enjoyment are often poles apart.

The Past Deserves to Be Left There

This, of course, is not true of Jesus. His work emanated directly from who he is. Nevertheless, though one may precipitate, or even be preparatory to, the other, knowing Jesus and knowing about him are not the same thing at all. Many political officials and religious leaders knew about what Jesus was doing in and around Jerusalem, either first-hand or by reputation, but relatively few came to know him as a person. There are clues to suggest that Saul of Tarsus may have found himself in the company of Jesus toward the end of his earthly ministry, but there is nothing beyond the speculative to that end. He certainly knew of him and had a Pharisaical zeal to destroy his legacy (Acts 7:54–58; 9:1–2) before his Damascene experience (vv. 3–22). However, this is what he had to say a few years later:

> But whatever was to my profit I now consider loss for the sake of Christ. What is more, I consider everything a loss compared to the surpassing greatness of knowing Christ Jesus my Lord, for whose sake I have lost all things. I consider them rubbish, that I may gain Christ and be found in him . . . I want to know

17. Epp, *Portraits of Christ*, 133.

> Christ and the power of his resurrection and the fellowship of sharing in his sufferings, becoming like him in his death, and so, somehow, to attain to the resurrection from the dead.[18]

I don't want to stray too far from our subject matter for this section, but a couple of things are especially worthy of note in this citation. I can speak only of my own experience, and perhaps that is not as typical as I imagine, but it is the only one with which I may make a valid comparison. First of all, the overwhelming majority of evangelistic messages I have heard seem not only to focus on the crucifixion, but terminate there with an abrupt suddenness, which is not exemplified in Scripture. Let me put it more bluntly: I challenge anyone to find biblical examples of the gospel being preached where the resurrection of Jesus is paid the same scant regard it finds from behind many of our pulpits today.

Secondly—and, again, by way of comparison—note how little Paul dwells on the past. Many of those I have heard professing to testify to the Lord's goodness in recent times expend so much effort convincing their audience how bad they used to be that it almost comes across as regrettable that God chose to intervene. I even heard one pastor recently declare with glee his creative ability to invent new sins where previously they had ceased to exist, before concluding with: "But I gave all that up, and it was such a sacrifice." No, the only thing he gave up was a different kind of eternity, which is hell without Jesus.

The mystery of the past clings to the present only that it might hitch a ride beyond tomorrow. Notice again Paul's estimation of what others might have thought to have been his illustrious past: "rubbish." The Greek word is *skybalon* and it appears in this form only here in the New Testament (once also in the Septuagint version of the Old Testament). It is not an entirely accurate translation, but on this occasion I reserve a little sympathy for the NIV. Suffice to say, the KJV is nearer the mark with "dung," though even that seems to be making allowances for readers with delicate sensitivities. Jim Packer has this to say of it:

> Nastiness and decay are the constant elements of its meaning; [*skybalon*] is a coarse, ugly, violent word, implying worthlessness, uselessness, and repulsiveness. Gnostics applied it to the human body to express their low view of it, as the tomb of the soul.[19]

18. Phil 3:7–11.

19. In Brown, *Dictionary of New Testament Theology*, 1:480.

Looking Out for Blood

The mercy seat (or atonement cover) shared more than one important construction feature with the lampstand: not only were they both made entirely of pure gold (Heb. *tahowr zahab*), but the respective decorative adornments were of one piece with the whole. Moreover, this was achieved not by cast molding, but by the skillful artisanship of the craftsman's hammer. It would not have been an easy task, but it was a necessary one if the divine directive was strictly to be observed: "See that you make them according to the pattern shown you on the mountain" (Exod 25:40).

This being the case, it seems incredulous that so many stylistic sketches misrepresent the most revered component. Over the years I have seen artists' impressions (most often in study Bibles) where the cherubim have looked to be either screwed down, welded on, wings tucked down by their sides, facing away from each other, facing in the same direction as they stand side by side, or even gazing adoringly into each other's closed eyes, as they seem to contemplate mutual respect for having been given such a shared honor. How difficult can it be to read the text: "The cherubim are to have their wings spread upwards, overshadowing the cover with them. The cherubim are to face each other, looking towards the cover" (i.e., downward—Exod 25:20). We shall return to this later.

Whatever symbolism we may attach to the mercy seat by way of its construction, I am more than a little resistant to the idea that the cherubim represent angelic protection of the divine. I concede that angelology is not my strong suit, largely because my chosen resource (i.e., the Bible) is not particularly forthcoming on the subject. It may well be that angels are entrusted with certain responsibilities as a matter of divine choice, as are humans, without necessarily implying any personal deficiency on God's part. What we do know is that the Almighty is precisely that: all mighty. He is, therefore, quite capable of self-preservation and self-protection without the need to engage the services of any ethereal hit beings. If that is, indeed, included in their functions, it can only be a matter of divine appointment by choice.

What we may deduce from the composite picture of the mercy seat is implied by its name and given value by its composition: it represents God's throne of judgment. We have already seen that bronze is the metal of judgment, as demonstrated at the altar of offering out in the courtyard. That is where judgment takes place, where sacrifice is made, and where blood renders atonement; but the throne of God is where judgment itself is judged as to its efficacy. Alec Motyer describes it thus:

> Sinners have standing before God only on the basis of, and by means of, those appointed substitutionary sacrifices by which the demands of divine holiness are met and satisfied.[20]

The altar is where sacrifice is made by way of offering; the throne is where satisfaction is meted out.

Features of the Throne

Although the idea of a throne is only implied here, the suggestion is sufficiently strong to remain beyond reasonable doubt. Objectively, a throne speaks of authority and government, but we cannot entirely dismiss the subjective aspects of those who willingly submit to that authority and embrace such governance. We should also be aware of the residual qualities of each. This is how the psalmist, traditionally thought to be Ethan the Ezrahite, put it:

> Righteousness and justice are the foundation of your throne;
> love and faithfulness go before you.[21]

The apostle John spoke in similar terms of what was revealed to him on the island of Patmos:

> The throne of God and of the Lamb will be in the city, and his servants will serve him.[22]

The hallmarks both of the throne of John's vision and those who serve it will be precisely the same as identified by the psalmist in the present tense, around seven hundred years earlier: righteousness and justice, love and faithfulness. (I am aware that most translations and commentators refer to the qualities of "love and faithfulness" as emanating from the throne's perpetual incumbent, rather than being symptomatic of those who gather around it in response to the dispensation of "righteousness and justice," but the Hebrew allows for both possibilities with equal conviction.)

20. Motyer, *Message of Exodus*, 263.
21. Ps 89:14.
22. Rev 22:3.

THE CONTENTS OF THE ARK

> Place the cover on top of the ark and put in the ark the Testimony, which I will give you.[23]

> When Moses set up the tabernacle . . . [h]e took the Testimony and placed it in the ark, attached poles to the ark and put the atonement cover over it. Then he brought the ark into the tabernacle and hung the shielding curtain and shielded the ark of the Testimony, as the Lord commanded him.[24]

The Tablets of Testimony

The above reading suggests that the original intention in the mind of God was that the tablets of Testimony were to be the sole occupants of the ark, thereby giving it the alternative name: ark of the Testimony. We shall hopefully clear up any misunderstanding in due course, though commentaries I have seen on the subject seem content to adopt a silent approach. For now, let us consider that which requires little clarification.

At the time when the instructions were given for the tabernacle's design, the tablets (here referred to simply as "the Testimony") had not yet been issued, though provision for their safekeeping was included. Strictly speaking, of course, the Testimony was the inscription upon the tablets, not the tablets themselves; therein lay their true value. It is a little like me keeping letters written to me by my wife from before we were married. The franked postage stamps, the scented notepaper, and the crushed, dried rose petals are not entirely without appeal, but none of them are the focus of my sentiment. Not that the keeping of God's law was in any way a matter of emotional expression. It was far too serious for that. In that respect, perhaps it is not the best comparison to make, though as the day of the wedding drew closer, there seemed to be a commensurate increase in the number of lines beginning: "Thou shalt not . . ."

The Hebrew word translated "the Testimony" is *ha'edut*, almost half its Old Testament uses being found in the book of Exodus. According to Alec Motyer, *ha'edut* relates to:

23. Exod 25:21.

24. Exod 40:18–21.

> . . . that which testifies to God and his requirements and is used of the Law as the Lord's "testimony" to himself. It comes from *'ud*, meaning "to attest, bear witness to/against." The ark, its cover and the Testimony are a single unity. The throne of the Lord rests on the foundation of the exact matching and mutuality of law and atonement. This is where God meets his people and speaks.[25]

It is true to say that these were the second issue of the tablets upon which were inscribed God's commands (i.e., the Decalogue), the original tablets having been broken by Moses on his way down the mountain to find its main precepts already breached (see Exod 32:19). But they were not a revised edition. God's standard of righteousness is intransigent. For this reason, humanistic attempts to formulate a code of secular morality can end only in failure. Societal trends are based on nothing more stringent than consensus of acceptance; thus, today's cause for consternation may well be tomorrow's normative behavior and/or vice versa. But again, God's ways are not our ways (Isa 55:8–9). Mitigating circumstances, temporary diminution of personal responsibility, and brownie-point balance sheets find no place in God's law. In fact, fall foul of just one small part of it, and the guilt for breaking it all is thereby incurred. Those who do not quite believe it to be so must stretch their credulity but a little further (Jas 2:10).

The typology is clear and clarified further by Scripture's declaration elsewhere:

> Sacrifice and offering you did not desire, but my ears you have pierced; burnt offerings and sin offerings you did not require. Then I said, "Here I am, I have come—it is written about me in the scroll. I desire to do your will, O my God; your will is within my heart."[26]

Here, "my heart" translates *me'ay*, which appears in other places as "my bowels," for which some translations offer "deep within me." In both type and antitype, the law of God resides in the ark of their respective covenants, expressed fully in Christ as the desire to do his Father's will (see also Heb 10:5–10).

From the Deuteronomic account (Deut 10:1–5), both grammatically and linguistically, it is possible to argue that both sets of tablets found

25. Motyer, *Message of Exodus*, 254.

26. Ps 40:6–8.

their resting place in the ark of the covenant (i.e., the original broken pair and the freshly inscribed replacement pair). Much depends on whether you read the word "them" as all-inclusive of what precedes it or subject dependent upon the opening clause only. But we must read the overt in the light of the obvious, not vice versa. No such ambiguity exists in the Exodus account. Moreover, it would be difficult to assign any typological relevance to the broken tablets being kept in the ark alongside the new ones.

The Pot of Manna

> The people of Israel called the bread manna. It was white like coriander seed and tasted like wafers made with honey. Moses said, "This is what the Lord has commanded: 'Take an omer of manna and keep it for generations to come, so they can see the bread I gave you to eat in the desert when I brought you out of Egypt.'" So Moses said to Aaron, "Take a jar and put an omer of manna in it. Then place it before the Lord to be kept for the generations to come." As the Lord commanded Moses, Aaron put the manna in front of the Testimony, that it might be kept.[27]

Although attached to a narrative description of an event that preceded the instruction to build the tabernacle, the narrator is describing it proleptically. In other words, writing from a later perspective, he is aware of the consequences of the instruction and how it was adhered to (see also Heb 9:4).

The word "manna" is an interesting one. It was the exclamation on the lips of those who discovered it on the first morning of its provision, and simply means "What is it?" (Exod 16:14–15a). Although not beyond description or similarization, all that was ever added to their understanding was Moses' reply to the question: "It is the bread the Lord has given you to eat" (v. 15b). So manna became its name; what is it was what it was!

The manna was provided with the morning dew and would not normally keep overnight without becoming what Kenneth Kitchen prosaically describes as "maggoty and malodorous."[28] The exceptions to this were but two: as no provision would be made on the Sabbath, double quantities were to be gathered the day before, its preservation beyond the

27. Exod 16:31–34.

28. In Douglas, *New Bible Dictionary*, 734.

norm being guaranteed by culinary preparation (Exod 16:4–5, 21–26). Secondly, as a perpetual reminder of God's provision for sustenance during their wilderness years of immaturity—and possibly also of the grumbling that originally precipitated it—a sample was to be taken and preserved (vv. 32–33).

If there is one phrase that amply describes both type and antitype, it is this: "bread of heaven" (see Neh 9:15). On this occasion, no linguistic expertise or subtle allusion is required to make the connection; Jesus himself provides it with sparkling lucidity:

> I tell you the truth, it is not Moses who has given you bread from heaven, but it is my Father who gives you the true bread from heaven. For the bread of God is he who comes down from heaven and gives life to the world.[29]

The events leading to Jesus' declaration suggest his enquirers were anticipating a sign greater than the divine provision of manna for their forebears in the wilderness (John 6:30–31). He did much better than that: he showed them that to which the sign had been pointing. That is the primary—sometimes only—function of a sign: to point us in the direction of something of greater import than itself. Signs are good, helpful, even necessary on occasion, but they are not—and should never be confused with—that to which they give direction.

In years that are not ravaged by pandemic, I am obliged to travel to London twice a year to meet with a group of fellow examiners. We discuss and agree on the mark scheme over two full days of arguing the toss about potentially tricky responses that might crop up. I have been doing this for almost twenty years, and even if we use the same venue as before, the corridors and floors remain a complete rabbit warren of mystery to me. For two principal reasons, I am grateful for the signage, and in no particular order: the one directing me to the dining hall, and those pointing out the nearest male bathrooms.

If two or three of us need to visit the facilities together, the lead person (usually the one most desperately in need) will follow the signs, and the rest will follow him. So single-minded is our purpose on such occasions that familiar passersby are completely ignored, ill-wisher and well-wisher both. What no one does (ever) is try to find a ladder so that we may all climb up the wall, one by one, and into the sign. That would

29. John 6:32–33.

be foolish, wouldn't it? Who on earth would think more of the sign than that which it had been designed to signify?

Aaron's Budding Rod

> The Lord said to Moses, "Put back Aaron's staff in front of the Testimony, to be kept as a sign to the rebellious. This will put an end to their grumbling against me, so that they will not die." Moses did just as the Lord commanded him.[30]

This declaration follows the incident whereby Korah led an insurrection against Moses and Aaron (Num 16:1–3). As God's delegated representative of his authority, Moses wasted no time in identifying the root of the protesters' challenge: "It is against the Lord that you and your followers have banded together" (v. 11a). It seems there were two complaints being registered under one banner: the right of Aaron's line to the priesthood and contempt for Moses' strategy in the wilderness. Each became subject to its own test (vv. 16–35; 17:1–9). Aaron's censer prevailed and his staff flourished, while those of the rebels were used to overlay the altar (16:39), and returned to their owners as dead as before (17:9).

As the eventual locus of the pot of manna was premeditated, so Aaron's budding rod was a belated addition. What they share in common is the word structure concerning the instruction for their placement: "Put (back) the manna/Aaron's staff in front of the Testimony" (compare Exod 16:34; Num 17:10). The main difference between the two is in parentheses in connection with Aaron's staff, suggesting a return to where it had previously been with the other staffs during the period of testing (vv. 6–7). It is possible to read this in two distinct ways: that the ark contained all three items (after this incident had taken place); or, that the ark contained only the Testimony (i.e., tablets thereof), with both the pot of manna and Aaron's budding rod placed within the Holy of Holies, but immediately outside the ark (i.e., in front of the Testimony).

I currently remain unconvinced by any claims to conclusive dogma in either direction. However, I must concede that, on the basis of Scripture's evidence (and my understanding of it), the weight of likelihood falls upon the latter possibility. The bulk of any counter-evidence to this position is made by the writer to the Hebrews:

30. Num 17:10–11.

> This ark contained the gold jar of manna, Aaron's staff that had budded, and the stone tablets of the covenant.[31]

Most English translations do not have "contained," but proffer "in which were" (e.g., NASB, NKJV) or "wherein" (RV). Not much difference, if any, you might think, but the "in" part translates the Greek preposition *en*, which can also mean "to be with, amongst, or in close proximity to."

For the purpose of this study, I don't think the precise location of the three items matter so much, though it would have been remiss of me not to mention it. What we do know is that they were all housed within the Holy of Holies, and each has something significant to say that extends much further than the tabernacle in the wilderness. The stone tablets preserve our understanding of the holy character of God through his revealed will, fulfilled in Christ by his obedience to that will; the manna would remind Israel of God's miraculous provision for sustenance in the wilderness, fulfilled in Christ as the bread of life; and the rod of Aaron would mark the validation of God's delegated authority, fulfilled in Christ through his resurrection (see also Jer 1:11). Ray Stedman puts it beautifully, when he says:

> Together they spoke of God's love, God's redemption and God's holiness. These find their counterpart in Christian experience: God's love for us initiates his redemptive activity (Jn 3:16); God's provision for us goes far beyond what any amount of human counseling or control can achieve (2 Cor 5:17); and God's sanctifying work within us produces at last a Christlike character that is fully acceptable to a holy God (2 Cor 3:18).[32]

One final note about the keeping of Aaron's budded rod as a sign. It was not for the benefit of the upright, but for the rebellious (Num 17:10). There is more than plenteous bounty implied by the fact that Aaron's staff "not only sprouted, but budded, blossomed and produced almonds" (v. 8). The Hebrew noun for *almond* (*seqed*) is very close in pronunciation to that for *righteousness* (*tsadiyq*), a connection that would not have been lost on those familiar with such idiomatic tendencies.

31. Heb 9:4b.

32. Stedman, *Hebrews*, 92–93 (footnote).

THE MERCY SEAT

When my grandfather died, as his next of kin, the responsibility fell to me to go through his personal documents and possessions. Some were passed to other relatives, such as photographs of parents when they were children, CDs and DVDs that were more likely to be appreciated elsewhere, and a stair-lift to an increasingly immobile great uncle. What could not be dispensed in that way was either handed over to charity shops or binned as of no practical use to anyone (e.g., unopened spice jars that were decades past their sell-by date).

The garage yielded the most junk. Tools for which their usefulness had long since evaporated in the mists of time, bargain purchases for the rainy day that never came (nor was ever likely to), and partially full containers of motor oil and garden pesticides that had not only become illegal, but in some cases required a permit for their registered disposal. In the spare bedroom, tucked behind a 1960s G-Plan teak sideboard, the ownership for which was being contested only by damp and woodworm, was an aged, framed print of a vase of peonies, alongside which, in Old English font, were the oft-quoted words of William Morris: "Have nothing in your home that you do not know to be beautiful or believe to be useful." Oh, the irony!

Beauty and usefulness can be subjective, and my appraisal of both often proved vastly different from that of my grandfather, in death as in life. They are also not necessarily mutually exclusive qualities. As we have seen so far in our journey through the tabernacle, something can be both stunning and practical. Although not quite synonymous terms, in the economy of God, purpose and functionality were also close companions. We need to look at both in relation to the mercy seat if we are more fully to understand its fulfilment in Christ.

Mercy Does Not Negate Justice

The lid of the ark of the covenant was the only "seat" in the whole tabernacle, and it was reserved for divine use only. In movie-making parlance, it was the director's chair. In truly typological fashion—though in an obviously limited sense—its purpose under the old covenant is reflected in its fulfilment under the new. Perhaps untypically, it might prove helpful to look there first and work backward. Paul broached the subject early on in his letter to the believers at Rome:

> God presented [Christ Jesus] as a sacrifice of atonement, through faith in his blood. He did this to demonstrate his justice, because in his forbearance he had left the sins committed beforehand unpunished—he did it to demonstrate his justice at the present time, so as to be just and the one who justifies those who have faith in Jesus.[33]

Most other English translations describe God's presentation of Christ Jesus here as "a propitiation" (e.g., KJV, NASB, ESV, HCSB), a more accurate reflection of the Greek *hilasterion*. Young even goes so far as to translate it "mercy seat" (YLT), for that is precisely Paul's point. So taken by them was he that the late Martyn Lloyd-Jones described these verses as "the classic statement of the great central doctrine of the Atonement . . . there are no more important verses in the whole range and realm of Scripture than these two verses."[34]

Just four verses earlier, the apostle had introduced his theme as the unveiling of "a righteousness from God, apart from the Law . . . to which the Law and the Prophets testify" (Rom 3:21). There is a strange—though legitimate—paradox at work here: the revealing of something that was never truly hidden . . . for those who had eyes to see. It may well have been disguised, it may have appeared only as a shadow awaiting its substantive fulfilment, but it was there all along.

Whatever position we take concerning the actual contents of the physical ark of the covenant, we must surely agree that the tablets of stone bearing God's inscription were kept there, the Testimony, or Law in summary form. I am of the opinion that the position of the mercy seat (as God's given residential address) in relation to these tablets is not without significance: he sits enthroned above the law.

Having established his law on the basis of his righteousness, however, any extension of mercy had to be on the basis that the demands of each were fully met. Forgiveness (or remission) is not unjust, but justly dispensed, God's just acts being an accurate reflection of his inherently just character. This is why I believe the correct position of the cherubim is so vitally important, for both the Law and the mercy seat lay in the direction of their gaze. Anyone attendant within the holiest sanctum of all (i.e., the high priest on the Day of Atonement) was thereby in the presence of God, wherein his law was established. To do so in the absence of blood on the mercy seat made one vulnerable to judgment without mercy. In

33. Rom 3:25–26.

34. Lloyd-Jones, *Atonement and Justification*, 95.

essence, the cherubim represented God's holiness, which demanded that the law be upheld; the blood-spattered mercy seat declared that a sacrifice had been made to that end.

A Theological Quandary

We must again distinguish between propitiation and expiation. They are both connected to wrongdoing, but the former is directed toward a person, whereas the latter concerns iniquitous conduct toward an object, such as a code or standard of behavior. Those who take exception to the idea of propitiation do so, not on linguistic grounds, but invariably because it offends their denial of divine wrath in need of satisfaction. Atonement not only achieves this, but in so doing also expiates the offense against God's moral code. So, propitiation includes expiation, whereas expiation stands alone in its satisfaction. Wayne Grudem outlines the apparent opposition thus:

> Many theologians outside the evangelical world have strongly objected to the idea that Jesus bore the wrath of God against sin. Their basic assumption is that since God is a God of love, it would be inconsistent with his character to show wrath against the human beings he has created and for whom he is a loving Father. But evangelical scholars have convincingly argued that the idea of the wrath of God is solidly rooted in both the Old and the New Testaments.[35]

One of the chief proponents of expiatory atonement only was C. H. Dodd (1884–1973). Having recently relinquished his position as Rylands professor of biblical criticism and exegesis to take the Norris Hulse Chair of Divinity at Cambridge in 1935, Dodd put forward a case for translating *hilasterion* as "expiation" and quickly garnered support for his proposal. So much so, in fact, that it was adopted by the panel of thirty-two scholars responsible for the translation of the Revised Standard Version of the Bible in 1946 (New Testament only). Dodd argued that in non-biblical Greek texts of the same period, *hilasterion* is, indeed, concerned with acts of a propitiatory nature, but its use in the Septuagint to translate *kapporeth* is often with nothing more attached to it than the idea of cleansing or removal.[36]

35. Grudem, *Systematic Theology*, 575.

36. See Dodd, *Bible and the Greeks*, 93.

Dodd's position (and that of the subsequent publication of the RSV) aroused a great deal of ill will among evangelical scholars, some seeing it as a back-door assault on the doctrine of penal substitution. The main protagonist for the propitiatory cause was Leon Morris (1914–2006), an Australian Anglican, whose first major work tackled the issue head on. First published in 1955, *The Apostolic Preaching of the Cross* has earned its place among the classics of its genre. Morris devotes two chapters to the biblical concept of propitiation, the gist of which is that only such a translation of *hilasterion* makes sense of the rest of Paul's letter to the Romans. Let me turn it around by saying this: if *hilasterion* is translated "expiation" in Rom 3:25, then it is entirely unsuited to its contextual environment, both immediate and in view of the lengthy introduction of chapter 1.

Although separated in the NIV by a panel-authorized subheading, the juxtaposition of Paul's quotation of the righteous living by faith and the wrath of God is not difficult to spot (Rom 1:17–18). Nor is it an accident or as sudden a shift of direction as some might have us believe: "I've dealt with that, so now let us move on to something completely different . . ." God's normal policy for generating/encouraging/growing faith is not on a weekend retreat in the picturesque hamlet of Goosebumpsville. For Gideon, it was in the Midianite camp; for Shadrach, Meshach, and Abednego, it was in the Babylonian furnace; for Ezra, Nehemiah, Haggai, and Zechariah, it was as returnees from exile. Not only does this cut right across the "faith equals comfortable existence" dictum, but it also demonstrates that God's assurance comes in the heat of the battle, not the slouching on the sofa.

Faith is no mere easy believism without any other end product. The so-called heroes of the faith, as identified by the writer to the Hebrews (Heb 11), could never have been accused of simply believing a truth that did not thereafter govern their way of living: they lived righteously by faith, to the very end. They availed themselves of the one implement at their disposal that would avert the wrath of God. For those who have failed to do so, there can be but one outcome. Paul's emphasis throughout the book of Romans is a righteousness from God. But a proper appreciation of what is at stake can only be gleaned by recognizing also where the alternative path leads. Righteousness has its own reward; and so does unrighteousness. Moreover, its perpetrators are without excuse (Rom 1:19–20). The immediate context is living by faith, but the wider context is Paul's unashamed desire to preach the gospel in Rome, and this is his opening gambit. No mention yet of experiential joy, or the delight of walking with God, or specific testimony to the Lord's goodness that he wants to share with others that they, too, might taste of the same beneficence. The urgency of the gospel Paul preached was driven by the very thing that many in more recent times have sought to deny on linguistic grounds.

Be Not Deceived

I happen to be of the opinion that something more sinister is afoot here than disagreement over textual implications. It is, I believe, of the same root as prosperity gospel preaching and strategic evangelistic approaches in accordance with the perceived marketing needs of the target audience. Our warning comes also from the pen of Paul, this time in his second pastoral epistle to Timothy:

> Preach the Word; be prepared in season and out of season; correct, rebuke and encourage—with great patience and careful instruction. For the time will come when men will not put up with sound doctrine. Instead, to suit their own desires, they will gather around them a great number of teachers to say what their itching ears want to hear. They will turn their ears away from the truth and turn aside to myths.[37]

Arguably the most startling thing about Paul's counsel here is that false teachers attract no apostolic hostility (though that is not always the case—see 1 Tim 1:4; Titus 14). Maybe it is because Paul is addressing Timothy as a fellow pastor, with the care of sheep under his care paramount, that they seem to be the focus of the problem to which he wishes to draw attention. More specifically, it is the willingness of the flock so easily to become hoodwinked. The unfolding sequence of events is also interesting. It is not simply that innocents are deceived into embracing unholy and ultimately unwholesome attractions, and so turn to them as desirable or convenient; the preparatory step that leads them to this turning aside is that they must first turn away from that which is holy and wholesome. In other words, it is a deliberate act of the will, promulgated by the yearning to fulfil "their own desires" (or fleshly lusts).

The idea that wrath and love are inconsistent is not thoroughly thought through. The wrath of God is exclusively—as far as it applies to us—in connection with his hatred for sin, itself commensurate with his

37. 2 Tim 4:2–4.

love for righteousness (Heb 1:9a). Again, we can invert that by saying that if wrath was absent from the divine Being, then we might thus conclude a toleration of or indifference toward sin. John Murray defines it accordingly: "wrath is the holy revulsion of God's being against that which is a contradiction of his holiness."[38] The effect is not that his love is thereby diminished or diluted; rather, it is the existence also of wrath as a divine attribute that gives real substance to his love and arrests the possibility of it being regarded by us as mere sentimentality. David Wells sums up the relational interplay perfectly:

> Man is alienated from God by sin and God is alienated from man by wrath. It is in the substitutionary death of Christ that sin is overcome and wrath averted, so that God can look on man without displeasure and man can look on God without fear. Sin is expiated and God is propitiated.[39]

Perhaps any objections to the idea of divine wrath are fueled by identifications of it with the kind of rage often viewed as outpourings of human anger. These are frequently precipitated by reaction to hostile provocation or spur of the moment temper tantrums. Morris is clear to distinguish between this and expressions of God's displeasure:

> The biblical writers habitually use for the divine wrath a word which denotes not so much a sudden flaring up of passion which is soon over [i.e., *thymos*], as a strong and settled opposition to all that is evil arising out of God's very nature [i.e., *orge*].[40]

THE *PEROCHET* HAS GONE

> Make a curtain of blue, purple and scarlet yarn and finely twisted linen, with cherubim worked into it by a skilled craftsman. Hang it with gold hooks on four posts of acacia wood overlaid with gold and standing on four silver bases. Hang the curtain from the clasps and place the ark of the Testimony behind the curtain. The curtain will separate the Holy Place from the Most Holy Place.[41]

38. Murray, *Romans*, 35.
39. Wells, *Search for Salvation*, 29.
40. Morris, *Apostolic Preaching*, 162–63.
41. Exod 26:31–33.

> And when Jesus had cried out again in a loud voice, he gave up his spirit. At that moment the curtain of the temple was torn in two from top to bottom. The earth shook and the rocks split.[42]

> Behind the second curtain was a room called the Most Holy Place . . . . The Holy Spirit was showing by this that the way into the Most Holy Place had not yet been disclosed as long as the first tabernacle was still standing . . . . Therefore, brothers, since we have confidence to enter the Most Holy Place by the blood of Jesus, by a new and living way opened for us through the curtain, that is his body, and since we have a great high priest over the house of God, let us draw near to God with a sincere heart in full assurance of faith . . . .[43]

Dealing with Incidentals

A couple of minor issues to deal with at the start. First of all, and before the weight of letters being sent in my direction places too heavy a strain on the international mailing system, of course I am aware that it was the curtain of the temple that was torn in two and not that of the tabernacle, but the symbolism remains valid. Just ask the writer of the letter to the Hebrews.

Secondly, I have thus far resisted the temptation to mention color and/or material symbolism beyond the actual furnishings under consideration. Here, however, is a good place to look at those relating to the curtain/veil (Heb. *perochet*):[44]

blue	–	heaven, heavenly authority, from above, Holy Spirit
purple	–	kingship, royalty
scarlet	–	blood atonement, sacrifice (as crimson)
fine linen	–	purity, holiness, righteousness of saints, sinless humanity
cherubim (as winged creatures)	–	swiftness, defense, strength, protection, flight
the veil	–	"his body" (Heb 10:20)

42. Matt 27:50–51.

43. Heb 9:3, 8; 10:19–22.

44. Conner, *Symbols and Types*, 21, 36, 61, 71.

What Lay behind the Rent Veil?

The significance of the removal of the veil is best viewed from the perspective of the original purpose: separation. The veil effected a two-way partition. Anthropocentrically, it prevented the Israelites from entering the holy immediate presence of God; theocentrically, it provided a barrier between that holy presence and the sin-tainted environment beyond. The exception to both was the annual duty of the high priest in office on the day of Yom Kippur (Heb 9:7).

Although it is usually inadvisable to argue from absence, we must revisit my opening minor issue. I stand by the premise that the veil that was rent on the day of Christ's crucifixion retains its symbolic value, but the fact remains that it thereby revealed something quite different to what would otherwise have been the case had it been the tabernacle in the wilderness. Alfred Edersheim describes the scene:

> [The Most Holy Place] was now quite empty, a large stone on which the high priest sprinkled blood on the Day of Atonement, occupying the place where the ark with the mercy seat had stood.[45]

The temple in existence at the time of Christ's death is often referred to as Herod's Temple. It was, in fact, the Second Temple, which became subject to an extensive refurbishment during Herod's Judean client kingship. This Second Temple had been built following the edict of Cyrus the Great to that effect, allowing a number of exiled Jews to return to their homeland to begin its construction. This only became necessary following the destruction of the First Temple (i.e., that of Solomon) by the Babylonians in 586 BC. The Second Temple was ready for consecration seventy years later.

Here is where the question of evidence from absence comes in: the ark of the covenant (and its contents) receives no mention in the Hebrew Scriptures after the destruction of the First Temple. According to the Mishnah, the foundation stone was located on the exact spot where the ark of the covenant had previously stood.[46] The Babylonian Talmud goes even further by insisting that the absence of the ark symbolized also the

45. Edersheim, *Temple*, 34.

46. Middot 3:6.

non-existence of the tabernacle's *Shekhinah* (i.e., the glory of God's presence) and the First Temple's *Ruach Ha'kodesh* (Holy Spirit).[47]

No Longer Partitioned from the Presence of God

So, what precisely did the removal of the veil achieve, and what are the implications of our understanding of that achievement? First of all, the renting of the veil was quite an accomplishment in itself. Lest we imagine the curtain to have been made of a lightweight economy fabric, the following insight dissuades us of such thoughts:

> The thickness of the veil was a handbreadth. It was woven of seventy-two cords, and each cord consisted of twenty-four strands. It was forty cubits long and twenty wide. Eighty-two myriads of damsels worked at it, and two such veils were made every year. When it became soiled, it took three hundred priests to immerse and cleanse it.[48]

As mentioned earlier regarding its original purpose, I believe there are two ways to view the achievements of the torn veil. The writer to the Hebrews correctly identifies Jesus' bloodshed body as the typological fulfilment of that which previously separated humanity from God, but now provides access by which we may enter boldly, yet reverently. Our confidence stems from our assurance of acceptance; our deference from an acknowledgment of the one toward whom access is made possible. This is clear and unequivocal. I make no attempt to disregard it. But does the physical renting of the actual curtain in Herod's Temple say nothing in its own right? I believe it does. William Hendriksen seems to think more may be implied than is often acknowledged, but is reluctant to say what or develop his consideration any further.[49]

The ark of the covenant represented God's presence among his covenant people, Israel. It is what distinguished the Most Holy Place from the Holy Place. The removal of the veil into the Most Holy Place revealed it to be an empty room. One thing I believe this symbolized was fulfilled three days later when the first disciples arrived at the tomb wherein Jesus had been laid following the crucifixion:

47. Yoma 21b.

48. In Harris, *Hebraic Literature*, 195–96.

49. Hendriksen, *Matthew*, 975.

> On the first day of the week, very early in the morning, the women took the spices they had prepared and went to the tomb. They found the stone rolled away from the tomb, but when they entered, they did not find the body of the Lord Jesus.[50]

One of the names ascribed to Jesus was Immanuel (Isa 7:14; Matt 1:23). It means "God with us." What the torn curtain and the rolled-away stone instruct us is that God is now with us beyond the parameters of previously self-imposed restrictions. Their removal was not only to let us in, but to allow us to see that access to him is no longer bound by the limitations of a time/space continuum. By implication, this also meant that all previous constraints had been declared null and void. What did they include? Paul puts it this way:

> You are all sons of God through faith in Christ Jesus, for all of you who were baptized into Christ have clothed yourselves with Christ. There is [now] neither Jew nor [Gentile], slave nor free, male nor female, for you are all one in Christ Jesus.[51]

The apostle speaks elsewhere in similar terms, also in connection with baptism (1 Cor 12:13). The tabernacle and the sepulcher speak of ritual and death. Baptism involves death, but only as a part of the process by which life might ensue. We are buried with Christ in the waters of baptism not to kill the old man, but as a public demonstration that he is dead, and are thereafter raised in the newness of Christ's resurrection life. It had long been a matter of intrigue to me that the writer to the Hebrews identified "the curtain" with Jesus' body (Heb 10:20). Or should the word structure lend itself more readily to "his body" being equated with "the new and living way"? With further consideration, I think it is as suggested by most translations. As much as it was necessary—even essential—for Christ's mission that he be endowed with a natural, physical body, it did act as a veil of sorts to those who were closest to him: it hid his Godness from them.

Revealing God through Christ's Body . . .

One of the many Pauline metaphors for the church—and arguably the most commonly used—is the body of Christ (see Eph 1:23; 4:25; 5:30;

50. Luke 24:1–3.

51. Gal 3:26–28.

Col 1:24). I'm fairly confident that such an allusion was far from the mind of the writer to the Hebrews when he/she penned those words about Jesus' body being a veil. But that does not mean that valid questions may not be asked of the church's performance down the centuries in relation to how it has hidden or revealed the presence of God to the generation in which it has found itself.

In many ways, how we view history—or, at least, what we perceive of the historical record—is regulated by personal convictions and individual churchmanship, which in turn dictate what aspects of God's Being we deem should be—or should have been—displayed to a watching world. These aside, few would find reasonable grounds to disagree that things began pretty well. The daily numbers of those attracted to the gospel in the book of Acts, for example, suggests that the early church was getting something right. The promised Holy Spirit had not only arrived but was welcomed by those to whom he was sent; God's purpose in his Son's death, burial, and resurrection may not have been fully understood by many, but as much as it was, it became the catalyst for growth, both numerically and spiritually; and godly structures of authority were rapidly implemented as the framework upon which God would both continue to add to the church and bring those within its confines to maturity. The *perochet* had gone, the *paraklete* had come, and God's program of new covenant transformation was well under way.

. . . or Concealing Him?

So, what went wrong? In a nutshell, the stream quickly became polluted. But let us crack open the nut and peer inside. Hierarchies began to develop within local church settings, this extended to inter-church rivalries as leaders began to covet elevation to the most authoritative positions, and ungodly models were introduced into the wider setting, such as the recognition of Rome as the center for government. Within three hundred years, the church was barely recognizable from the one at its initiation . . . and things were about to become decidedly worse before there was any sign of improvement. The veil, which is his body, was being slowly but surely re-erected, and from the bottom up.

One of the key verses in the New Testament concerning the basis of the early church's growth comes toward the end of the same chapter that describes Pentecost:

> They devoted themselves to the apostles' teaching and to the fellowship, to the breaking of bread and to prayer.[52]

Although there is no direct suggestion in Scripture of cause and effect, it would be difficult to argue against such an inference. From personal experience, I would have to say that the most effective methodologies I have seen for local church governance have been those that most closely resembled this pattern. The converse is equally true. The condition of the church in history seemed to deteriorate from the point at which these essentials of the faith were superseded by factors that were considered to be of greater importance. Policy became directed by extrabiblical sources and a reimposition of shadow-like ideals, which Christ had come to fulfil.

Arguably the single most contributory factor toward the church's decline was its association with the state. The salvation of Emperor Constantine, followed by his victory over arch-rival Maxentius at the Battle of the Milvian Bridge in 312 AD, was hailed as the promise of a new dynamic in the history of the church. Prior to the battle, Constantine is alleged to have seen a vision of a cross in the sky, bearing the inscription: *In Hoc Signo Vinces* ("in this sign thou shalt conquer").[53] He won, of course, and thereafter Christianity was imposed on imperial subjects at the point of the sword. Constantine was responsible for a great many reforms, both administrative and economic, but it was the relationship he oversaw between church and state that had the most impact, and not necessarily for the good.

Constantine's reign and the effective paganizing of Christianity coincided, but it was no coincidence in the widely acknowledged use of the term. Sunday became the day of rest and worship (and had little to do with it being the day of Jesus' resurrection), festival dates like Christmas and Easter took over preexisting pagan celebrations on the Roman calendar, and the emperor retained his title of *pontifex maximus* (high priest). Things grew ever more bleak and it would require radical reformation to allow the light in once more.

Shine, Jesus Shine

Despite the gloomy picture, every age has also had its share of those for whom the purpose of God for his church is paramount. Whatever

52. Acts 2:42.

53. See Barnes, *Constantine and Eusebius*, 43.

condition it finds itself in, and whatever some of us may think of it from time to time and in various expressions, the church is a primary agent of God for establishing his kingdom rule, as Christ's body on earth. If the stakes were considerably lower, the world might be excused for failing to acknowledge the existence of God, given that his presence has been somewhat obscured by those responsible for making it known: Christ's body, the church. Division parading as diversity continues to impede it in its mission. And yet, the sole commandment of the new covenant era is that we should love one another, as Jesus has loved us, so that the world may see and know that we belong to him (John 13:34–35). We only need to invert the condition ("if you do not love one another") to realize how disastrous its consequence has been ("the world will see and not know").

An impossible dream? Well, if it is, then the implications are incredulous, for it will mean that the Father's response to Jesus' heartfelt prayer for believers to be one, as they are one, was an unequivocal "No!" (John 17:20–21).

SUMMARY

The ark of the covenant is probably the one piece of tabernacle furniture that receives something approaching its fair share of pulpit time. However, that does not necessarily make it the most sufficiently or satisfactorily understood. I once heard the ark referred to as "an ordinary wooden chest with a lid," which is about as inaccurate a description as it is possible to be. It was much more than that, both to the eye and in essence. It was far more glorious than any of us can grasp, because the source of its glory is beyond human comprehension, even that of a certain Mr. Spielberg.

Such glory was never seen among God's old covenant people after the destruction of the First Temple (see Jer 3:16), and yet it was prophesied that the latter glory would be greater than the former (Hag 2:9). How could this be? In every meaningful way imaginable, the Second Temple was only a shadow of its predecessor. But we do not find true glory by gazing at shadows, especially absent ones. The promise finds fulfilment only in the substance of Christ, who challenged his oppressors: "Destroy this temple and I will raise it again in three days" (John 2:19).

Conclusion

As implied in the introduction, I have wanted to tackle a work of this nature for quite some time—well over forty years. The seed to do so was planted with a gift from a friend, which nearly died of thirst, until it was watered by a series of seminars by another friend almost twenty years later. I have refrained from taking on the project until now because I was never truly confident about my capacity for the task. Even now, I'm not sure I have done it justice, but I'm even less sure that I'll be better equipped.

The opening chapter allowed us briefly to postpone our search for meaning in the specific items of furniture, but provides a useful background against which they are all set. The tabernacle as a complete unit can be described as many things according to what we understand to be its primary purpose. Function and purpose should always bear some correlation, but this is not always the case. There may also exist a number of underlying objectives, each coming under the grand scheme of the overall aim. As far as I can see, the tabernacle was nothing if it was not a place of worship. But seeing that, articulating it as I see it, and conveying it to the reader in a way that accurately represents how I see it are not as easy as might be imagined. It can only really come about if both parties are in agreement concerning their respective definitions of the word *worship*. For me, in this context, it is the intimate expression of relationship between the believer, either as an individual or in a corporate setting, and the Creator, God.

Finding ourselves in the presence of God whereby such worship is possible requires progression. Although the old covenant system has now been rendered obsolete by those of us who are beneficiaries of Christ's once-for-all sacrifice, the principle it underscores is one I believe would enhance our experience of worship, if only it finds expression in a moment of reflection to appreciate the cost involved in providing us with access. For Israel of old, it began at the brazen altar. The sacrificial requirements for temporary atonement from sins meant that when the tabernacle was *in situ*, the altar was constantly in use. The contrast between the type and its fulfilment was never more stark: Christ offered one sacrifice for all sins and sat down (Heb 10:11–12). The similarities included the shedding of innocent blood: that of a sacrificial substitute. I realize, of course, that talk of such things is currently unfashionable, but fashions change; truth does not.

Proceeding through the outer court, we then came to the brazen laver. In so doing, we ventured into priestly territory. With that privilege came responsibility. The priests functioned on the basis of their having been consecrated, but that one-time event did not negate the requirement to maintain a cleansed condition as servants of the Most High. Some have seen such ritual purification under the old covenant to be equated with justification in the new. Justification for believers, however, is not a process whereby they are made justified, but a declaration of the fact that they are regarded as just on the account of another. If ritual purification finds any New Testament equivalent, then it must surely be in the process of sanctification.

We then took our leave of the outer court as we proceeded into the Holy Place. Away from the slaughterhouse conditions of the outer court, but still conscious of its proximity, we took in our surroundings. The Table of Presence was the first item to arrest our attention. The bread upon it was rich in symbolism, but we saw also that the table itself is not without significance. Aside from any religious inference, a table is a place of trust, of communion, of common values, as well as a shared meal. In many ways, the meal consumed is secondary to the company with whom fellowship is expressed. At this table, the meal represented that company, the closest most priests would ever be to God's presence digested with every crumb. It could point to only one thing: the Bread of life (John 6:35).

Directly opposite the table of shewbread stood the golden lampstand. It is then we realize that when we entered the Holy Place a strange thing occurred. Our attention was not immediately attracted to the lampstand, but our gaze could have fallen nowhere without its effect. The purpose of the lampstand was to direct our focus elsewhere. Light illuminates its surroundings wherever it may reside or be placed. The more reliable the source of that light, the more effective its enlightenment. Our responsibility is to avail ourselves of its portability by bringing it to bear on those things we more keenly desire to see. A light kept under the bed might help you to locate your slippers in the night, but little else (Luke 8:16).

As we made our way toward the veiled doorway opposite the one wherein we entered, we noticed the last item in the room: the altar of incense. Its location as described by the writer to the Hebrews is not without controversy. The issues raised by that are, in my opinion, currently beyond our capacity to resolve with entire satisfaction. However, I believe I have posited reasonable solutions that do not require of us that we should doubt the inerrancy of Scripture. Neither should we allow the unknown—and probably unknowable—to impede our understanding of what can be known. Where the shewbread provided sustenance and the lampstand gave sight to the eyes, the incense appealed to the sense of smell, giving off a fragrant aroma. Who says so? Moses, Aaron, the Levites, the Pharisees, more recent rabbis, or latter-day Bible teachers? No, it is the divine evaluation. This is how God delights in the prayers of the saints.

Within the veil we then did come; and what did we see there? Something far more beautiful than "Itchycoo Park": the ark of the covenant in all its splendor. What the ark contained were reminders of God's goodness: a code of conduct whereby we might live righteously, a sample of his provision for sustenance during the wilderness years of immaturity, and a token of his miraculous life-giving fruitfulness. But the Most Holy Place is where we see the importance of godly covering, for it is the ark's lid—or, just above it, between the cherubim—wherein God chose to invest his localized Presence. This was the true source of the *Shekhinah* glory, for without it the curtain over the entrance veiled only a richly ornamented room. Nice, but not glorious! A bit like an empty tomb, really. But why would we want to look for the living among the dead?

Bibliography

Allen, Robert E, ed. *Concise Oxford English Dictionary*. Oxford: Clarendon, 1990.

Baldwin, Joyce G. *1 and 2 Samuel*. Tyndale Old Testament Commentaries 8. Leicester, UK: InterVarsity Academic, 2008.

Barnes, Timothy D. *Constantine and Eusebius*. Cambridge, MA: Harvard, 1981.

Berkhof, Louis. *Systematic Theology*. Edinburgh: Banner of Truth, 1988.

Best, Ernest. "1 Peter II 4–10—A Reconsideration." *Novum Testamentum* 11.4 (1969) 270–93.

Bridges, Charles. *Proverbs*. The Geneva Series of Commentaries. Edinburgh: Banner of Truth, 1998.

Brown, Colin, ed. *Dictionary of New Testament Theology*. 4 vols. Carlisle, UK: Paternoster, 1992.

Bruce, F. F. *1 & 2 Corinthians*. London: Marshall, Morgan & Scott, 1981.

Calvin, John. *Genesis*. The Geneva Series of Commentaries. Edinburgh: Banner of Truth, 1992.

———. *Institutes of the Christian Religion*. Edinburgh: Banner of Truth, 2014.

Childs, Brevard S. *The Book of Exodus: A Critical, Theological Commentary*. London: SCM, 1974.

Cole, R. Alan. *Exodus*. Tyndale Old Testament Commentaries 2. Leicester, UK: InterVarsity Academic, 2008.

Conner, Kevin J. *Interpreting the Symbols and Types*. Portland, OR: City Christian, 1992.

Culverwell, Nathanael. *Spiritual Optics or a Glass Discovering the Weakness and Imperfection of a Christian's Knowledge in This Life*. Whitefish, MT: Kessinger, 2003.

Dodd, Charles H. *The Bible and the Greeks*. London: Hodder & Stoughton, 1954.

Douglas, J. D., ed. *New Bible Dictionary*. 2nd ed. Leicester, UK: InterVarsity, 1992.

Edersheim, Alfred. *The Temple: Its Ministry and Services*. Peabody, MA: Hendrickson, 2006.

Epp, Theodore H. *Portraits of Christ in the Tabernacle*. Lincoln, NE: Back to the Bible, 1976.

Friedman, Richard E. "The Tabernacle in the Temple." *The Biblical Archaeologist* 43.4 (1980) 241–48. https://doi.org/10.2307/3209799.

Gilders, William K. *Blood Ritual in the Hebrew Bible: Meaning and Power*. Baltimore: Johns Hopkins University Press, 2004.

Girdlestone, Robert B. *Synonyms of the Old Testament.* Peabody, MA: Hendrickson, 2000.

Grudem, Wayne A. *Systematic Theology: An Introduction to Biblical Doctrine.* Leicester, UK: InterVarsity, 1994.

Harris, Maurice H., ed. *Hebraic Literature: Translations from the Talmud, Midrashim and Kabbala.* New York: Tudor, 1946.

Hendriksen, William. *John.* New Testament Commentary. Edinburgh: Banner of Truth, 1998.

———. *Luke.* New Testament Commentary. Edinburgh: Banner of Truth, 1997.

———. *Matthew.* New Testament Commentary. Edinburgh: Banner of Truth, 1989.

Horton, Henry. *The Tabernacle of Moses: The Prototype for Salvation in Jesus.* Bloomington, IN: WestBow, 2014.

Hughes, R. Kent. *Genesis: Beginning and Blessing.* Wheaton: Crossway, 2004.

Jensen, Irving L. *Jeremiah and Lamentations.* Everyman's Bible Commentary. Chicago: Moody, 1974.

Johnson, Alan F. *1 Corinthians.* New Testament Commentary Series 7. Leicester, UK: InterVarsity, 2004.

Kidner, Derek. *Genesis.* Tyndale Old Testament Commentaries 1. Leicester, UK: InterVarsity Academic, 2008.

———. *Proverbs.* Tyndale Old Testament Commentaries 17. Leicester, UK: InterVarsity Academic, 2008.

Lloyd-Jones, D. Martyn. *Authentic Christianity: Acts 7:30–60.* Vol. 5. Edinburgh: Banner of Truth, 2006.

———. *Romans: Atonement and Justification: An Exposition of Chapter 3:20—4:25.* Edinburgh: Banner of Truth, 2003.

Longman, Tremper III. *Psalms.* Tyndale Old Testament Commentaries 15–16. Leicester, UK: InterVarsity Academic, 2014.

Milgrom, Jacob. *Leviticus 1–16.* Anchor Bible Commentaries. New Haven, CT: Yale University Press, 2007.

Milne, Bruce. *Know the Truth: A Handbook of Christian Belief.* Leicester, UK: InterVarsity, 1982.

Morris, Leon L. *The Apostolic Preaching of the Cross.* Grand Rapids: Eerdmans, 1965.

Motyer, J. Alec. *Isaiah.* Tyndale Old Testament Commentaries 20. Leicester, UK: InterVarsity Academic, 2009.

———. *The Message of Exodus: The Days of Our Pilgrimage.* Leicester, UK: InterVarsity, 2005.

Murray, John. *The Epistle to the Romans.* Grand Rapids: Eerdmans, 1968.

Packer, James I. *God Has Spoken.* London: Hodder & Stoughton, 1979.

Ritzer, George. *The McDonaldization of Society.* Thousand Oaks, CA: Pine Forge, 1992.

Robertson, O. Palmer. *The Christ of the Covenants.* Phillipsburg, NJ: Presbyterian & Reformed, 1980.

Selman, Martin J. *1 Chronicles.* Tyndale Old Testament Commentaries 10. Leicester, UK: InterVarsity Academic, 2008.

Sklar, Jay. *Leviticus.* Tyndale Old Testament Commentaries 3. Leicester, UK: InterVarsity Academic, 2013.

Soltau, Henry W. *The Tabernacle, The Priesthood and The Offerings.* Grand Rapids: Kregel, 1972.

Stedman, Ray C. *Hebrews*. New Testament Commentary Series 15. Leicester, UK: InterVarsity, 1992.

Stulac, George M. *James*. New Testament Commentary Series 16. Leicester, UK: InterVarsity, 1993.

Sweet, Leonard I., and Frank Viola. *Jesus Manifesto: Restoring the Supremacy and Sovereignty of Jesus Christ*. Nashville: Nelson, 2010.

Towner, Philip H. *1–2 Timothy & Titus*. New Testament Commentary Series 14. Leicester, UK: InterVarsity, 1994.

Trench, Richard C. *Synonyms of the New Testament*. Peabody, MA: Hendrickson, 2000.

VanGemeren, Willem A., ed. *New International Dictionary of Old Testament Theology & Exegesis*. 5 vols. Carlisle, UK: Paternoster, 1997.

Vine, William E. *Expository Dictionary of New Testament Words*. Iowa Falls: Riverside, 1975.

Wells, David F. *The Search for Salvation*. Leicester, UK: InterVarsity, 1978.

Woodall, Chris. *Covenant: The Basis of God's Self-Disclosure*. Eugene, OR: Wipf & Stock, 2011.

Milton Keynes UK
Ingram Content Group UK Ltd.
UKHW022329070124
435591UK00005B/36